THE COMPLETE IDIOT'S GUIDE® TO

Grilling

by Barbara Grunes and Virginia Van Vynckt

alpha
books

A Division of Macmillan General Reference
1633 Broadway, New York, NY 10019

To Jerry, and to Marv, Lian, and Daniel, our happy eaters

Development Team

Publisher
Susan Clarey

Editorial Director
Anne Ficklen

Managing Editor
Cindy Kitchel

Marketing Brand Manager
Felice Primeau

Editor
Jim Willhite

Production Team

Production Editor
Arun K. Das

Copy Editor and Indexer
Helen Chin

Cover Designer
Mike Freeland

Illustrator
Kevin Spear

Designer
Nathan Clement

Layout/Proofreading
Melissa Auciello-Brogan
Marie Kristine Parial-Leonardo
Lisa Nicholas

Contents at a Glance

Part 1: For Starters   **1**

1 The Smell of Success   3
Just what is "barbecue," anyway, and what's the big deal about grilling? Also, how to best set up cooking, storage, and eating spaces for outdoor food preparation and entertaining.

2 All-American Grills   11
The various kinds of charcoal, gas, and electric grills, plus smokers. Find out how they work, their advantages and disadvantages, and how to keep them clean and in good working order.

3 The Extra Touch   23
Tongs and mitts, grill screens, fish baskets, charcoal chimneys—if you can use it with a grill, you'll find it here.

4 The Proper Provisions   35
Which ingredients you'll want to keep on hand to grill successful meals. Plus, a guide to herbs and spices and how they can lift dishes from good to extraordinary, and basic tips on choosing, storing, and preparing food for the grill.

Part 2: Getting Warmer   **45**

5 Fire and Smoke   47
A guide to choosing charcoal, briquets, smoking woods, and other aromatics. How to start a fire and keep it going, and how to judge when the coals are just right for cooking.

6 Techniques That Really Cook   55
The art of cooking over direct heat, indirect heat, or even in the embers. Plus, the joys of smoking (food, that is). Basic cooking methods, and how to tell when foods are done.

7 Safety First   63
Why you need to treat your grill with respect, and why you'd better cook those hamburgers through. And what's all this business about cancer-causing substances in grilled foods?

8 It's Your Party   73
Using the book's recipes to plan successful themed menus for outdoor parties, from a casual summer get-together to an all-out graduation bash. Plus, charts on when to do what, and how much food to buy.

9   Chew the Fat—Not   83
    Tips for producing balanced, healthful menus with plenty
    of flavor and little fat. Plus, catering to vegetarian tastes.

Part 3: Ladies and Gentlemen, Start Your Grills   91

10 There's the Rub   93
    How sauces define the region. Also, how to make basic
    marinades and rubs, what they do, and how long to
    marinate various foods.

11 The Meat of the Matter   99
    Which popular meat cuts fare best on the grill and how
    best to cook them, how to make the perfect burger, and
    flavors that go well with red meats.

12 Birds of a Feather   107
    The answer to that burning question: With the skin or not?
    Plus, a guide to poultry types, how to bone a chicken
    breast, and flavors that go well with birds.

13 The Angle on Fish   115
    How to prepare and cook fish and shellfish, and flavors
    that go well with seafood. Plus, a chart showing which fish
    can be substituted for which.

14 Fruits, Vegetables, and Grains   123
    Choosing and preparing vegetables, fruits, legumes, and
    grains for the grill. Also, making a great meatless "burger."

15 A Second Life   131
    Cool ideas for turning leftover grilled foods into great
    sandwiches, soups, and salads.

Part 4: Hot Stuff: The Recipes   139

16 Here's the Rub   141

17 Appetizers   151

18 Meats   165

19 Poultry   179

20 Fish   193

21 Shellfish   207

22 Vegetables and Grains   219

23 Sweet Stuff   231

24 Smoked Foods   243

A What's Wrong, and How to Fix or Prevent It   257
   Common grilling mistakes and problems, and how to
   prevent or correct them.

B Glossary   261
   Grilling and barbecuing terms, and what they mean.

C Resources   267
   Where to get equipment, supplies, food, and further advice.

   Index   273

Contents

Part 1: For Starters   **1**

1 The Smell of Success   **3**

Getting It Together 5
Eating/Entertaining Space 6
Cooking/Prep Area 7
Serving Utensils 8

2 All-American Grills   **11**

What Kind of Grill? 12
Charcoal Grills 13
    Choosing One 13
    Pros and Cons 14
    Cleaning and Maintenance 15
Gas Grills 16
    Choosing a Grill 16
    Pros and Cons 18
    Cleaning and Maintenance 18
Electric Grills 19
    Pros and Cons 19
    Cleaning and Maintenance 19
Tabletop and Portable Grills 19
Specialty Grills 20
Build-Your-Own Pits 20
Smokers 21
    "Real" Wood Smokers 21
Water Smokers 22
    Choosing One 22
    Pros and Cons 22
    Cleaning and Maintenance 22

3 The Extra Touch   **23**

The Core Collection 23
    Tools 24
    Pot Holders and Mitts 24
    Grill Screen 24
    Grill Brush 24

Basting Brushes 24
Skewers 25
Food Thermometer 25
Knives 26
Cutting Boards 26
Charcoal Dividers or Holders 26
Fire Starters 27
Work Table 27
Ice Bucket and/or Cooler 27
Tray 28
Tool Holder 28
Drip Pans 28
Aluminum Foil 28
Small Watering Can 28
Spray Bottle 28
Scoop for Briquets 28
Garbage Bags 29
Fire Extinguisher 29
Nice, But You Can Live Without Them 29
Hinged Cooking Grid 29
Grill Lifter 29
Smoker Box 29
Cart 29
Rotisserie 30
Food Holders 30
Warming Rack 30
Cooking Bags 30
Burger Press 31
Oven Thermometer 31
Grill Baskets 31
Condiment Shelf 31
Flashlight 31
Vinyl or Canvas Grill Covers 31
Grillers' "Toys" 31
Poultry Shears 31
Barbecue Glasses 32
Silly Aprons and Hats 32
Cast-Iron Griddle 32
Heat-Resistant Gloves 32
Baking Tiles or Stone 32
Pizza Peel or Paddle 32
Light Strings 32
Citronella Candles or Torches 33

4 The Proper Provisions   35

The Griller's Spice Rack 36

  Allspice 36

  Basil 36

  Bay Leaves 36

  Chives 36

  Cilantro 36

  Cinnamon 37

  Coriander 37

  Cumin 37

  Dill 37

  Fennel 37

  Garlic 37

  Green Onions (Scallions) 37

  Marjoram and/or Oregano 38

  Mint 38

  Onions 38

  Parsley 38

  Pepper (Black) 38

  Pepper (Red) 38

  Rosemary 38

  Sage 39

  Shallots 39

  Spice Blends 39

  Tarragon 39

  Thyme 39

Oils, Vinegars, and Condiments 39

  Balsamic Vinegar 39

  Rice Vinegar 40

  Wine Vinegars 40

  Flavored Vinegars 40

  Olive Oil 40

  Sesame Oil 40

  Canola Oil 41

  Vegetable Oil 41

  Nonstick Cooking Spray 41

  Barbecue Sauce 41

  Hoisin Sauce 41

  Ketchup 41

  Mayonnaise 41

  Mustard 41

Salad Dressing 42
Soy Sauce 42
Teriyaki Sauce 42
Worcestershire Sauce 42
The Perishables 42
Storing and Handling Foods 42
Food Prep 101 43

Part 2: Getting Warmer   45

5   Fire and Smoke   47

How Wood Burns 47
All About Charcoal and Briquets 48
Starting the Fire 49
When Is It Ready? 50
Keeping It Going 51
Preheating Gas Grills 52
Where There's Smoke, There's Flavor 52
Putting It Out 53

6   Techniques That Really Cook   55

Directly to the Point 55
Indirectly Speaking 57
Rotisserie Grilling 59
Cooking in Embers 59
Smoking 59
Done to a Turn 60

7   Safety First   63

Grills First 64
Fending Off the Bad Bugs 66
Keep It Clean 66
Keep It Cold (or Hot) 67
Cook It Through 67
So What Are These Awful Bugs, Anyway? 68
E. coli 68
Campylobacter jejuni 69
Salmonella 69
Botulism 70
Hetero What? 70

8 It's Your Party 73

A Grilling Timetable 75
Several Days to a Week Before 75
A Day or Two Before 75
Several Hours to a Day Before 77
Just Before the Party 78
*Anywhere from 30 Minutes to an Hour and a Half
Before You Plan to Serve Food* 78
When the Food Is Nearly Finished Grilling 78
After the Party 78
The Wine (Well, Beverage) List 78
Some Suggested Menus 79
Picnic in the Park 79
Backyard Family Barbecue 79
Fourth of July Celebration 79
Pacific Rim–Style Dinner Party 80
Just Appetizers 80
Shore Grill Dinner 1 80
Shore Grill Dinner 2 80
Grilling Party for Kids 81

9 Chew the Fat—Not 83

Pyramid Power 84
Other Guest-Pleasing, No-Fuss Strategies 84
Lowfat and Vegetarian Recipes in the Book 87
Appetizers 87
Main Dishes 88
Vegetables and Grains 88
Desserts 89
Vegetarian But Not Necessarily Low in Fat 89

Part 3: Ladies and Gentlemen, Start Your Grills 91

10 There's the Rub 93

Marinades and Pastes 94
Rubs 96
Basting and Finishing Sauces, and Condiments 97

11 The Meat of the Matter   99

Steaks and Burgers 99
A Juicy Steak, Texas Style *100*
The Perfect (and Safe) Hamburger *101*
Fajitas 103
Ribs and Brisket: Take Your Time 103
Spareribs *104*
Baby Back Ribs (Loin Ribs) *104*
A Beautiful Brisket *104*
Pork Chops, Tenderloin, and Roast 104
Lamb *105*
Veal *105*
Flavors That Go Well with Meats 105

12 Birds of a Feather   107

Poultry on the Grill 107
So, What About That Thanksgiving Turkey? 109
Types of Poultry, and How to Prepare and Grill Them 111
Broiler/fryer *111*
Free-Range Chicken *111*
Chicken Wings *111*
Capon *112*
Cornish Hen *112*
Duck and Goose *112*
Quail *112*
Squab *112*
Ground Turkey or Chicken *113*
Turkey or Chicken Sausages *113*
Flavors That Go Well with Poultry 113

13 The Angle on Fish   115

Freshness Is Everything 116
Buying It *116*
Storing and Thawing It *117*
Great Catches on the Grill 118
Marvelous Mollusks *120*
Crispy Crustaceans *121*
Soft-Shell Crabs *122*
Flavors That Go Well with Fish and Shellfish 122

14   Fruits, Vegetables, and Grains   **123**

Vegetables 124
  Artichokes *124*
  Asparagus *124*
  Beets *124*
  Carrots *124*
  Corn *124*
  Eggplant *125*
  Garlic *125*
  Mushrooms *125*
  Onions *126*
  Peas *126*
  Peppers *126*
  Potatoes *126*
  Summer Squash *127*
  Sweet Potatoes *127*
  Tomatoes *127*
  Winter Squash *127*
Vegetables You Can't Grill 127
Fruits 127
  Apples *128*
  Bananas *128*
  Cantaloupe *128*
  Citrus Fruits *128*
  Kiwifruit *128*
  Mangoes *128*
  Papayas *129*
  Peaches or Nectarines *129*
  Pears *129*
  Pineapple *129*
Legumes and Grains on the Grill 129
  Breads *129*
  Cake *129*
  Tofu *130*
Flavors That Go Well with Vegetables and Grains 130

15   A Second Life   **131**

Storing Leftovers.. 131
Heating Them Up 132

Creative "Recycling" 132
Poultry 132
Beef 133
Pork 134
Sausage or Ground Meats (any kind) 134
Lamb 134
Fish and Shellfish 135
Vegetables 136

Part 4: Hot Stuff: The Recipes   139

16 Here's the Rub   141

Cajun Spice Rub 142
Two-Mushroom Dust 142
Tennessee Whiskey Barbecue Sauce 143
Herb Marinade for Fish 144
Orange or Tangerine Marinade for Poultry or Pork 145
Ginger Marinade for Chicken or Pork 145
Red Wine Marinade for Meat 146
Rosemary Brushing Marinade for Lamb 147
Cranberry Raisin Ketchup 148
Pineapple Salsa 149
Tartar Sauce 149

17 Appetizers   151

Turkey Sausage on a Stick 152
Five-Minute Mussels 153
Glazed Polish Sausage 153
Spicy Chicken Dogs 154
Sweet and Sour Lamb Ribs 155
Greek Cheese with Garlic Pita Chips 156
Garlic Pita Chips 157
Focaccia 158
Walnut-Stuffed White Mushrooms 159
Grilled Garlic Potato Skins 160
Crostini 161
Grilled Antipasti 162

18 Meats 165

Skirt Steak with Grilled Peppers
and Shallot Marinade Sauce 166
Grilled Sliced Meat Loaf with Chopped Tomatoes 167
Jerk Strip Steaks 168
Flank Steak Strips on Salad Greens
with Lemongrass Mopping Sauce 169
Cheeseburger Deluxe 170
Beer-Basted Short Ribs 171
Pork Tenderloin in Flour Tortillas 172
Pork Chops with Apple Slices 173
Greek-Style Lamb Chops 174
Lamb Rib Chops with Fresh Mint 174
Lamb Burgers 175
Shish Kebabs 176

19 Poultry 179

Cantonese-Style Sweet and Sour Chicken Breasts 180
Whole Grilled Chicken with Apricot Sauce 181
Chicken Yakitori 182
Chicken Pieces with Molasses Barbecue Sauce 183
Paella 184
Chicken Dogs with Caramelized Onions 186
Pesto Chicken 187
Grill-Roasted Turkey Breast 188
Turkey Burgers with Dried Cranberries 189
Yogurt-Marinated Turkey Legs 190
Grilled Quail 190

20 Fish 193

Swordfish in Buttermilk Marinade 194
Tarragon-Scented Striped Bass 195
Red Snapper with Olive Salad 196
Halibut Steaks au Poivre 197
Orange Roughy with Salsa 198
Bluefish Piccata 199
Minted Flounder on Lime Slices 200
Grilled Whitefish with Spinach
Pasta and Fontina Cheese 201
Mackerel with Tangerine Brushing Sauce 202

Salmon Steaks with Asian Marinade 202
Very Simply Salmon 203
Red Snapper Margarita 204
Scrod with Grilled Apple Slices 205

21 Shellfish   207

Sea Scallops and Mashed Potatoes
   with Jalapeño Mayonnaise 208
Sea Scallop Kebabs 209
Soft-Shell Crabs on the Grill 210
Soft-Shell Crabs with Garlic Crumbs 211
Whole Maine Lobsters 212
Lobster Tails with Sherry Sauce 213
"Poor Man's Lobster" (Monkfish)
   with Grapefruit Relish 214
Coastal Shrimp in Beer 215
Prawns with Honey Brushing Sauce 215
Down Maine Clambake 216
Crab Cakes 217

22 Vegetables and Grains   219

Pizza Crust 220
Buffalo Cheese and Tomato Sauce Pizza 221
Asparagus and Mushrooms with Sage Brushing Sauce 222
Mixed Grilled Vegetables in a Pita Pocket 223
Tortellini Vegetable Salad 224
New Potatoes with Garlic and Cilantro 225
Mixed Greens Topped with Grilled Vegetables 226
Baked Potatoes with Vidalia Onions 227
Grilled Tomatoes and Green Onions 228
Baby Artichokes with Rosemary 229

23 Sweet Stuff   231

Glazed Mixed Fruit Grill 232
Blueberry-Apple Cobbler on the Grill 233
Wine-Brushed Pears 234
Warm Apple Cinnamon Slices with Cheddar Cheese 235
Fruit Kebabs on Grilled Chocolate Pound Cake 236
Campfire-Style S'Mores 238
Honeyed Papaya Strips with Warm Brie 239

Apricots Topped with Raspberries
and Raspberry Sherbet 240
Grilled Angel Food Cake and Pineapple 240

24 Smoked Foods   243

Smoked Shrimp with Chili-Orange Mopping Sauce 244
Individual Smoked Whitefish 245
Whole Smoked Salmon
with Pecans and Dried Cherries 246
Carolina-Style Slow Smoked Pulled Pork 247
Smoked Beef Short Ribs 249
Mesquite-Smoked Turkey Thighs 250
Smoked Turkey Sausages 251
Honey-Brushed Smoked Chicken
with Mandarin Orange Sauce 252
Smoked Pork Sandwiches with
Bourbon Barbecue Sauce 253

A What's Wrong, and How to Fix or Prevent It   257

B Glossary   261

C Resources   267

Index   273

Foreword

I didn't become a grilling fanatic until I had two children under the age of five and a teenager in the house. I got a gas grill. Here was an appliance that saved more time than my microwave oven. In less than half an hour I could marinate some fish or chicken, season some vegetables, heat the grill, and have a glorious meal ready for my family. An added bonus was that it was all done outside. We don't have air conditioning, so getting out of that hot kitchen was a real plus. There is also far less clean-up with grilling than with oven or stove-top cooking. No wonder that when winter came, I was still grilling. We have photos of me standing in snow on the deck, turning those kebabs.

I wish that I'd had *The Complete Idiot's Guide to Grilling* when I purchased my grill. There are lots of hints and tips for the grilling neophyte. Even after a few years of grilling, I found useful information throughout the book. Recipes are simple, yet interesting—just the way grilling should be. Grill-Roasted Turkey Breast with a Tangerine Marmalade can be done in a flash. Red meat lovers will find what they want, but for something a little different, why not try the Turkey Burgers with Dried Cranberries?

Barbara Grunes and Virginia Van Vynckt know that grilling and casual parties are made for each other. They share their knowledge and approach to entertaining to ensure that having guests over is both relaxing and fun. And they make sure that it is safe; there are helpful sections on everything from preventing food contamination to what to do with hot coals and flare-ups.

This book will add to your use and enjoyment of your grill, whether you have a gas grill, a charcoal kettle, or a small hibachi. And, you might just find yourself, like me, standing in the snow to fire up that grill.

—Terry Golson

Terry Golson is the author of *1,000 Lowfat Recipes,* and is a regular contributor to the *Boston Herald* food pages.

Introduction

Just moved to the suburbs and planning to buy your first grill? Or perhaps you already have a grill, but every time you use it, you feel as though the food is burned, your hair is singed, and you'll be divorced if your spouse doesn't quit offering useful advice on how to stack the coals. Maybe you can grill basic stuff, but need some recipes and tips to get you out of that hot-dog rut. Or you're pretty proficient at the actual grilling, but need some help in getting organized and planning, so you don't end up running the equivalent of a marathon between your refrigerator and the grill.

You're no idiot, of course, but the vast array of grills, accessories, utensils, woods, charcoals, sauces, and spices—not to mention terminology—are beginning to make you wonder if this whole barbecuing thing isn't beyond you. Or at the very least, a lot more work than it's cracked up to be.

Relax. This book is for you. By the time you finish reading *The Complete Idiot's Guide to Grilling*, you will know just about everything there is to know about choosing a grill and other equipment, selecting foods for grilling, and cooking them to perfection. You'll be able to put together the sort of casual, outdoor parties that everyone loves, and wow your guests with entire menus cooked on the grill. You'll be able to turn out juicy steaks, "wood-fired" pizzas, roasted vegetables, and even grilled desserts with ease.

With our help, you can be confident that when you shell out the money for steak or seafood or exotic vegetables, they'll arrive on your guests' plates grilled to perfection. You'll soon win the kind of acclaim reserved for those who are deemed not "complete idiots," but accomplished pros.

Before You Get Started

Hold your fire! Before you take a match to the coals, we recommend that you read *The Complete Idiot's Guide to Grilling* all the way through. There's a lot more to grilling than just slapping a piece of chicken on the grid. You need to learn how to best organize your kitchen, eating and grilling spaces, storage—and time—so you don't waste effort or charcoal.

A meal is only as good as its ingredients, so you also need to know how to select the best foods for grilling. Also you need to know how to prepare them so that grilling enhances, rather than obliterates, their flavors.

Even beginning grillers will have fun practicing with various rubs, marinades, and sauces to find the ones that hold the greatest personal appeal. Learn to understand the workings of the grill, so you'll know how best to use its dry, intense heat to advantage.

Although grilling recipes tend to be fairly simple, some do require more sophisticated techniques and/or equipment. If you're a novice griller, start with the most basic recipes—those that we have marked "easy"—and gradually expand your repertoire. Remember, grilling is the cooking method most associated with summertime fun but after reading this book, you'll be so at ease with it that you'll be grilling year-round. The goal is to create great grilled fare, and also to have a good time.

What You'll Find in This Book

Part 1: For Starters explains how to set up grilling, eating, and food preparation spaces to best advantage, details grills and accessories, and lists what you'll need in your pantry.

Part 2: Getting Warmer tells you how to start a perfect charcoal fire and keep it going. You'll learn how to cook over direct and indirect heat, and how to keep you, your family, and your yard safe from everything from flying sparks to food poisoning. We'll also clue you in on how to plan and host successful outdoor parties, and tailor menus to appeal to different tastes.

Part 3: Ladies and Gentlemen, Start Your Grills tells you everything you need to know about marinades, rubs, and sauces; explains the basics of selecting, preparing, and cooking meats, poultry, seafood, vegetables, and grains, and shares great ideas for "recycling" grilled leftovers.

Part 4: Hot Stuff: The Recipes is an assortment of tested recipes that run the gamut from appetizers to desserts. Whether it's the perfect barbecue sauce or the most luscious shellfish, you'll find it here.

We've included three appendices, which will tell you how to troubleshoot various grilling problems, help define common grilling terms for you, and point you to resources for equipment and further advice.

Extras

We've also sprinkled various sidebars throughout the book, which highlight information we especially want you to have.

What's What

Read these boxes for definitions of important terms.

Hot Tip

Look here for information on how to accomplish a task more efficiently or make a food taste better.

Don't Get Burned!

These boxes caution about potential hazards, or mistakes that could ruin your meal.

Tasty Tidbit

These are interesting morsels of extra information we thought you'd enjoy reading.

Acknowledgments

A big thanks to Jim Willhite, who guided this book through the process, and Helen Chin, who tweaked our copy into final shape. We want to thank our agent, Martha Casselman, for her steady support. A Texas-size thank you to Brad Blumenthal, for his advice on cooking steak. And we extend our appreciation to the folks who happily shared information on grills, charcoal, and techniques with us, including Don Hysko of Peoples Woods.

Trademarks

All terms mentioned in this book that are known to be or are suspected of being trademarks or service marks have been appropriately capitalized. Alpha Books and Macmillan General Reference cannot attest to the accuracy of this information. Use of a term in this book should not be regarded as affecting the validity of any trademark or service mark. The following trademarks and service marks have been mentioned in this book:

Weber	Kamado
Kingsford	Big Green Egg
Nature's Own	

Part 1
For Starters

In grilling more than almost any other kind of cooking, organization is vital. With the right foodstuffs, tools, and equipment on hand, you'll discover that barbecuing is a breeze.

We begin at, well, the beginning. Before you start cooking, you need to set up your food preparation and eating spaces, buy a grill if you don't have one (or clean the old one if you do), collect all the accessories and utensils you need—and maybe a few that you simply want—and make sure you have all the provisions to make grilling and entertaining a success.

Chapter 1

The Smell of Success

In This Chapter

➤ The meaning of barbecue

➤ Setting up a pleasant outdoor eating area

➤ Organizing cooking and storage spaces

Why do we love grilling and barbecuing so much?

When asked that question in surveys, most people say it's because the food tastes great and because they like to eat outdoors.

But you knew that, didn't you?

We think another reason that North Americans love grilling is that we don't *have* to cook that way. Instead of a chore, grilling is a sport, an art, a hobby. Folks who wouldn't be caught dead lighting a stove and cooking an omelet will fire up the coals and nurse a brisket for 12 hours.

Tasty Tidbit

The word "barbecue" dates far back in American history, and was already in common use, at least in the Carolinas, in the 17th century. The word "barbecue" comes from the Americas as well. The Taino, a native Caribbean people, used the word *barabicoa* for a raised stand of sticks, on which they cooked meat. *Barabicu*, another Taino word, means "the sacred fire pit." The Spanish translated it to *barbacoa*, which in turn evolved into the English *barbecue*.

Yet another reason to love barbecuing is that it touches something fundamental in us. Archaeologists reckon that early humans probably stumbled onto cooking meat by accident, when a forest fire charbroiled the animals they'd been using for food. People have been cooking all sorts of foods over fire ever since. Barbecuing over fire is the oldest form of cooking, and truly universal. Heck, in a lot of countries they still cook most of their meals that way.

In modern America, what we like to barbecue depends on who you talk to. Some surveys put chicken on the top; others vote for hamburger. Steaks are second in line, with hot dogs not too far behind.

One thing is for certain: Americans are particularly fanatical about styles of barbecuing. Cooking foods over fire is the subject of almost religious-like reverence and intensely heated debates. Everyone seems to have their favorite method, as well as their favorite menu choices—the fun part is discovering your own.

What's What

There's a difference between *grilling* and *barbecuing,* at least to true fans of these culinary arts. *Grilling* means cooking food fairly quickly over medium-hot coals. Most of the recipes we offer in this book are for grilled foods. Barbecuing means slow-cooking foods over a low fire. For our purposes, *smoking* is basically barbecuing, with the use of wood chips or chunks to create extra flavor.

North Carolinians swear by their *pig pickin's*. New Englanders have their clambakes, a cooking method that dates back to the original inhabitants of the region. As you move westward, to Memphis and St. Louis, the ketchup predominates and the vinegar lessens, and "sloppy barbecue"—fatty ribs glistening with sauce, pork piled high on a sandwich with coleslaw—takes over. In the Midwest, chicken joins the ranks of frequently barbecued foods. Finally, when you move far enough west to, say, Texas, an honest-to-gosh barbecue will feature beef rubbed in a mixture of seasonings and served as is. Sauce on the side is strictly optional, and don't you even think about drowning the meat in it.

Go even farther west, to California, and suddenly grilling takes on an almost European flavor, with vegetables and pizzas and polenta starring alongside the meat, and with smoke provided by dried grapevines and bits of recycled wine barrels. In the north-western United States and southwestern Canada, salmon is the choice, lightly seasoned in spices and smoked over the delicate sweetness of alder. Go even farther west, to Hawaii, and the pig reappears, as the star (and main course) of the luau.

What's What

One of the most classic—and probably earliest—of the American barbecues is a Carolina *pig pickin'*. Pork is slow-cooked, then pulled into shreds with forks, moistened with a vinegary sauce that probably owes its origins to English-style ketchups, and piled high on buns. North Carolinians make a plain vinegar sauce, South Carolinians add mustard, and in western Carolina, they add a touch of ketchup.

While regional food styles may vary widely, the love of cooking outdoors spans the continent. More than three-quarters of U.S. households have a barbecue grill and, every year, we hold more than 2.6 million cookouts. And that doesn't even count the many people who cook outdoors in Canada and Mexico.

Not surprisingly, families barbecue more often than single people. After all, if you're going to fire up the grill, might as well cook enough for three or four or more. That's not to say that single people don't appreciate the grill as well—what better way to prepare a whole bunch of grilled foods for the week, from leftover steaks for sandwiches, to grilled chicken breast for a spectacular Caesar salad.

Getting It Together

The joys of grilling are obvious. The frustrations are less obvious—until you find yourself standing at the grill and realizing that you're out here and the salt and your basting brush are inside.

A little thought to get organized can keep grilling from becoming a real hassle. You'll often need to prepare food in the kitchen and bring it outdoors to cook, and still have the energy left to carry the dirty dishes back inside. If you don't have everything you need at the ready, you'll be running inside while the shrimp kebabs cook—which, of course, is not a good idea.

That's why successful grilling depends so much on getting yourself, your work and storage spaces, and your serving/entertaining area in order.

If you are wealthy (and/or in the restaurant business), you can stop reading right here. Call your contractor and designer and have them design and build you one of those lovely outdoor kitchens. While you're at it, hire a chef to do the cooking.

If you're like most of us, you gaze longingly at those ads for outdoor kitchens and $5,000 grills, and try to figure out how you can approximate it with your beat-up old kettle and something nice in, say, recycled plastic. The good news is that while you cannot bask in luxury, you can put together a tidy, pleasant eating area and efficient cooking space for not that big an outlay.

Eating/Entertaining Space

Ideally, you already have a decent deck or patio, or the wherewithal to build one. Of course, if you live in a condo or town house with a little balcony, you're probably planning to eat inside, or hosting a smaller gathering.

The major things you need in the eating area are comfort, a shield against the elements, and the ability to serve and clean up easily. The eating area needs to be as close to the kitchen as possible—or even in the kitchen or dining room, if outdoor seating is simply an impossibility. If you can, screen in the deck or patio; it's so much nicer to enjoy a good meal and conversation if the mosquitoes aren't making hash of you and if you don't have to swat flies off your steak. If your deck is large enough and not screened, you can burn citronella torches to help keep mosquitoes at bay; just make sure the smoke isn't going to get in your guests' eyes.

You also want the eating area to be near the grill, but not close enough that your guests choke on the fumes. Take into account the prevailing winds, and which way they're most likely to blow in late afternoon. One of the pleasures of grilling food is the anticipation that the smoky aromas incite—but that doesn't mean you want to smoke your friends.

Tasty Tidbit

You probably won't be surprised to learn that more men than women grill (61 percent compared with 39 percent, according to the Barbecue Industry Association), but you may be surprised to hear that grilling is most popular in the Northeast. Neither rain, nor sleet, nor snow . . .

Since the majority of barbecues tend to take place in the afternoon or evening, try an awning or roof to protect the eating area if it has a western or southern exposure. It can be very uncomfortable to eat while you're steaming in your sweat, or squinting to make out your partner across the table. It can also spell the end of a party when the thunderclouds roll in just as you're serving the Cornish hens with a flourish. If an awning or roof is out of the question, a big umbrella's the next best thing.

The actual eating arrangements need to be comfy as well. Those molded plastic chairs are OK for emergencies, but can get pretty uncomfortable during a three-hour party. Padded chairs or benches and, if you can afford it, a glass-topped or other easy-to-clean table make sense. If you're likely to be entertaining older people most of the time, skip the picnic tables where you have to crawl over the bench. After the age of 40 or so, legs don't bend quite as easily.

Unless the table you have for guest seating is large, you'll need an extra table or cart for serving. Get an enclosed one if possible; then you can store plates, silverware, pitchers and other serving utensils in it.

The cart really should be on wheels so you can load it with dirty dishes and wheel it into the kitchen, clean it off, load up the clean dishes and wheel it back out to the patio. (Needless to say, this doesn't work if you have stairs.)

Cooking/Prep Area

This one's easy, you say. My "cooking area" is the grill.

Well, yes. But there are several factors to keep in mind. For a start, there's safety. First things first: The grill must be outdoors. (Don't even think about using anything but a small electric tabletop model in the house.) At the same time, it must be reasonably sheltered from the wind. It has to be on firm, flat ground with little or no vegetation. It can't be too close to the house, yet it has to be close enough so that you don't feel you're traveling to outer Mongolia to turn the steaks. It should be situated where it won't blow smoke through the windows and into the house, or constantly in the guests' faces.

Getting a bit more complicated, eh?

Once you figure out where the grill goes, then you have to take care of storage and work space.

If you've got one of those everything-but-the-kitchen-sink gas grills with condiment racks, enclosed storage, and pullup side tables, you're probably all set. At the other end of the spectrum, if you've got a no-frills kettle, you can buy tool racks, work tables, and condiment shelves that hang over the side of it. You might find it more handy, though, to just buy a tall, rolling, enclosed cart and slap a cutting board on top of it.

Another possibility is to build in storage. You're in luck if there's a sheltered nook or cranny near the grill where you can put up hooks, or shelves and doors, or all three. You'll need ample space to hold the barbecuing tools, pot holders and mitts, grill

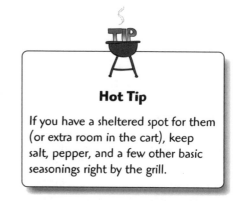

Hot Tip

When you're shopping for a food storage or preparation cart, don't confine your search only to barbecue or cookware shops. Workshop carts designed for tools might offer better storage options. You'll find them in home-building centers. If the top surface isn't conducive to food preparation, just set a cutting board on top of it.

Hot Tip

If you have a sheltered spot for them (or extra room in the cart), keep salt, pepper, and a few other basic seasonings right by the grill.

Hot Tip

While it's tempting to store your carving knives near the grill, don't do this if children—yours or someone else's—would have access to them.

screens, thermometers, kitchen towels, and all the other accessories.

Keep your charcoal and smoking woods in a dry place. Unless you live in a dry climate, that usually means keeping them in the garage, or even in the house. To make it easier to haul them around, you can put the bags in a wheelbarrow.

If you're into gardening as well as grilling, try growing containers of herbs such as rosemary or thyme right on the deck or outside the patio. It's so satisfying to snip off a few leaves of fresh basil or rosemary to sprinkle right on the grilling chicken or fish.

Serving Utensils

For outdoor dining, plastic is the way to go for dinnerware and glasses. These days, you can get plastic cups and glasses in a rainbow of stunning, casual colors that look great in an outdoor setting. In fact, you can buy a set just for outdoor entertaining; if you have a good enclosed serving cart, keep it there.

For really casual parties, you can use paper or disposable plastic plates. Do make sure they're sturdy. Just envision the tandoori chicken somersaulting into your boss's lap, and you'll agree the extra cost is marginal.

When it comes to silverware, plastic doesn't cut it, literally. Real flatware just works better unless you're hosting a big party and need 50 forks and knives. Plastic is fine for the kids, but give the adults real stainless. If you can, it's also great to have a second set of forks and knives just for outside dining. This will lessen the chance that your good forks end up in the flower garden. Be sure the flatware is stored where it'll stay clean.

Hot Tip

For casual outdoor parties, who cares if the silverware's fancy or the plates match? Hit the garage sales or discount outlets, and you should find flatware for next to nothing. Check out similar sources, or party-supply stores, for plastic dishes, serving platters, and whatever else you need.

Make sure you have plenty of serving platters and bowls. A couple of meat platters stored near the grill can keep you from running back and forth to the kitchen. You'll also want a pitcher or two for iced tea, lemonade, sangria, or juice.

If you have a wood picnic table, you'll want to protect it from grease stains and spills. Vinyl tablecloths are ideal. You can buy reusable ones in pleasing patterns or, for less work, throwaway ones in bright colors.

There's no need for cloth napkins. The paper ones come in festive patterns and colors, and can be tossed in the trash.

The Least You Need to Know

➤ Barbecuing and grilling are not the same.

➤ Barbecuing is a truly universal form of cooking.

➤ Your eating space should be comfortable.

➤ Cooking and storage spaces should be designed with the goal of having the cook run back and forth between the kitchen and the grill as little as possible.

Chapter 2

All-American Grills

In This Chapter

➤ Types of grills

➤ Cleaning and maintaining your grill

➤ Smokers and how they work

As civilization evolved, so did grilling equipment. People discovered that meat tasted better if it wasn't covered with ashes, so they stuck it on sticks. Then they realized that meats could be cooked on flat stones heated in the fire. After that, they cooked it in grills woven of green wood. On the other side of the world, grillers cooked meat more quickly by cutting it into chunks and sticking it on sword and dagger blades. Finally, people started putting the fire in clay jars, brick ovens, and fireplaces.

The modern grill essentially is still little more than a glorified, enclosed campfire. Of course, that's like saying the automobile is an internal combustion engine on wheels. In case you haven't noticed, the grill has gone upscale. In fact, the market for upper-end grills has been spreading like wildfire. Suddenly, those stainless-steel outdoor kitchens are no longer just for the very rich.

Of course, increasing choices bring increasing confusion. While you'll still find plenty of charcoal kettles in American backyards, you'll also see gas grills, ranging from your basic box-and-burners-on-wheels to gleaming wonders that could double as restaurant kitchens. Even if you're not quite ready to trade in the car for a new grill, you'll still find plenty of decisions confronting you. Should you buy charcoal or gas? What's the difference between lava rocks and flavoring bars? Does it matter what the cooking grid is made of? And how do you maintain the grill once you've lost the owner's manual in that jumble of papers in the kitchen drawer (or is it the garage)?

What Kind of Grill?

Before you even head out to the store, there are a few basic questions to ask yourself:

➤ How often do you barbecue? Twice a summer? You'll want a very basic charcoal grill. Every other weekend during the spring, summer, and fall? Look for a more deluxe charcoal grill or a medium-range gas grill. If you're the type who stands out in the cold grilling the Thanksgiving turkey, you want the best grill—either gas or a genuine smoker-type grill—that you can afford.

➤ If you currently have a grill, how and when do you use it? If you think you would grill more often if only you didn't have to lug around the charcoal and clean out the ashes, it may be time to switch to a gas grill. If you're constantly juggling to find room for the chicken and steaks, you'll need a larger cooking grid.

➤ Which is more important to you: flavor or convenience? Honest-to-gosh charcoal-grilled flavor comes only from charcoal. If you're the sort who can tell that there's a touch too much alderwood in the salmon, you won't be happy with gas. On the other hand, if you're tired of cursing at briquets that don't light and long for a turn-it-on-and-go experience, you should definitely consider a gas grill.

➤ What size grill do you need? If 90 percent of your barbecuing will be for you and your spouse, a tabletop model may suit you fine. If "grilling" usually means entertaining 40 of your closest friends, you'll need the biggest cooking surface you can afford.

➤ Where do you do most of your barbecuing? If nearly all of it is on your patio or deck, you want an average to large-size grill. If you're a roaming, in-the-park griller, you'll find a tabletop model useful. And of course, if you're one of those super-serious sorts who enter every barbecuing contest in the country, you're talking something that can be hauled on a trailer.

➤ Are there any restrictions on grilling where you live? If you live in a condo or apartment, you may not be allowed to have an outdoor grill at all—in which case, you should get a stovetop grill. Or you may be confined to a small electric grill.

What's What

Cooking grids are made of different materials:

➤ Chrome-plated. Foods tend to stick, and the grid can rust.

➤ Stainless steel. Most common. Doesn't hold heat well, but is rustproof and easy to clean. Foods can stick.

➤ Porcelain-enameled steel. Nonstick and easy to clean. Doesn't hold heat well.

➤ Cast iron. Holds heat well; great for searing meats. Heavy, and prone to rust. Must be kept oiled if it's not porcelain-coated.

➤ Which niceties do you want? Add money if you want a cart or side table (well worth paying for, in our opinion), warming baskets or shelves (nice, but you can live without them), a grease catcher (something else that's important), wood instead of plastic shelves, and so on.

By the way, in a Barbecue Industry Association survey, the features that gas-grill owners rated as most important were: a large cooking surface, shelves, side burners, grease catchers, and a fuel gauge. Charcoal owners voted for ash catchers, smoking capability, and shelves.

Charcoal Grills

Although gas is catching up, in sheer numbers the most popular grill is still the kind that burns charcoal. Most households that have a grill at all own a charcoal one—including more than half of the folks who own gas grills as well.

Choosing One

Although charcoal grills come in all shapes and sizes, the most popular shape is the kettle, introduced in the 1960s by Weber. Its rounded shape allows for good airflow. You pile coals on the bottom grate and cook food on the top grid. The temperature is determined by the heat of the coals and by the vents, top and bottom.

Nearly all kettle grills have a baked enamel finish and ash catchers underneath to make cleanup easier. You can buy tables and carts that the grill fits into to make two side shelves. Extra features include adjustable racks, bigger ash catchers, lids that tuck in a pocket on the side of the grill, and hinged cooking grids (standard on newer models). They come in various sizes, from 14^1/$_2$-inch-diameter tabletop models to huge models designed to grill for a crowd. Far and away the most popular sizes, though, are the 18^1/$_2$- and 22^1/$_2$-inch-diameter kettle grills. On a 22-incher, you can easily cook enough chicken breasts or hamburgers to feed six to eight people.

Hot Tip

One of the easiest maintenance tips for keeping the cooking grid in good shape: Oil it before cooking. This will keep food from sticking to it, and make cleanup much easier. You can use your basting brush to lightly wipe on a thin coating of oil, or simply coat it with nonstick cooking spray.

Although you'd never guess it from the sea of kettles on backyard decks, charcoal grills do come in other shapes. Some are shaped like horizontal barrels; others, like rectangular boxes. Many of these non–kettle grills are designed for serious barbecuing, and may feature extra-large cooking surfaces, heavy-gauge steel construction, adjustable racks, and the ability to smoke or grill in the same box. Highly popular, these are the kinds of grills you'll see at the annual church picnic.

Another grill is the brazier, a shallow round grill without a lid that once was found everywhere in suburbia but has largely vanished, except for a few small models (see Tabletop Grills).

Some charcoal grills allow you to adjust the cooking grid. Big, commercial-size grills often have a pulley allowing you to raise or lower the rack. Home grills may just have brackets inside in two different places, so you can choose where to put the rack. Unless you're a serious barbecuer (in which case you'll probably have a serious, smoker-type grill), adjustable racks probably aren't that important. Nearly all food is grilled 4 to 6 inches from the coals, which is just where the standard rack sits.

Pros and Cons

The advantage of charcoal is that, for aficionados, it's the only way to get that true, smoke-kissed, wood-grilled flavor. It's also inexpensive. The initial grill costs anywhere from $80 to $200. Deluxe kettle models can run $400 and up, but that includes a gas ignition system and a deluxe cart. Charcoal is cheap, too, even if you use the pure hardwood charcoal we recommend. (See Chapter 5, "Fire and Smoke.")

Charcoal grills are reliable; since there are no moving parts, ignitions (except in a few high-end grills), and other potential trouble spots, they last practically forever with little maintenance. Buying one is as simple as running down to the hardware or discount store and looking for the best price. The only choice you have to make is size and, sometimes, shape.

The disadvantages of charcoal grills? They are dirtier than gas—you have to clean up the ashes. They can be a hassle to get started, controlling the cooking temperature is much more of an art than a science, and they're easily affected by the whims of weather, as anyone who's tried to grill during a cold rainstorm can attest. They tend to require more hands-on attention, especially for indirect cooking, in which you have to replenish the coals every 45 minutes or so. However, this makes little difference for most types of grill foods, which cook up relatively quickly (precisely why planning ahead is so important).

The charcoal grills' very simplicity also limits the extras you can have. Forget side burners. You've either got heat or no heat.

Cleaning and Maintenance

Besides choosing and installing your grill, it's important to maintain it and keep it clean.

For kettle grills, at the end of the season, use a brass-bristled brush to clean off the cooking rack and any flaking, baked-on grease on the inside of the kettle lid. Never use the brush on the outside; it'll scratch the finish. You also can use very fine (000) soapy steel wool.

Empty out all the ashes. Get a big bucket of warm water with some dish soap in it and a big sponge. Sponge down the grill with soapy water, inside and out. Then just hose it down completely to rinse it off. Let it sit outdoors in the sun until totally dry, then stick it in the garage or another covered storage space away from the elements. If you have a canvas or vinyl grill cover, use it to keep off spider webs and dust. When it's time to pull the grill out for the season, all you'll need to do is dust or hose off the outside.

If you have a porcelain-enamel coating on the outside, never paint, wax, or use a metal brush on the exterior. Don't use caustic cleaners, such as bleach or dishwasher detergent, on either the inside or outside of the grill. They can ruin the finish.

If you live in one of those climates where you can grill year-round comfortably in the outdoors (though for hard-core grillers, weather is no obstacle), clean your grill this way a couple of times a year.

Don't Get Burned!

When you store your grill for the season, be sure to put the lid on and close all the vents. Otherwise, little critters attracted by the food smells may decide a nice, big kettle is a great place to set up housekeeping.

For day-to-day maintenance, the most important thing is to keep the ashes emptied. If they build up, they can obstruct airflow through the vents.

You should clean off the cooking grid every time you get ready to cook. It's easiest to just burn the gunk off. Stick the cooking grid over the coals while they're still red hot, and cover the grill for about 5 minutes. Then scrape the residue off the grid with a brass-bristled brush.

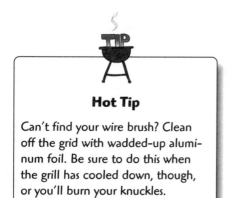

Hot Tip

Can't find your wire brush? Clean off the grid with wadded-up aluminum foil. Be sure to do this when the grill has cooled down, though, or you'll burn your knuckles.

Every once in a while, you may want to scrub down the grid with hot soapy water, then give it a good rinse.

Clean the brass-bristled brush by soaking it in hot water to which you've added a bit of dishwasher detergent. Be sure to rinse well; dishwasher detergent residue can give your chicken a pretty foul flavor.

Gas Grills

Gas grills are becoming more popular every year. They've come a long way from the "scorch it" school of cooking. They're more expensive than charcoal grills, but not outrageously so. You can easily spend thousands for a top-of-the-line grill, but you also can get a perfectly decent grill for $200 to $300.

While the high-end grills generally do a great job, price is not the only indicator. The best way to buy a gas grill is to ask various friends and colleagues for recommendations. Ask them what kinds of foods they grill most often, and what they like and don't like about their grills.

Choosing a Grill

Nearly all gas grills run on liquid propane. The tank sits underneath the grill. You no longer need tools to assemble most of them, but check. Some models also have a natural-gas hookup, so if you have a gas line handy, you can utilize this. Obviously, your grill isn't portable, so make sure it's where you want it.

Gas grills work pretty much like stoves. Fuel flows through a flexible hose into the grill, and you push a button or turn a knob to produce a spark. Some newer grills have electronic ignitions, like gas ranges. They usually require a battery to run, but are more reliable than grills with the old ignitions.

Most gas grills have two or three burners. Some cheaper models have only one, while upper-end models may have six or more. Some have one burner with individual controls for each side, which you can count as two burners. Because it's important to good grilling to be able to move the food off direct heat, we recommend a grill with at least two burners or burner controls. The ones with three burners give better cooking control, but may cost a bit more. Most burners are made of stainless steel and should last a long time, usually the life of the grill.

Gas grills use various types of heat distributors, which sit atop the flame and also act as flavoring elements. Some use metal plates or bars; others use briquets made of ceramic or pumice, a porous stone. These materials help distribute the heat evenly from the burners, and as the juices from the food drip onto them, they create smoke, helping to give grilled foods a charcoal flavor. Briquets or lava rocks need to be turned occasionally, and are more subject to flare-ups. Bars shaped like upside-down Vs do a good job of letting grease run off, reducing the chance of flare-ups. Plates that cover the bottom of the grill are best at keeping flare-ups to a minimum.

Obviously, the heat distributors catch a lot of grease and smoke buildup, so if you keep the grill a long time, plan on replacing them sooner or later. As long as they don't get chipped, porcelain-enameled bars are easy to clean and hold up well.

Cooking grates on gas grills may be the standard skinny rods found on typical charcoal grills, or wide bars set close together—the best for keeping foods from dropping through. Porcelain-coated steel is easiest to clean; stainless steel holds up well.

Don't Get Burned!

While it's possible to convert some propane grills to natural gas, never do so without consulting the manufacturer. Propane is under pressure, and uses a smaller hose and connection than natural gas, which must flow freely. Converting a grill to natural gas usually requires new parts and connections.

Cast iron can rust if you don't season it properly (follow the manufacturer's directions) and keep it coated with oil. An adjustable rack is a nicety that allows you to raise or lower the food from the coals.

Paying more for a gas grill will get you more features, such as a sturdier cart, better performance at grill-roasting and slow cooking, and more optional features. One of the most popular of these additional features is a side burner, so you can cook side dishes while you grill other foods, or reheat the marinade to enhance the flavor of your grilled food while keeping food safety in mind. Other upgrades include a warming rack, to keep one batch of foods hot while you grill another; shelves—a great convenience; fuel gauges; electronic ignitions; smoking boxes, to hold wood chips; extra burners; larger work surfaces or storage space; condiment racks; and stainless-steel finishes.

Burners come in various shapes and materials. The most common burner shape is an "H." Some are oval; others are long, thin rectangles. If you need to replace the burners, make sure they're the same shape as the original. Aluminized steel, similar to galvanized steel, is used in less expensive grills. Porcelain-coated steel is sometimes used, but the most common is stainless steel in varying thicknesses. Some grills have cast-iron burners, which must be oiled so they don't rust. Cast brass, which lasts the longest, is used on some very expensive grills.

To clean the burners, use the wire grill brush to scrape off corrosion or oily residue. If any of the holes are clogged, you can open them with a metal paper clip bent straight. If the burners are really corroded, you should replace them.

Always keep long matches handy; if the igniter goes out, you'll have to light the grill manually. Check the instruction book for directions.

Pros and Cons

Gas grills have several advantages over their charcoal counterparts. They're cleaner, are less of a hassle to start, heat up faster, and are less dependent on weather. It's no coincidence that people with gas grills are more likely to cook year-round (64 percent, compared with 41 percent of charcoal-grill owners).

The disadvantages are that gas grills can be a pain to assemble, they're generally more expensive than charcoal grills, and you have to deal with replacing the propane tank. Like all gas appliances, they can pose a danger if not installed and maintained properly.

Perhaps the biggest disadvantage, to true barbecue aficionados, is that you don't get the same flavor. Gas grills flavor foods by juices dripping onto the briquets or flavor bars, so they're actually more like broilers than real barbecues.

Cleaning and Maintenance

To keep gas grills in good working order, follow the manufacturer's instructions. Models that use pumice or ceramic briquets will often require that you turn them occasionally to clean them. Another important thing with a gas grill is to check that the fuel pipe does not get clogged. Some gas grills have insect guards, to keep your friendly neighborhood spider from building webs or nests in your gas pipe.

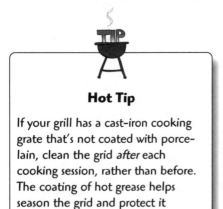

Hot Tip

If your grill has a cast-iron cooking grate that's not coated with porcelain, clean the grid *after* each cooking session, rather than before. The coating of hot grease helps season the grid and protect it from rust.

To clean the cooking grid, turn the burners to high, close the lid, and wait until the grill stops smoking, about 5 to 10 minutes. Then use the wire brush to scrape off the residue. When the grid cools down, you can remove it and clean it with warm, soapy water.

Keep the bottom tray and grease catch pan clean. This will help prevent grease fires, and also discourage visits from four-legged neighborhood critters.

Fairly often, you should change the liner for the catch pan. If the grill lid has smoke stains, use fine soapy steel wool to clean it off. Don't scrub too vigorously; a light touch will do it. (Note: To clean a cover over the side burner, use warm soapy water and a sponge, never steel wool.)

If you have porcelain-coated metal bars as heat distributors , most of the residue will burn off. Just scrub them every now and then with a brass-bristled brush. If your grill has lava rocks or ceramic briquets, you need to turn them every now and then to clean them, and occasionally replace them. Follow the manufacturer's instruction booklet.

Clean the outside of the grill occasionally with warm, soapy water, and try to clean up grease spills immediately, preferably while the grill is still slightly warm—not hot! Don't use harsh cleaners, which can ruin the finish.

If you have cast-iron cooking grids, lightly oil them after cleaning to keep them from rusting.

Electric Grills

Electric grills range from the high-end, indoor cooking grates found on fancy cooktops to outdoor grills that plug into a handy outlet. They're still pretty rare compared with gas and charcoal grills; only about 3 percent of U.S. households have an electric grill.

Because they don't tend to get as hot as gas or charcoal grills, electric grills often feature nonstick cooking surfaces.

Pros and Cons

In general, grilling mavens don't like them compared with gas and charcoal. They don't get as hot. They don't come in the assortment of sizes (and often tend to be small). They're more expensive to run.

They are, however, a good choice—and often the only choice—if you live in a 23rd-floor apartment with a small balcony, or if you go camping a lot with your RV. They also are cleaner than both charcoal and gas.

Cleaning and Maintenance

You clean electric grills like any other electrical appliance. Obviously, you cannot submerge or hose down any of the electrical parts. But the cooking grid can be cleaned with soapy water. Wipe down the grill now and then with a cloth.

Tabletop and Portable Grills

Tabletop grills come in charcoal, gas, or electric versions. The electric ones can be used indoors. They don't offer much of a cooking surface and are good for cooking only quick cuts, but they're very portable, which makes them great for picnics and camping.

What's What

One of the most famous of the tabletop grills is the Japanese *hibachi*. A small, rectangular grill, it has a stand, rather than legs, so it won't tip over, and a fairly heavy cooking grid that can be adjusted by fitting it into notches on the side.

If you're tight on space (grilling on that balcony, for example), a tabletop grill might be all you want. Note that they're really only suitable for grilling enough for one to two people.

Of course, you can also just buy a grill pan—a heavy pan with evenly spaced ridges that produce grill marks on food—and use it on your stove.

Specialty Grills

Two specialty grills with devoted followings are the Kamado and its cousin, The Big Green Egg. Both are inspired by the kamado, a ceramic cooker that originated in China 3,000 years ago and was popular in Japan, where U.S. servicemen discovered it after World War II. Their manufacturers and devotees say the extra-thick, ceramic walls and bell (or egg) shapes of these grills provide more precise control over cooking temperature.

The Kamado is larger and prettier than The Big Green Egg—its outside is decorated with tiles in various colors. It also has thicker walls. But essentially, both grills are very similar.

Tasty Tidbit

Another famous clay grill is the tandoor, used in India and in Indian restaurants here. The tandoor looks much like a bell-shaped clay jar, which sits in the ground or another enclosure. The interior walls of a tandoor can get as hot as 900°F, which explains how your favorite Indian restaurant can serve you a tasty half of a tandoori chicken only 15 minutes after you order it.

Cooking in clay retains moisture, so a water pan is not needed. The manufacturers also claim that because of the insulation provided by the thick clay walls, you get a wider range of temperatures—from very low to very high, making the kamado-type grill suitable for both slow-smoking and searing.

The disadvantages? Both grills are pretty expensive, not widely available, and very heavy (the large Kamado weighs 248 pounds). Ceramic can weaken or even crack if you drop it or if you splash water on it when it's hot.

Another specialty grill, which is still pretty rare, is the pellet grill. Pellet stoves, which are popular in some Western states, burn small pellets made of wood, compressed sawdust, and fillers. Pellets burn more efficiently than whole wood, with fewer emissions and less smoke. A couple of the stove manufacturers have started making these types of grills. They're similar to convection ovens. The pellets are fed through a hopper and ignited.

True barbecue aficionados, the people who roam the country from one grilling contest to another, often construct their own grills. Some of these contraptions are wondrous to behold.

Build-Your-Own Pits

For true grilling rituals, such as cooking for a crowd, you usually have to build your own grill. Some folks dig an actual pit—this is easy to do if you're grilling clams on the beach—but that may not always be possible or desirable. Instead, you can build your own grill on the spot with cement blocks. The dimensions depend on how big the pig, lamb, or side of beef is, or how many you're roasting, but it should be at least 3 blocks wide by 5 blocks long, and 18 inches deep. You make a cooking grid out of metal rods inserted into the cement blocks, and top that with a metal screen to hold the meat.

You must start with real wood (often oak) and burn it down until it's mostly charcoal before you can start cooking. Needless to say, pit barbecuing is not something you do on the spur of the moment—though it does make for a great party.

You can build a simple barbecue box in the backyard using this method. If you have trouble visualizing it, you can buy plans at home-building centers and some hardware stores.

Smokers

A word about jargon here: What manufacturers and most of us call "smoking" is actually what most true barbecue fans (and there are a lot of them out there) call "barbecuing." When you order the baby back ribs or pulled pork at your favorite barbecue joint—you know, the one with all those fragrant trailers or the smoke shack out back—you're getting meat that is cooked in a long, slow process that involves smoke. You can't duplicate this at home on a standard grill. You have to use a smoker, or a deep grill that's capable of both grilling and smoking.

"Real" Wood Smokers

These are for serious barbecuing, the kind that involves cooking a brisket or three turkeys for 25 of your closest friends. They're used mostly for large cookouts. If you are a serious barbecuer, the kind who roams the country looking for contests to win, this is what you need.

These babies weigh a minimum of 200 to 300 pounds, and some much more. There's one big difference between a smoker and the standard grill: the firebox is separate from the cooking

Tasty Tidbits

About 1 out of 10 grill owners owns a water smoker as well. One in 20 owns a horizontal wood smoker in addition to a regular grill.

area. It's off to one side. The cooking chamber has a chimney in it. A baffle between the firebox and cooking chamber forces the smoke and heat underneath the food before it escapes out the chimney. The food cooks slowly in this "bath" of smoke and heat. The firebox may have a lid that can be raised, turning it into a grill. Some wood smokers also have a water chamber beneath the cooking grid(s), which helps keep foods from drying out.

The advantage to this kind of smoker is that the slow, gentle cooking makes meats taste out of this world. The disadvantage is that you need a trailer to haul these smokers around, and you may have to experiment a lot to master this type of cookery.

Water Smokers

The most common smokers for home use are water smokers, which come in charcoal, electric, and, less commonly, gas versions. They are shaped like a big upright cylinder on legs. The bottom is the firebox, where you put the charcoal and/or wood chunks. Above that or next to it is the water pan, and the food sits on a rack above that. Some smokers have two racks, which gives them a bigger capacity. The food is tightly covered and often spends hours, rather than minutes, in the smoker. As the water boils, it creates a flavorful, smoky steam that bastes the food as it cooks.

Choosing One

This is pretty easy since there really aren't that many different water smokers and they're pretty basic. Your basic choice is usually between charcoal or electric, and various capacities. Some smokers have only one rack, others have two. Most have a door in the side so you can easily feed in additional charcoal.

Pros and Cons

Water smokers are easier to use than wood smokers. However, wood smokers impart a better flavor. Electric smokers are easier to use, since you don't have to keep replenishing charcoal.

Cleaning and Maintenance

Again, follow the manufacturer's directions. Since a smoker is basically a specialized charcoal grill, the cleaning and maintenance is much the same. (For an electric smoker, consult the owner's manual. Because the water pan is permanent, it should be cleaned frequently in hot, soapy water so it doesn't get all grimed up.

The Least You Need to Know

➤ Charcoal gives a more "authentic" flavor to barbecued foods, but gas is more convenient.

➤ Cleaning and maintaining the grill is as important as choosing the proper one.

➤ For long, slow barbecuing, you need a smoker.

Chapter 3

The Extra Touch

In This Chapter

➤ Tools that are essential to good grilling

➤ Tools that are helpful, but not necessary

➤ "Toys" for the griller with money to spare

➤ Kitchen tools to make food preparation easier

You didn't really think you would just buy a grill and be done with it, did you? Like any other sport, grilling requires an assortment of specialized equipment. Some of it is absolutely vital to smooth grilling and outdoor entertaining, and some is merely helpful. Then there's the category of grilling "toys," fun items that you don't need at all—at least until you've convinced yourself (and your spouse) that you really, truly cannot grill without them.

Nearly all of these accessories are inexpensive and readily available in supermarkets, cookware stores, discount or department stores, hardware stores, and/or home-building centers. For less common accessories or those, such as rotisseries, that are specific to certain grills, you might have to look in a shop devoted to barbecuing supplies, or contact the manufacturer of your grill.

The Core Collection

This handy list of all of the must-haves of grilling includes several items already in your home that you'll simply not want to forget when planning your grilling session.

Hot Tip

Most barbecue tool sets come with one pair of tongs. But you'll need a second set. That way, you'll have one pair of tongs for the coals, and one for the food.

Tools

Why can't you just use your kitchen tongs and spatula? Because their handles are too short to offer you protection against the searing heat of hot coals. Barbecue utensils have extra-long handles. They're cheaper by the set: fork, tong, spatula. Get a good stainless-steel set with flameproof plastic or composite handles. Wood handles tend to scorch and can look ratty when they're kept outside for any length of time.

One handy variation on the spatula combines a spatula and tongs. The top lever is tongs; the bottom is a spatula.

Pot Holders and Mitts

To keep your hands away from the heat, you should use barbecue mitts, extra-long, flame-retardant "mittens" that protect your hands and lower arms from the coals' intense heat. Because the mitts can be fairly clumsy, you'll also want a pair of extra-thick pot holders with a flame-retardant coating.

Grill Screen

A flat, portable metal grid designed to sit atop the grill's cooking grid, the grill screen has mesh or holes set closely together. It's designed to keep small foods such as sliced onions and shrimp from taking a nosedive through the wires of the grid and into the coals. Most grill screens have handles and nonstick surfaces, making them easy to move around and clean. A variation on the flat grill screen has deeper, sloping sides, similar to a wok's, making it easier to turn or toss foods.

Hot Tip

Haven't gotten around to getting a grill screen yet? You can mimic one by folding foil to make a double thickness, and punching holes all over it with a fork or knife. Set the foil on the cooking grid, and the food on top of that.

Grill Brush

You can clean the cooking grid with wadded-up foil, but a grill brush works much better. It has stiff metal bristles that easily scrape cooked-on grease off the wires of the grid. There's no need to spend a fortune on this implement—it's going to get pretty grimy, and you'll just want to replace it anyway at some point.

Basting Brushes

You should also have at least two brushes for basting food. Having more than one allows you to baste different foods with different sauces at the same time. Among those we find useful:

➤ An all-purpose basting brush with a long handle and wide, angled bristles. This makes it easy to spread sauces over large amounts of food.

➤ A basting mop. Made of cotton string attached to a wooden handle, these brushes are basically a miniature version of your kitchen mop. They're ideal for slathering foods with thin sauces, like those wonderful vinegar-based sauces that are essential to a Carolina pig-pickin'.

➤ A round brush for brushing small game birds and long skewers of meat and kebabs and for dabbing a bit of sauce into hard-to-reach cavities.

Whichever brushes you buy, be sure to clean them thoroughly in hot soapy water, both to keep them from getting gummed up and to prevent the growth of bacteria.

Hot Tip

Appalled by the prices the cookware store wants for decent basting brushes? Check out long-handled, narrow paintbrushes at the local hardware store for an alternative. Don't get the really cheap kind, though—they'll shed bristles into your food.

Skewers

It's one of the unwritten laws of grilling: sooner or later, you will cook kebabs. That means you will need either bamboo or metal skewers to thread through the chunks of meats and vegetables. Bamboo skewers are inexpensive, have a rough surface that grips food well, and can be discarded when you're through with them. However, they do have to be soaked in water for 20 to 30 minutes and drained before you use them, so they don't catch fire.

Metal skewers can be used over and over again, and usually are longer, so they'll hold more food. They are slippery and don't grip foods well, so the meat tends to spin when you turn the skewer. The exposed surfaces also get very hot during cooking.

If you make kebabs often, you might want to spring for double skewers, which look like giant bobby pins and help keep the food in place, or even a kebab rack, a whole set of skewers set in a rack, with a rod in the middle that turns them. Or, you can just thread the meat and vegetables on two skewers, instead of one, to keep them from slipping off.

Food Thermometer

For thicker cuts of meat, a thermometer is the best way to tell if the food is really cooked through. Some meat thermometers are intended to stay in the food during cooking, but they tend to get gunked up with grease and hard to read. We recommend an instant-read thermometer. You stick it in the cooked food, wait for about a minute,

Tasty Tidbits

Shish kebab originated in the Middle East, probably with meat skewered on swords.

or until the needle stops moving, and get a reading. Some grills come with thermometers.

Knives

You'll also need at least one good knife, and preferably three or four. These are not just for grilling, of course, but are essential kitchen tools. The best knives are made of forged carbon steel. They hold up well as long as you keep them dry. If they stay wet, they can rust.

What's What

Choose the right knife for the job. *Chef's knives* have thick, heavy blades, and are all-purpose chopping and slicing utensils. *Carving knives* have very long, fairly thin blades, and are strictly for slicing. *Boning knives* have thin, curved blades designed to cut meat off the bone. *Paring knives* have short blades suitable for peeling and other detail work.

Cutting Boards

You'll need at least one good cutting board, in acrylic or solid wood. Besides having a cutting board in your kitchen, you might want to keep a second one handy to the grill. For best results, use a board with a trench around the outside to collect juices. Just be sure to clean the cutting board thoroughly with hot, soapy water (or in the dishwasher, if it's acrylic) after each use.

Though experts were at one point saying that acrylic boards were safer against collecting harmful bacteria from raw meats, there is now some disagreement on the subject. Knife ridges in acrylic can apparently host bacteria just as well as wood—whatever you choose, it's just important to keep it clean by washing carefully after each use.

Charcoal Dividers or Holders

These help keep briquets in a neat pile and stop them from tumbling into the drip pan when you're cooking over indirect heat. Some are simply standup racks that sit between the water pan and charcoal; others are actual containers that you fill with charcoal. Obviously, you can skip these if you have a gas grill. Many charcoal grills come with these racks as standard equipment.

Fire Starters

If you have a gas grill, the fire starter is that little spark that ignites the propane when you turn that handy knob. If you have a charcoal grill or smoker, you'll need one or more of these:

➤ Charcoal chimney. This ingenious but simple device offers a very efficient way to light charcoal. Basically, it's a metal can with a shelf inside and a heatproof handle outside. You fill the top with charcoal and the bottom with wadded-up newspaper, and light the newspaper. As it burns, it ignites the coals in the bottom, which in turn gradually ignite the coals above them.

➤ Electric starters. These glowing wands are very efficient for lighting coals, and are very tidy. You just put the starter in the grill, pile charcoal on top of it, and plug it in. Obviously, this kind of starter will do you no good unless you have an electrical outlet near the grill.

➤ Long fireplace matches. To light the charcoal, and to light your gas grill if you need to do so manually. Don't use regular matches, which aren't long enough to keep your hands free of any flaring flame. As an alternative, you can use a utility lighter, which works like a cigarette lighter, but has a long wand that allows you to light the coals without getting your hands too close to them. Some lighters have a child-resistant guard.

Tasty Tidbit

The charcoal chimney started out life as a coffee can. Generations of Boy Scouts and cowboys knew that if you punched holes around the bottom part of a coffee can, filled the can with charcoal and lit it, you'd have glowing coals in no time.

Work Table

If your grill didn't come with one, better get one. You'll need something handy for carving meats, cutting into chicken to see if it's done, slicing foods into serving portions, and so on. For kettle grills, you can get a work table that hooks onto the side of the grill. Or, get a small, freestanding table.

Ice Bucket and/or Cooler

This is not directly related to grill-cooking, of course, but since by its nature, most grilling is done for outdoor parties, you can either have something to store ice in, or run back and forth to the freezer—and who needs that? A cooler can be used both for ice and for storing cans of soda and such, but an ice bucket adds a bit more class.

Don't Get Burned!

If your tray has a smooth surface, things can slide right off, especially if you need to go up or down stairs to get to the deck or patio. Get a piece of the bumpy vinyl that's used to keep dishes in place on shelves or to keep throw rugs from slipping, and cut a piece to fit the inside of the tray.

Tray

Carrying foods and dishes in and out of the house gets old fast. A large tray makes the toting much easier.

Tool Holder

One popular tool rack has three or four hooks, and hangs from the side of the grill. While these are handy, they do tend to lift up when you tug a tool off. A better bet, if possible, is to use screw-in hooks and hang the tools in a place handy to the grill.

Drip Pans

You'll need these for indirect cooking on charcoal grills, to keep the food moist and away from the coals. Disposable cake pans are ideal for this. They're not too sturdy, so use two of them, one nested inside the other. The bigger the surface area, the better. We recommend the 12-by-8 or 13-by-9-inch foil cake pans for most purposes.

Aluminum Foil

You'll need this to wrap delicate foods such as fish or vegetables, and to cover already-grilled foods while you finish cooking the rest of the batch. It also can come in handy if you've misplaced your grill brush. Crumple the foil into a ball and use it to scrub the grease off the cooking grid. (Caution: don't do this when the grid is hot.)

Small Watering Can

The spout makes it easy to replenish the water in the drip pan without splashing water on the hot coals. You'll need this only if you're using a charcoal grill or a smoker.

Spray Bottle

Fill it with water and keep it by the grill, so you can easily put out minor flare-ups. Again, you'll need this only if you grill over charcoal.

Scoop for Briquets

A large plastic flour scoop is ideal. With a scoop, you don't have to plunge your hands into the charcoal bag, getting soot up to your elbows.

Garbage Bags

This is something that's easy to overlook. There you are, standing at the grill, holding a wadded-up greasy paper towel or ball of foil, and realizing that there's no place to toss it. And, of course, your guests need someplace to throw away the paper plates. Actually, it's not a bad idea to have a small wastebasket or garbage can designated just for outdoor parties. Put it somewhere where it won't collect water when it rains (or turn it upside down when it's not in use). And be sure to change the bag after every grilling/eating session, or you'll have raccoons or other "friends" rooting around on the deck.

Fire Extinguisher

If you've set the grill away from flammable objects and take care in grilling, the chance that you'll need a fire extinguisher handy is about nil. However, you should definitely have one in the kitchen. And if your kitchen is handy to the grill . . . well, it's nice to know the extinguisher is there, just in case.

Nice, But You Can Live Without Them

Hinged Cooking Grid

These look like a standard round cooking grid, except that they're hinged on two sides. They make indirect cooking much easier. You simply lift up the hinged ends of the grid and drop more into the fire. Hinged grids are standard on many new charcoal grills.

Grill Lifter

This implement is designed to slip under the wires of the cooking grid and lift it up, so you don't have to handle it when it's hot. Frankly, we think a combination of a barbecue mitt and a barbecue fork (slide it under a handle) works fine. A hinged cooking grid is even handier.

Smoker Box

This metal container holds wood chips used to impart flavor to foods. It sits in the base of a gas or electric grill. It contains the ashes so they can't clog the starter.

Cart

If your grill doesn't come with one, consider buying one. It makes moving the grill around, as well as storing the charcoal, easier.

Rotisserie

If you often cook whole chickens or other poultry, roasts, and other big pieces of meat, a *rotisserie* can come in handy. It turns the meat as it cooks, so that it roasts more evenly. You must have an electrical outlet handy. Be sure to get a rotisserie designed for your make of grill, so it will fit.

What's What

A *rotisserie* consists of a long rod, or *spit,* with prongs on either end to hold the food in place. At one end is a small motor, which rotates the rod with the food on it, helping larger cuts of meat and poultry to cook more evenly.

Food Holders

Vertical roasters are small racks that keep a chicken or an ear of corn upright. A horizontal rack is designed for roasts. None of these are essential, but help in cooking the meat evenly and, in the case of the vertical roasters, you don't have to turn the meat or vegetables while they cook.

Warming Rack

This fits on the side of a charcoal or gas grill over the cooking grid. It's ideal for warming hamburger buns and quick-cooking vegetables. A lot of grills come with warming racks as standard equipment. Bear in mind, though, that a hamburger bun can also be heated quickly right on the grill, toasting it up and adding attractive grill marks.

Cooking Bags

Reynolds Aluminum makes heavy-duty foil bags that you fill with meats and vegetables, then put on the grill. They eliminate cleanup, and are especially suitable for more delicate foods that might not stand up that well to direct grilling.

You also can buy perforated aluminum bags that contain wood chips and sugar. You put the meat inside the bag and lay it on the grill. The chips and sugar flavor the meat, and the sugar also helps brown it.

Burger Press

If you've got a thing about perfectly round (or square) burgers, better get one of these. At least one burger press puts spiral grooves in the meat, which supposedly make it cook faster. It will also keep the kids from fighting over the bigger burger.

Oven Thermometer

If your grill or smoker does not have a built-in thermometer, setting an oven thermometer on the cooking grid can give you at least a rough idea of the interior temperature.

Grill Baskets

These hinged, long-handled metal baskets make turning more delicate foods, such as fish or vegetables, easier. They come in different shapes, with square being the most popular. A fish basket is a grill basket shaped like a fish. As the name implies, it's for grilling fish, especially whole fish. There's nothing more frustrating than having your perfectly grilled fish fall through the grid.

Condiment Shelf

This hangs from the side of the grill and holds barbecue sauce, ketchup, salt and pepper, or whatever.

Flashlight

Sooner or later, you'll probably be grilling in the dark, whether you intended to or not. If your deck or patio (or fancy grill) doesn't have a light that will illuminate the grilling area, having a flashlight handy is essential. Of course, if you want to get fancy, you can clip a halogen light to the grill table.

Vinyl or Canvas Grill Covers

They can help keep dirt, leaves and bird droppings off your grill. That is, if you remember to put them over the grill once it's cooled down.

Grillers' "Toys"

Poultry Shears

Few folks outside of the food professions have these, but they can come in handy if you have a sudden urge to butterfly your own Cornish hens. (Butterflying your poultry speeds the cooking time—see Chapter 12, "Birds of a Feather," for details.)

Barbecue Glasses

For toy value, these rank up there with those onion-flower makers you see on TV. They're goggles designed to keep the smoke out of your eyes when you grill. For those who lack that final grill accessory, and enjoy the serious look of "grill expert" that the goggles naturally impart to the wearer.

Silly Aprons and Hats

You don't need these at all, but hey, they're a tradition. What's suburban barbecuing without silly slogans on Dad's apron? Also recommended are the logo T-shirts your cousins sent you from their last vacation.

Cast-Iron Griddle

This can be nice for fajitas and such, but unless you're into making pancakes on the grill, you really don't need one.

Heat-Resistant Gloves

The gloves come in two varieties, one for picking up food and one for picking up a hot grill by the handles. A little more nimble than those oversize mitts, they can come in handy if you cook a large cut, such as a whole turkey or a roast, which is easiest to turn with your hands. They're also good for turning metal skewers.

Baking Tiles or Stone

For those times when you want to recapture that woodburning pizza experience. Baking tiles are basically thick, unglazed, high-fired quarry tiles; baking stones are, indeed, made of a light stone. You'll want these if you plan to make pizza or similar breads on the grill. Some cookware stores sell baking tiles and a grilling screen as a set.

Pizza Peel or Paddle

This is basically a long-handled giant spatula, made of all wood or of metal and wood, used to transfer pizza or focaccia to the grill and to remove it when it's done. Again, you only need this if you like to grill pizza or other breads.

Light Strings

Somewhere along the line, some savvy marketing type realized that Christmas lights needn't be confined to the holidays. You can buy lights in the shape of pumpkins, ears of corn, chiles, fish—you name it. Definitely not essential, but they add a festive atmosphere to evening parties.

Citronella Candles or Torches

If you don't have a screened-in patio, these can help keep mosquitoes at bay, more or less. And they're much trendier and smell nicer than bug-repellent spray. Just make sure the smoke won't be blowing in your guests' faces.

The Least You Need to Know

➤ Regular kitchen tools don't cut it for most barbecuing purposes—get grilling utensils.

➤ Along with standard grilling accessories, don't forget the other, easily overlooked indispensables, such as garbage bags, foil, and a good knife.

➤ You need only a few "core" accessories, but there are plenty of other tools and gadgets that can make grilling easier or more fun.

The Proper Provisions

In This Chapter

➤ Basic food preparation

➤ Spices, and what they go with

➤ Buying and storing perishable foods

Now that you've got the grill and all the accessories set up, all you need is the food. If you like to fire up the barbecue but have never turned on the oven, bread flour probably isn't high on your list of priorities. So we've confined the list to the sorts of foodstuffs you're most likely to use in grilling and smoking. We've also added a minisection on food preparation, in case you're a kitchen novice.

Herbs and spices play a big role, since they are frequently used as both seasonings and *aromatics* on the grill.

What's What

An *aromatic* is an herb, spice, or other ingredient that you sprinkle onto the coals or into the drip pan to perfume the smoke and enhance a food's flavor.

The Griller's Spice Rack

Spice and smoke—ah, what a combination. Barbecue means spice: the rub on a Texas brisket, the secret ingredients in a Memphis barbecue master's sauce. Here are some you may find useful.

Allspice

A bit like cloves, but not as sharp and a bit sweeter. Allspice is a key component in Jamaican cooking and in jerk, a Jamaican rub for grilled meats.

Basil

Sweet-sharp and with undertones of anise, basil goes with almost anything. Use it fresh if possible. Dried basil is not bad, but just doesn't have the full flavor.

Bay Leaves

A wonderful aromatic tossed onto the coals, or placed in the cavity of a whole chicken or fish. Remember to remove the bay leaf before eating, though, because it is inedible.

Chives

This mildly onion-flavored herb was born to go with fish and potatoes.

Cilantro

This is the fresh leafy herb; coriander is the seed of the same plant. It has a very assertive minty-peppery flavor that is commonly found in Southeast Asian, Mexican, and U.S. Southwestern cooking. Great in salsas, with potatoes, corn, most meats, poultry, and fish. Use it fresh; it loses a lot of its flavor when dried.

Cinnamon

Although it's usually associated with sweets (just think cinnamon rolls), cinnamon is used for savory dishes in the U.S. Southwest, and some parts of the Mediterranean. It's lovely with beef. Toss some cinnamon sticks onto the coals for a delicious smoke.

Coriander

Citrusy-peppery, this fairly assertive spice is good with poultry, and also makes a good aromatic.

Hot Tip

Dried herbs and spices make wonderful aromatics for grilling. Soak them for about 5 minutes, squeeze out the moisture, and sprinkle them either directly on the coals, or in the water pan if you're cooking over indirect heat. Watch out for seeds such as mustard and coriander, though; heat makes them pop.

Cumin

Sharp and a little musty, cumin is used around the world. In the United States, it's probably used most heavily in the Southwest, where it helps gives sauces and rubs that distinct "Tex-Mex" flavor. It is commonly a flavor component of chili.

Dill

With its grassy-citrus flavor, dill seed or fresh dill was born to go with fish, but is also nice with lamb and poultry.

Fennel

This licorice-tasting spice is nice with fish or pork sausages (it's a key seasoning in Italian sausage), and sprinkled over the coals or in the water pan. It is a seed that actually resembles a cumin seed very much. Also, distinguish between fennel the spice, and fennel the vegetable, which is a celerylike bulb, popular in Italian cooking.

Garlic

Ah, where would the world be without it? Fresh garlic is superb when it's roasted on the grill (see Chapter 14). Don't toss garlic on the coals, though, because it turns acrid when it burns. You can put fresh, granulated, or powdered garlic in the drip pan when you smoke foods or cook them over indirect heat.

Green Onions (Scallions)

Supermarkets label them "green onions," but they're actually scallions. (Green onions are more bulbous on the bottom.) These are not only good in marinades, but are fabulous brushed lightly with oil and grilled until they're lightly charred and softened.

Marjoram and/or Oregano

The pizza herb, and it's great with any tomato-based sauce. It also enlivens poultry, especially with lemon, and goes well with mushrooms. Don't toss it on the coals; it smells remarkably like another herb that is illegal.

Mint

Fresh spearmint or peppermint makes a lovely seasoning for fish, lamb, poultry, and yogurt or citrus-based sauces.

Hot Tip

One delightful way to use herbs, especially fresh ones, is to finely chop them and mix them with a bit of softened butter to make herb butter. A dab of herb butter is wonderful on fish.

Onions

Like garlic, onions are wonderful roasted on the grill. They also turn acrid when burned, so leave them off the coals. You can put fresh, granulated, or powdered onion in the drip pan when you smoke foods or cook them over indirect heat.

Parsley

Peppery but pleasant, it enlivens nearly any dish. Italian (flat-leaf) parsley has a stronger flavor than curly parsley. Use it fresh; it doesn't retain much of its flavor dried. It doesn't do much as an aromatic.

Pepper (Black)

It adds a pungent-hot-fragrant note to just about anything, but is especially nice with more assertively flavored foods such as beef and salmon. It's great in rubs.

Pepper (Red)

An extra dose of fruity heat. Don't sprinkle red pepper on the coals; the smoke may burn your eyes. But do use it in rubs and sauces. Remember to wash your hands before touching your face.

Rosemary

Piney and sweet, this is a wondrous herb, both as a flavoring agent and an aromatic. It goes with pork, lamb, poultry, vegetables, and fruit. Use it on the food and on the coals. With the needles pulled off, a twig of rosemary also works great as an impromptu kebab

Tasty Tidbit

Greek fishermen use rosemary to preserve their catch. Scientists say those fisherman have the right idea, and rosemary is indeed a preservative. All the more reason to use it in that marinade.

skewer. If it's very dry, remember to soak it in water for 20 minutes before using it this way.

Sage

It has a strong but pleasant smoke, making it a good aromatic. Flavor-wise, this gray-green herb has a strong, almost medicinal flavor that's great with "autumn foods" such as pork, poultry, tomatoes, mushrooms, and squash. Sage is a common ingredient in the stuffing for the Thanksgiving turkey.

Tasty Tidbit

Some Native Americans in the Southwest burn sage (actually, a relative of the culinary herb) to purify their surroundings. It does have a cleansing, incenselike aroma.

Shallots

This member of the onion family grows in bulbs like garlic, and tastes like an onion with garlicky undertones. Shallots are superb with anything, and essential to Southeast Asian–style pastes and marinades.

Spice Blends

Blends of various spices or herbs can be quite convenient. Some popular ones for grilling include Cajun-style blend, Italian seasoning, chili powder, herbes de Provence, fines herbes, and lemon pepper.

Tarragon

Another anisey-flavored herb, French tarragon is sweet and delicious with fish, poultry, and most vegetables. You also can toss it onto the coals or in the water pan with white wine.

Thyme

Pungent and minty, this small-leafed herb goes nicely with beef, pork, poultry, tomatoes, and mushrooms.

Oils, Vinegars, and Condiments

Balsamic Vinegar

Traditionally, this vinegar is aged for years in barrels in Modena, Italy, until it turns dark, sweet, and utterly delicious. Nearly all the "balsamic vinegar" you buy in the states is actually balsamic vinegar mixed with red wine vinegar. (It's easy to spot genuine balsamic vinegar: It costs way, way more than you're ever likely to pay for a bottle of vinegar.) However, even this pale imitator is a very nice vinegar. It's good with all foods, either in the marinade or sprinkled on them just before serving.

Rice Vinegar

Its low acidity makes this an ideal vinegar for marinating more delicate foods. If you can find it (some Asian markets carry it), aged rice vinegar is truly mellow and delicious.

Wine Vinegars

White wine, red wine, and sherry vinegars are, of course, made from wine. Any of them are suitable for marinades.

Flavored Vinegars

Vinegars flavored with fruits or herbs make great marinades, and also are lovely sprinkled lightly on foods before serving. Try blueberry vinegar on fruit kebabs, or a dill-garlic vinegar on fish. Yum.

Olive Oil

For marinades, any regular olive oil, or *virgin olive oil* (a cold-pressed olive oil that's more acidic and slightly less flavorful than extra-virgin), is fine. For salads and finishing sauces, you might prefer the full, fruity flavor of *extra-virgin*. Olive oil is good for brushing lean foods such as chicken breast or fish so they don't stick to the grill or dry out during cooking.

What's What

Extra-virgin olive oil, from the first pressing of olives, is low in acid and rich in flavor. Drizzle it over foods such as cooked fish or vegetables. *Virgin olive oil* is also made from the first pressing, but is higher in acidity. Plain *olive oil,* which is fine for marinades and general cooking, is a blend of refined and extra-virgin or virgin olive oil.

Sesame Oil

Pressed from sesame seeds, this comes in two varieties: a clear yellow oil that's fine for cooking, and a dark reddish oil made from toasted sesame seeds. The latter, with a robust, nutty flavor, is usually drizzled on foods as a condiment.

Canola Oil

A clear, flavorless oil that's popular because it's lowest in saturated fat of all the vegetable oils. It tends to have a fishy odor when it burns, which of course makes it ideal for fish, but a bit less desirable for foods such as fruits. You can buy blends of canola and other vegetable (usually corn) oils.

Vegetable Oil

A flavorless, all-purpose oil that's usually made of soybeans. It's fine for marinades and for brushing foods.

Nonstick Cooking Spray

This mixture of oil and propellants is the quickest way to coat the cooking grid or grill screen with oil. If you're a purist, you can use special spray bottles that you fill with your own olive oil.

Barbecue Sauce

Face it—plenty of times you won't have the time or inclination to make your own. Experiment with different brands to get one with the flavor you prefer.

Hoisin Sauce

Another dark, fermented sauce, this sauce made of soybeans is sweet and makes a great Asian-style barbecue sauce for fish, pork, or poultry.

> **Hot Tip**
>
> For a quick sauce that's your very own, jazz up store-bought barbecue sauce by adding chopped chiles, a little more Worcestershire, a splash of extra vinegar, some chopped fresh onions or garlic, or whatever you have a taste for.

Ketchup

Well, you need something for your burgers. Ketchup also is the base of most home-made barbecue sauces.

Mayonnaise

You'll need it for the leftovers and all those sandwiches. Also, add some chopped pickles or pickle relish, some capers if you like, and voilà—tartar sauce.

Mustard

Many supermarkets carry a treasure trove of mustards, especially if you live in the Midwest, which is a veritable Mustard Land. The sharp bite of mustard perks up marinades and makes the condiment a great companion to beef, pork, poultry, and, especially, sausages. Don't forget—if you serve hot dogs, the mustard had better be yellow.

Salad Dressing

You'll need something to put on the salad, of course. Plus, ready-made salad dressings make great emergency marinades. Your in-laws are arriving a day earlier than planned? Pop a couple of chicken breasts in Italian dressing, marinate, and slap them on the grill.

Soy Sauce

Rich, dark, and salty, this sauce can be thought of as an all-purpose condiment. Use it in marinades, pastes, and as a table seasoning. Don't confine it just to Asian foods. It's wonderful on hamburgers.

Teriyaki Sauce

Soy sauce mixed with sugar, wine, and seasonings. It's a very popular sauce for grilled foods. Use it in marinades, or just brush it on the food during grilling.

Worcestershire Sauce

This fermented sauce of English origin is a must in most barbecue sauces. It rounds out the ketchup, sugar, and vinegar with an intriguing tang.

Don't Get Burned!

Buy meats, poultry, fish, and other perishables last, just before you're ready to check out of the supermarket. And don't stop to run other errands on the way home. That way they'll still be cold when you get them home.

The Perishables

Because of its very simplicity—the best grilled foods taste of themselves, with a hint of seasoning and a wisp of charcoal—grilling requires top-notch ingredients. The grill is no place to try to resurrect that chicken breast that's been sitting in the back of the freezer for a year. Fresh meats are better than frozen, though frozen are acceptable, and you should always select the freshest fish, poultry, and seasonal vegetables.

As for meats and poultry, those that are best for the grill are tender without being overly fatty (fat causes flare-ups). However, remember that very lowfat meats can easily dry out on the grill, so be careful not to overcook.

Storing and Handling Foods

To keep perishables at their very best, keep them well-wrapped (except for live crabs or shellfish, which need to breathe) and store them in the coldest part of the refrigerator—usually the bottom shelf. Use them as quickly as possible, or freeze. Don't refrigerate or freeze them too long; they'll spoil, or at the very least, suffer in flavor and texture.

Table: How Long Can You Keep Them?

Food	Refrigerate (40°F)	Freeze (0°F)
Meats, raw (steaks, roasts)	3 to 5 days	6 to 12 months
Meats, cooked	3 to 4 days	2 to 3 months
Poultry, raw	1 to 2 days	6 to 12 months
Poultry, cooked	3 to 4 days	4 months
Hot dogs (beef, pork, or poultry)	2 weeks	1 to 2 months
Hot dogs, opened package	1 week	1 to 2 months
Ground meats, raw	1 to 2 days	4 months
Ground meats, cooked	3 to 4 days	4 months
Fish, raw	1 to 2 days	1 to 6 months*
Fish, cooked	2 to 3 days	Don't freeze
Shellfish, raw	1 day	1 to 2 months
Shellfish, cooked	2 to 3 days	Don't freeze

Lean fish, such as cod, will keep for 6 months; somewhat more fatty fish, such as trout or bass, for about 4 months, and very fatty fish, such as salmon, for only a month or two. Never refreeze fish that has been previously frozen and thawed; it will turn mushy.

Food Prep 101

If you're a novice, here are a few definitions of basic terms you'll encounter in this book's recipes.

Boil: To cook a liquid on medium-high or high heat until the liquid is very active, with large bubbles breaking the surface.

Chop: To roughly cut food into fairly small pieces, using a chef's knife or food processor. To chop onions, peppers, and similar vegetables, lift and drop the blade of the knife rapidly, using a bit of a rocking motion.

Core: To remove the woody or seedy center of a fruit, such as a pear, apple, or pineapple. If you don't have a special tool called a corer, the easiest way to do this usually is to cut the fruit in half lengthwise, and cut out the core.

Dice: To cut a food into little cubes, about $1/2$ inch or smaller. It's neater than chopping, and is often used for hard foods such as carrots. To dice, you slice the food one way, then the other way to make small squares.

Don't Get Burned!

Keep your knives well-sharpened. Contrary to what you might think, dull knives are actually more dangerous—because they don't cut as easily through the food, you have to use more force when cutting, so they're more likely to slip.

Grate: To shred a food such as ginger or cheese by rubbing it against the holes on a grater. Used interchangeably with shredded.

Marinate: To tenderize and flavor meats by soaking them in a liquid, usually a mixture of acid and oil, for a long time—anywhere from an hour to overnight.

Mince: To chop into very fine pieces. Garlic, ginger, and herbs are often minced.

Oil or spray: To coat a food or the cooking grid lightly with a vegetable oil (use a brush or a paper towel for this), or to spray it with a nonstick cooking spray.

Peel: To remove the skin of a fruit or vegetable. The easiest way to peel hard vegetables such as potatoes or carrots is to use a vegetable peeler. The easiest way to peel soft fruits such as peaches or tomatoes is to put them in boiling water briefly, then slip off the skin (see Chapter 14). We also use *peel* to refer to the colored part of the rind in citrus fruits, commonly referred to as *zest*.

Pit: To remove the large seed in a fruit such as a plum or peach. Cut the fruit in half lengthwise, then pry out the seed.

Process: To grind, chop, or blend foods in a blender or food processor.

Simmer: To cook foods at just below a boil. The liquid will have small bubbles coming to the surface, but will be "calmer" than a boiling liquid.

Slice: To cut crosswise or lengthwise through a food to make thin, fairly large pieces.

Trim: To cut off and discard parts of a food that you don't normally eat. That includes such things as the woody bottoms of asparagus, the ends of green beans, or the fat and gristle on meats.

Turn: To use a spatula or tongs to flip a food onto its other side.

The Least You Need to Know

➤ The right herbs, spices, and condiments can make the difference between a so-so grilled dish and a great one.

➤ Choose the freshest meats, fish, and poultry, and refrigerate or freeze them no longer than recommended.

➤ Chopping is rough; dicing is neater; mincing is small.

Part 2
Getting Warmer

So you've got your grill. You've got your accessories. You've got a cupboard full of flavored vinegars and boutique barbecue sauce from somewhere in the heart of Texas, and a refrigerator that's just waiting to receive the best of the best in meats and vegetables.

Now the learning begins in earnest. In this section, we show you how to build a great fire, prepare your grill for direct and indirect cooking, keep your family and your food safe, plan successful outdoor parties, and gracefully juggle the demands of cooking for varied tastes, including lowfat and vegetarian.

Chapter 5

Fire and Smoke

In This Chapter

➤ Types of charcoal

➤ Getting the fire lit

➤ Keeping it at the proper temperature

➤ Putting out the fire

When it's time to light a charcoal fire, you quickly realize why we label grilling an art rather than a science. Many a weekend barbecuer has stood around cursing as the coals don't light (then get too hot), or the wind comes up, or humidity turns the fire into a wimpy, smoking mess.

However, with a little practice, some attention to coal and grill temperature, and the help of good charcoal and accessories, you'll find that it is quite simple to keep frustration to a minimum.

First, here's a quick lesson in wood combustion 101. Of course, most folks don't grill over plain wood, but pure charcoal is nothing more than burnt hardwood.

How Wood Burns

The hardwoods used in barbecuing are made up primarily of wood fibers (cellulose, hemicellulose, and lignin), extractives (tannins, starches, resins, oils, dyes, alkaloids, and sugars), and ash. Green wood is mostly water, which is why it smokes, rather than burns. It's the extractives that give various woods their distinctive characteristics and that make pecan wood smell like, well, pecan.

When wood is heated, it releases water and volatile gases such as carbon monoxide, sulfuric acid, carbon dioxide, hydrocarbons, hydrogen, acids, ketones, alcohols, aldehydes, and tar, which comes from the sugar residues.

What's What

Hardwood is the solid, compact wood of various, usually deciduous trees. Hardwoods commonly used in grilling include oak, cherry, maple, hickory, and mesquite. *Softwoods* come from conifer trees such as pine, spruce, fir, and cedar. They contain a lot of resin, making them unsuitable for barbecuing, although you can use small twigs for kindling.

If oxygen is present and the temperature is high enough, the volatiles burn off. This is why you should light the briquets or charcoal, then let them burn to ash with the grill uncovered. When temperatures are too low or when there is not enough oxygen for the volatiles to burn off completely, the wood smolders and gives off creosote, an icky, oily substance that will give foods a bitter flavor.

This is why if you are starting from scratch with dried wood (as you might if you're pit-barbecuing or cooking foods in a large smoker), you must burn it down to embers before you start cooking.

Once it's dried, hardwood consists of about 20 to 25 percent moisture, 50 to 55 percent volatile compounds, and 25 percent char.

Commercial hardwood charcoal is produced by heating wood for several days in closed ovens to get rid of noxious fumes, water, and just about everything except the pure char—that dry, black, porous stuff we know as charcoal. (The coal in this case is a misnomer, and manufacturers of pure charcoal often prefer to label it charwood.) Char has few volatile compounds and only about 3 percent moisture. It burns cleanly, with little smoke.

Of course, damp wood produces plenty of smoke. That is why you soak wood chips or chunks in water before you put them on the coals.

All About Charcoal and Briquets

Charcoal briquets are not pure charcoal. They do contain charcoal that has been ground to a powder, but may also contain binders, cardboard, borax, actual coal, limestone, sawdust, and other materials, even motor oil. The better-quality briquets contain a high percentage of charcoal to other ingredients, which is why they catch faster and burn better. This is one area where you get what you pay for.

We highly recommend pure hardwood charcoal for grilling. It imparts no "off" flavors to the food, and burns very well. But we realize that it is not as widely available as briquets, and costs more. Good-quality briquets are acceptable for most grilling purposes.

Instant-lighting briquets have been soaked in lighter fluid, and have that unpleasant petrochemical smell. We recommend avoiding them and using a charcoal chimney to get the charcoal started.

Whatever type of charcoal you use, store it in a cool, dry area such as the basement or garage. When charcoal absorbs moisture, it can be hard to light. If you live in a dry area such as the Southwest, you can probably keep it outside, but you should still cover it. If you buy charcoal in large bags and have to store it some distance from the grill, put the bag in a wheelbarrow or cart to make transporting the charcoal easier. And don't forget a large scoop, so you don't have to dig the charcoal out with your hands.

The lighter fluid in instant-lighting charcoal can evaporate, so keep the bag tightly closed.

For tailgate parties and other occasions, you can buy briquets in a bag that's meant to be ignited right along with the charcoal. These are expensive, but convenient.

According to Kingsford, makers of charcoal briquets, a 5-pound bag of charcoal contains 90 to 100 briquets, a 10-pound bag between 180 to 200, and a 20-pound bag 360 to 400. As a rule, the company says, allow about 30 briquets per pound of food you're grilling.

Starting the Fire

First, sweep any old ashes out of the grill so they won't block any of the air vents.

Be sure to burn the coals with the lid open until you're ready to cook. This feeds plenty of oxygen to the fire to keep it going, and also allows any volatiles to burn off.

Tasty Tidbit

Back in the good old days, charcoal wasn't something you trucked out to buy for weekend parties—it was a cooking necessity. Charcoal vendors used to roam the streets and sing ditties to attract customers. One common chant from 19th-century Philadelphia:

Charcoal by the bushel

Charcoal by the peck

Charcoal by the frying pan,

Or any way you lek!

Tasty Tidbit

Some guy named Kingsford invented the charcoal briquet, right? Nope. It was none other than Henry Ford, better known as the inventor of the mass-produced automobile. Ford used wood in the Model Ts, and started burning the scrap to make industrial charcoal at his plant in Kingsford, Michigan. To reduce storage and shipping costs, he compressed the charcoal into briquets. The supply was greater than the demand, so Ford tried selling the briquets to the public at car dealerships. The business never truly "caught fire," though, until the Kingsford Company acquired it.

There are several ways to light the fire:

➤ Kindling method. Pile some kindling—wadded-up newspaper that has had 1 teaspoon vegetable oil added to it, a few pine cones or some twigs—in the bottom of the grill. Mound the coals in a pyramid shape atop the kindling, leaving some gaps for air to come in and so you can light the kindling. Light the kindling material with a long-handled match or utility lighter. Once it catches, it will heat the coals and get them started. This method works for wood as well as charcoal fires.

➤ Charcoal chimney method. Fill the chimney with briquets or lump charcoal. Place wadded-up newspaper in the bottom of the chimney, and light it in a couple of places through the air holes, using a long-handled match or utility lighter. When you see the charcoal on top is alight, carefully pour the charcoal out into the grill.

Don't Get Burned

Pouring coals from a charcoal chimney to the charcoal grid creates sparks. Put the rim of the chimney as close to the grid as possible, and pour the coals slowly and gently, standing as far back as you can. Be sure to wear long mitts to protect your hands and forearms.

➤ Electric starter method. Plug in the starter, place it in the bottom of the grill, and arrange the briquets atop it in a pyramid shape. When the starter glows red and ignites the coals, remove it and unplug it (be sure you put it on a fireproof surface until it is thoroughly cool).

➤ Solid starter method. These white cubes are made of a nontoxic wax. Pile the charcoal in a pyramid, tuck some of the starter cubes between the charcoal pieces, and light.

➤ Lighter fluid method. This is our least favorite method, because lighter fluid not only gives off obnoxious fumes, but if you don't burn the coals long enough to get rid of the residue, it also imparts an unpleasant flavor to your food. Plus, in some localities, using lighter fluid is illegal because of its polluting emissions. Pile the charcoal in a pyramid. Squirt the equivalent of about $1/4$ cup of lighter fluid onto the coals, and let sit for a minute, then light with a long match or utility lighter. *Never* squirt lighter fluid onto coals that are already burning.

➤ Just plain coals method. You simply pile the charcoal or briquets up in a pyramid, and light them. Unless you're using instant-lighting coals (which have been saturated with lighter fluid), this method is the least reliable.

When Is It Ready?

Charcoal goes through three stages before it's ready for cooking. First, it's literally aflame. Then the flames die down, but the charcoal is still glowing red hot. Finally, the charcoal is mostly covered with ash and will have only a slight glow. That's what we call medium hot, and it's the proper temperature for most foods.

Since charcoal grills, unlike ovens, don't have handy little lights that go off when they're preheated, you'll have to use your eyes and your hands to tell when the charcoal is ready for cooking.

First, you should look at the coals. Then, for a further check, you can hold your hand, palm down, about $1/2$ inch above the cooking grid (or about 6 inches above the coals). Count off how many seconds ("one thousand one," "one thousand two," and so on) you can comfortably hold your hand there. Here's what you're looking and feeling for:

Tasty Tidbit

From 1987 to 1997, the sales of grills stayed steady. In the same period, however, the sales of charcoal briquets climbed by 14 percent and the number of "barbecue events" doubled, according to the Barbecue Industry Association. In other words, people have been buying grills all along, but in the '90s they've actually been *using* them.

➤ Glowing or red hot coals. The coals will still be very red and glowing. You will be able to hold your hand over the grid for only about 2 to 3 seconds. The charcoal is still too hot for cooking most foods, but is ideal for searing meats.

➤ Medium-hot coals. The coals will still have a bit of a red glow, but they'll be about 70 percent covered with a medium-thick layer of gray ash. You'll be able to hold your palm over the grid for about 4 to 5 seconds.

➤ Cooling coals. The coals will be thickly covered with gray ash. You'll be able to easily hold your hand over the grid for 5 seconds or longer. At this stage the charcoal is too cool for most cooking, but OK for warming foods, or gently grilling fruit for dessert.

Of course, if you have a gas grill, this process is much easier; just read the thermometer.

Keeping It Going

If you're cooking over direct heat, you shouldn't have any problem getting all your cooking done well before the coals die down. If you're slow-cooking foods over indirect heat, though, you will have to add some lit charcoal to the fire every 45 minutes or so, to keep the fire fueled.

Generally coals are ready anywhere from 20 to 45 minutes after lighting. Really narrows it down, doesn't it? But the fact is, coals are very dependent on temperature, humidity, wind, what you use to start them, and so on. With a little practice you'll have no trouble whatsoever telling when the coals are ready for grilling.

Preheating Gas Grills

For a gas grill, you always want to preheat it before cooking. Set all the burners on high and close the lid. Heat for 10 minutes, or until the thermometer registers 500 to 550°F.

Open the lid, which will immediately start to lower the heat. Some manufacturer's directions call for turning off a burner or two, but we've found it usually works better, at least in a three-burner grill, to turn all the burners to medium, unless we're cooking over indirect heat. Each grill is different, however, so experiment to see what seems to work best.

Don't Get Burned!

Never pour water on a flare-up in a gas grill. Water can make a grease fire spatter dangerously, and it also can wet the ignition, making it impossible to light the gas until the igniter dries out. If the fire flares up, cover the grill to smother it.

Where There's Smoke, There's Flavor

Smoking woods and aromatics won't cook your food. Instead, they're designed to create a fragrant smoke that enhances foods so they get that distinctive barbecued or smoked flavor.

You can use a wide variety of herbs, spices, and woods to create a nice smoke (see the table below for some ideas). You can buy wood chips or chunks in hickory, mesquite, pecan and oak, as well as more offbeat "flavors." You should soak wood chips for 20 minutes in cool water, or wood chunks for an hour. Drain them well, then put them on the coals. In a gas grill, you can put them on the ceramic briquets or other heat dispersers, but it's even better if you put them in a smoking box, to keep ashes from clogging the burners.

Table: How Many Briquets?

Generally, for direct grilling, you need enough briquets to extend 1 to 2 inches beyond the food. Or, follow these guidelines. For indirect grilling, remember that you need to pile half the briquets on each side of the drip pan.

Grill size	Indirect grilling	Direct grilling
14^1/$_2$ inches	30 (15 per side)	25
18^1/$_2$ inches	40 (20 per side)	30
22^1/$_2$ inches	50 (25 per side)	35
26^1/$_2$ inches	60 (30 per side)	40

If you're using fresh herbs in a recipe, toss the stems or leftovers on to the fire. They won't give as strong a flavor as dried herbs, but will perfume the smoke a bit.

You can mix and match woods, or woods and spices, to get different flavors. Try oak with a fruit wood, for example, or mix mesquite with sage or cumin.

Be careful not to put too much smoking wood on the fire. It can make foods bitter.

"Shop" in your garden for woods. When you prune the grapevine or lilac bush or maple tree, save some vines or branches for grilling. Most herbs, especially the woody types such as thyme and rosemary, can be used as aromatics. (Do make 100 percent sure that the twig you use is not from a poisonous plant—it's possible the smoke could make you sick.)

Hot Tip

Next time you have corn on the cob, put the cobs out in the sun to dry. Once they're completely dry, store them in a paper sack that's out of the reach of raccoons or other curious creatures. Next time you barbecue, tuck the cobs among the lumps of charcoal. They produce a sweet smoke that gives foods a fabulous flavor.

Putting It Out

The easiest, and safest, way to put out the fire is to cover the grill, close the top and bottom vents, and let the coals burn out. Let the ashes cool for at least 48 hours before you dispose of them. Natural charcoal ashes can be used in the garden or compost heap. (It's probably best not to do this with the ashes from briquets, which may include petroleum products.)

Any lumps of charcoal that did not burn completely can be saved for your next grilling session. Just add them to the new briquets.

Don't use water to put out the fire—either by dumping water into the grill or dumping the coals into a pan or bucket of water. This can create potentially dangerous hot steam. And dumping water into ashes creates a mildly corrosive paste that's bad for the grill's finish and definitely a pain to scrape up.

Don't Get Burned!

Be careful what you use as aromatics. Chile peppers can be fairly potent when burned. Garlic and onion turns acrid. Pine is very resinous and gives off a greasy smoke that can lend an unpleasant flavor to foods. Some shrubs, such as dogwood, are too flowery and can literally "perfume" the food.

The Least You Need to Know

➤ Pure charcoal burns cleanly and gives the best flavor, but good-quality briquets are acceptable for most purposes.

➤ The coals are medium hot, the preferred temperature for most foods, when they are covered with ash and you can hold your hand over the grid for 4 to 5 seconds.

➤ For extra flavor, use smoking woods or other aromatics, such as herbs.

Chapter 6

Techniques That Really Cook

In This Chapter

➤ Using direct heat to quickly grill foods

➤ Using indirect heat to cook larger cuts

➤ Smoking (barbecuing) foods

➤ Tips for turning out perfectly grilled dishes

You're smart enough to realize that you don't grill-roast a whole chicken the same way that you grill a hot dog. But how, exactly, *do* you grill them? Besides, roasting a chicken or turkey on the grill seems pretty complicated.

Relax. With this book to guide you and a bit of practice, you'll realize that grill roasting a turkey, or just about anything else, is not complicated at all. It simply requires a slightly different technique. Before long, you'll be able to grill anything short of a whole suckling pig. Actually, if you have a large enough grill, or a pit and a bunch of willing neighbors and friends, you can even do that.

Directly to the Point

By far the most popular method of grilling is over direct heat. That means just what you think it does: You stick the piece of meat, fish, chicken, vegetable, pizza, or whatever grilled fare you've a mind to try on the cooking grid, right over the hot coals. When it's browned, you turn it over and cook the other side.

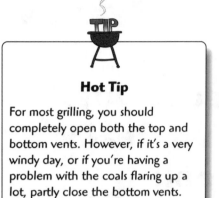

Hot Tip

For most grilling, you should completely open both the top and bottom vents. However, if it's a very windy day, or if you're having a problem with the coals flaring up a lot, partly close the bottom vents.

This method is ideal for chicken breasts, thin hamburgers, fish fillets, portobello mushrooms, or any other food that will cook in 20 minutes or less. It's also great for precooked foods, such as hot dogs or sausages, that you just want to char a little. Thin foods will brown nicely on the outside, but not burn, before they are cooked through in the center.

You can sear really thin foods on an uncovered grill. But most foods cook more evenly if you keep the grill covered for most of the cooking time. Open the vents in the lid and in the bottom of the grill.

Although we talk about cooking food directly over the coals, foods with any fat on them, such as chicken breast with the skin, actually fare better if you set them slightly off center, away from the coals. That way, the fat is less likely to drip into the fire and cause flare-ups, which can burn the food and, possibly, you. It's also important to cover the grill when cooking fatty foods. By putting the lid on, you feed a bit less oxygen to the fire, thus making it less likely to flare.

The way you arrange the coals also affects cooking and the likelihood of flare-ups. For very thin and/or quick-cooking foods—for example, precooked sausages that you're just charring, or cutlets—keep the coals slightly mounded for very hot heat, and put the food directly over them. For slightly thicker cuts, such as boneless chicken breast or thick beef patties, put the coals in a single layer and, if the food seems to be charring too quickly on the outside, move it off center, so it's not over the hottest coals.

Nearly all foods are grilled over medium-hot coals, which means the coals are no longer red-hot and glowing, but mostly covered with a layer of white ash. One exception is steaks or other foods that you want to *sear* before cooking through. They should be seared over red-hot glowing coals. Then, finish cooking the meat over medium-hot coals. One easy way to accomplish this is to separate the coals slightly, with most of the still-glowing ones on one side of the grill, and the mostly ashy ones on the other, before you set the cooking grid in the grill.

What's What

To *sear* a meat, you cook it quickly on both sides over very high heat. This forms a crust on the surface, which helps seal in the juices.

If flames are licking out of the coals, never place the food directly over them. Wait until the flames have died down. If flames shoot up while you're grilling, move the food to one side and cover the grill. A notable exception is marshmallows—some connoisseurs like them really black and gooey.

Indirectly Speaking

We know several folks who like to grill their Thanksgiving turkeys. It's a great way to free up the oven for all those side dishes, and with some care, the turkey turns out moist, juicy and slightly smoky—in a word, luscious. These people know the secrets of indirect grilling, or grill-roasting.

When you grill-roast, you're basically using your grill like an oven. The standard covered kettle-shaped grill works quite well as an oven. It gets plenty hot and provides lots of air circulation around the food. Do note, though, that your grill must have a lid for you to use the indirect method.

Indirect cooking is ideal for larger foods, such as beef roasts, whole chickens, and turkeys, that would char to a crisp over direct heat long before their insides were done.

To keep foods moist, add a drip pan to the grill. Place the drip pan—you can use a couple of disposable foil pans nested inside each other—in the middle of the grill, on the bottom rack. Fill the pan half full of water. If your grill is 18^1/$_2$ inches in diameter, pile about 18 to 20 coals on each side of the drip pan; if it's 22^1/$_2$ inches, use 24 to 26 coals. Add or subtract a few coals if your grill is larger or smaller than that. If your grill came with two charcoal holders or dividers, by all means use them. They'll keep the coals from spilling all over (like into the water pan).

Hot Tip

If you do a lot of grilling, a hinged top rack can come in handy. Its sides lift up, making it a cinch to add extra coals when you're cooking over indirect heat.

Hot Tip

Got an old cake or bread pan that's too battered or grease-stained to use for baking? Turn it into your drip pan for the grill. Reserve it just for that purpose, and wash it in hot, soapy water between uses.

Light the coals. When they are covered with a thick layer of ash, replace the top rack and put the food in the center of that, over the drip pan. The drippings from the meat or poultry will drip into the pan, flavoring the food and keeping the coals from flaring up.

To perk up the flavor of grill-roasted foods, you can toss some soaked wood chips or dampened herbs such as rosemary sprigs on the coals. Or, you can put wine, broth, or water with dried herbs in it in the drip pan.

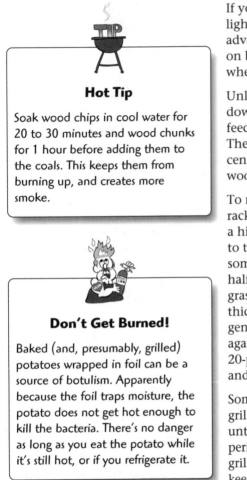

Hot Tip

Soak wood chips in cool water for 20 to 30 minutes and wood chunks for 1 hour before adding them to the coals. This keeps them from burning up, and creates more smoke.

Don't Get Burned!

Baked (and, presumably, grilled) potatoes wrapped in foil can be a source of botulism. Apparently because the foil traps moisture, the potato does not get hot enough to kill the bacteria. There's no danger as long as you eat the potato while it's still hot, or if you refrigerate it.

If you have an extra grill or a charcoal chimney, you can light the coals before you pile them in the grill. The advantage of this is that the coals will be burning evenly on both sides. Be sure to very carefully pour the coals where they're needed, and not into the drip pan.

Unlike your oven, your grill relies on fuel that burns down. This means that for longer roasting, you need to feed fresh coals to the grill every 40 to 45 minutes. There, doesn't that make you appreciate those 19th-century women who cooked three meals a day on a woodstove?

To replenish the coals, gently lift the food off the top rack and onto a plate. (This assumes you do not have a hinged grill rack; see "Hot Tip.") This is preferable to trying to pull up the rack and the food; there's something really heartbreaking about watching your half-cooked capon slide head (well, neck) first into the grass. With the food safely aside, remove the rack. Wear thick, extra-long barbecue mitts on both hands, and gently lift the rack by its handles. Set it on or prop it against a level, heatproof surface. If you're cooking a 20-pound turkey, better get someone to help you lift it and the rack.

Some recipes require low heat. If you're using a charcoal grill, keep the heat low by using fewer coals, waiting until they are ashen, and adding only enough coals periodically to keep the fire going. In a three-burner gas grill, it may mean turning two of the burners off and keeping the remaining burner on medium.

Cooking indirectly on the gas grill is much easier. Just follow the manufacturer's directions. Usually, that means preheating the grill to about 500 to 550°F, with the lid down. Two of the burners, in a three-burner grill, or one burner, in a two-burner grill, are turned to medium, and the other burner is off. The food is placed over the burner that's turned off. You may have to experiment a bit, perhaps turning off two burners instead of one, for example, to find a "comfortable" temperature for indirect cooking.

If your gas grill has only one burner, without dual controls, you can't cook foods by the indirect method.

Rotisserie Grilling

This is the way those roasted-chicken restaurants cook their birds to a golden turn. It's a great method for whole poultry or large poultry pieces with the skin, as well as large beef, pork, or lamb roasts, because as the bird turns, it bastes itself with its own fat. It also cooks more evenly. You can use a rotisserie over direct or indirect heat. Rotisserie attachments are sold for gas and charcoal grills.

The first thing you'll need is an electrical outlet handy to the grill, so you can plug in the rotisserie. Put the meat on the spit (rod), carefully fastening the forks in place. The meat can be anywhere from 5 to 10 inches from the heat, depending on how slowly you want to cook it. Start the rotisserie and check to make sure the meat or poultry isn't loose or wobbling. If it's rotating unevenly, take it off the spit and start over.

Cook the meat, occasionally checking on it and the coals, and replenishing the charcoal as necessary.

Cooking in Embers

This is down-and-dirty cooking, the way our ancestors did it. While the cavemen and women cooked wild boars right in the fire, you've probably only explored this culinary avenue with marshmallows.

Cooking in embers also works for some dense foods, usually vegetables, where you want long cooking and a smoky undertone. You wrap the food in foil and place it directly in the coals. Potatoes and sweet potatoes are great cooked this way.

> **Hot Tip**
>
> Obviously, you don't want to add unlit coals to your fire. You can use a charcoal chimney to heat more coals (set it on a heatproof surface, such as concrete). If you frequently cook over indirect heat, you might want to buy a small, cheap tabletop grill and use it just for lighting those extra coals.

Smoking

You might think you can't really smoke foods at home. It's true that making, say, bacon, is an art best left to the professionals. But if you want to smoke a little fish, poultry, or meat, all you really need is a water smoker. This is a tall, narrow grill shaped like a silo. The coals sit in a pan at the bottom of the smoker. Over them lies a water pan, and the food sits directly over that, with a lot of air above it to give the smoke room to rise. The combination of hot air, smoke, and steam cooks the food.

To smoke foods, you first light the charcoal, then wait for it to burn down to ash. You cook the food the same way you grill by the indirect method, adding another 12 to 14 coals, plus additional wood chunks, to the fire every 30 to 45 minutes. Most smokers have a door on the front so you can easily add more coals.

Tasty Tidbit

Commercial smoking is a more complex process than home-based water smoking. Take traditional ham. It starts with fresh pork, which is cured with a rub of salt, sugar, and spices, or brined (soaked in water with salt, sugar, and spices). It is then hung in a smokehouse for several months (if it's made the old-fashioned way) or several weeks (more likely these days). It picks up flavor from the rub or brine, and from the wood used to smoke it. Processors either cold-smoke foods at 70 to 90°F, or hot-smoke them at 100 to 190°F. Commercially smoked foods may or may not be fully cooked—check the label.

Hot Tip

If your smoker is getting a bit hotter than you like, or if you need an extra-low temperature to smoke something like cheese, add a few ice cubes to the water pan.

Unlike grills, water smokers have a permanent drip pan that slides into brackets.

The usual temperature range for smoking is 200 to 250°F, with 225 being the optimum. Don't peek at the food too often; you'll only increase the cooking time.

Sprinkle soaked wood chips over the coals to help perfume the smoke and flavor the food. Don't go overboard on the wood chips, though, or the smoke flavor will be overpowering. Two to 3 cups of soaked chips often is about right, but for best results, follow the individual recipe or the smoker manufacturer's directions. To further enhance the flavor, you can use cider or wine, instead of water, in the pan, or use water and add a handful of dried herbs.

Although we don't recommend starter fluid for any grilling, we especially caution against using it to light the coals in a smoker. The smoke gets more concentrated in the smoker than it does in a grill, and starter fluid can leave an unpleasant aftertaste. For the same reason, we strongly recommend using pure charcoal, rather than briquets, in your smoker.

If you're really serious about barbecuing (smoking), you can use a wood smoker. Use either real hardwood charcoal, or actual wood—three sticks is about average—for the fuel. The air intake (vent) on the firebox should stay open to release smoke; close it partway if the fire is too hot or flaring up frequently. A wood smoker will cook food more quickly than a water smoker.

Done to a Turn

Okay, so you've got the grill going—now, how do you handle the cooking? Here are some general tips that apply to grilled or barbecued foods in general. You'll find more tips, geared specifically to certain foods, in Chapters 10 through 14.

➤ Don't overcook. While you do want foods to be cooked through, grilling is a dry heat. Overcooking lean foods, especially, is a good way to ruin their flavor and texture. Remember, foods continue to cook after they're removed from the grill. When in doubt, it's better to undercook a bit; if the food turns out to be under done, you can put it back on the grill. Once it's overcooked, there's not much you can do except drown it in sauce.

➤ Lightly brush very lean foods such as skinless chicken breast or vegetables with a bit of olive oil before grilling, to help keep them moist.

➤ Baste foods, especially if they're lean. Baste the food every 5 minutes or so during cooking with the marinade or barbecue sauce. If you have soaked raw meat, poultry, or fish in the basting sauce, you should quit basting it at least 5 minutes before the expected end of cooking, so that the food will get hot enough to kill any bacteria on the surface.

Don't Get Burned!

It's best not to salt meats, poultry, or fish before grilling. Salt draws out the natural juices, further drying out the food.

What's What

Basting is a fancy name for brushing or drizzling a liquid over a food as it cooks. You can baste with a kitchen brush, a clean paintbrush (with bristles that don't shed), a spoon, or a bulb baster, which is a tool designed for the purpose. The bulb baster works only with thin liquids. Use a brush or spoon for thick liquids such as barbecue sauce.

➤ Plan ahead, so you know the cooking times for various foods, and can grill them in succession or simultaneously, as appropriate. For more on timetables, see "A Grilling Timetable," in Chapter 8.

➤ Soak bamboo skewers in cool water for 20 to 30 minutes before using them. This will help keep them from charring or even catching fire, burning the food along with them.

➤ Turn foods grilled over direct heat at least once, and more frequently if the fire's a bit too hot or if the food has a sauce on it. The exception is delicate fish, which should not be turned at all.

➤ To make kebabs, cut the meat, poultry, or fish, and your vegetables or fruit, into chunks about 1 to $1^1/_2$ inches. Thread the skewer through a chunk of meat. Alternate the meat with vegetables (if you're using vegetables). Alternating, say, beef with a cherry tomato, then a piece of pepper, then a piece of onion, then another piece of meat, makes for an attractive arrangement.

Don't Get Burned

When you pull up the lid of your charcoal grill during cooking, lift it to the side. When you lift it straight up, you can create a draft that draws ashes up unto the food.

Don't cram the ingredients too tightly on the skewer; you want a touch of air circulation so the meat will cook. Because the skewer can push surface bacteria into the center of the meat, kebabs, like hamburgers, should be cooked until they're no longer pink in the center.

➤ Drain marinated foods thoroughly, and brush any sauce on grilled foods toward the end of the estimated cooking time. The sugars, garlic, and other ingredients in sauces can burn, while the oils in marinades can drip into the fire and cause a flare-up. Usually the sauce is added to smoked ribs and meats during the last 30 minutes of grilling. For chicken, the sauce is brushed on during the last 10 to 15 minutes; for steaks and chops, just the last 5 minutes, and for sausages and hot dogs, the last 5 minutes.

➤ Keep the vents open during grilling to feed oxygen to the fire. You can adjust the bottom vents if necessary, but the top vents should always stay open to release the smoke. Remember, metal vents get hot! Use barbecue mitts or pot holders to adjust them.

The Least You Need to Know

➤ Quick-cooking foods should go directly over (or very near) the coals.

➤ Thicker cuts, roasts, and foods that need longer cooking should be roasted away from the coals, over a drip pan.

➤ For any but the thinnest cuts, keep the grill covered for even cooking.

Chapter 7

Safety First

In This Chapter

➤ Cooking and eating safely outdoors

➤ Handling and storing perishables properly

➤ Making sure foods are cooked through

➤ Reducing any risks associated with high-heat cooking

Cooking and food safety are always important, of course. But they can be especially important when grilling. Because grills deal with open flames (in the case of charcoal, anyway), get very hot, and are out in the open, they pose greater risks than the average kitchen appliance.

Food safety can be a big concern, too. The foods you are most likely to grill are meats, poultry, and seafood—foods that are at higher risk of bacterial contamination. Toss in the fact that grilling is more art than science, and it can be harder to make sure foods are cooked through as much as they should be.

To top it off, you're usually eating grilled foods outdoors. Which means foods sitting outside, maybe in the hot sun. And yellow jackets buzzing around the food. And kids buzzing around the grill.

So, here's all that stuff you'd rather not hear about, but need to know. Once you've had a little experience, though, this stuff will be second nature.

Grills First

Grills are wonderful. They also can be very dangerous. Not only do they get very hot, but unlike stoves, they don't have safety knobs to keep kids from playing with them. So it's important to follow some basic safety rules:

➤ Pick a level spot away from dense vegetation. That's especially true for smaller or lighter charcoal grills, which can tip easily.

➤ Never use a grill inside the house, garage, or any other enclosed space. Grills can give off carbon monoxide, a poisonous, colorless, odorless gas.

➤ Don't put the grill too near the house. If it's too close to a window, it could send fumes and sparks into the house.

➤ Try to keep the grill out of the way of where the kids usually play and run through the yard, or where guests are likely to be walking.

➤ Never leave the grill unattended if there are young children around. You should also keep an eye on pets, which may be attracted by the food smells.

➤ Don't wear loose, long sleeves or flowing clothing when you grill.

➤ Try not to use a charcoal grill when it's really windy. Besides the fact that it's difficult to light the fire and the food may not cook well, the wind can whip the flames and sparks around—or, in a real gust, possibly knock the grill over. If you've already started grilling when the wind gets gusty, close the bottom vents most of the way.

What's What

Propane is a colorless, flammable (but of course) gas that's a component of petroleum and natural gas. It burns more cleanly than gasoline, and, unlike natural gas, can be toted around, making it the ideal fuel for gas grills and camp stoves.

➤ Keep a spray bottle of water nearby in case of a minor flare-up. *Note:* This applies only to metal charcoal grills. Never use water to put out a flare-up in a gas grill, or in a ceramic charcoal grill. In fact, the method should be used only as a last resort in charcoal grills, since water mixed with ashes makes quite a mess. Always try to smother the flare-up first by covering the grill and closing the vents.

➤ Never use kerosene, gasoline, or other liquids in place of charcoal lighter fluid, or try to run a gas grill on anything other than the fuel it's designed for. The results can be explosive.

➤ Never dump out the coals while they're still hot. Cover the grill and close all the vents, and let the coals cool for at least 48 hours before you dump them.

➤ If your gas grill flares up, turn all the burners off and move the food to another area of the cooking grid, away from the flames. Once the flames die down, light the grill again. Never use water to put out a fire in a gas grill.

➤ Do not line the bottom of a grill, especially a gas grill, with foil. This can collect grease, which might catch fire.

Don't Get Burned!

You do know you should never, *ever* squirt starter fluid into lit charcoal, right? If you're like most impatient grillers, you've probably done it anyway. Do not do it again. The flame could travel back up the stream of liquid and burn you.

➤ If you have a gas grill, it's a good idea to check it for leaks whenever you remove and reconnect the propane tank. Consult the owner's manual to see which connections you should check, how you should check them (usually you brush on soapy water and look for bubbles), and what to do about it if you find a leak. When in doubt, don't try to fix it yourself; turn off the gas and call the company that made the grill.

➤ If you have any reason to believe the fuel lines are clogged or leaking or the gas jets aren't working properly on your gas grill, and simple maintenance or cleaning procedures don't help, do not operate the grill until you have checked with the manufacturer.

➤ Keep the grilling area clean; it can attract unwanted critters. Usually this means mice, cats, and maybe raccoons, but depending on where you live, it could also include mountain lions or bears.

➤ Exercise caution during that unwelcome ritual at cookouts and picnics throughout much of the United States: the swarming of the yellow jackets. Earlier in the summer, these yellow-and-black-striped insects prefer a diet of bugs, but in late summer and early fall, they start foraging for other foods, especially sweets. Yellow jackets alone are responsible for about half of the "bee" stings annually in the United States.

If you're planning a cookout in August or September and have been having problems with yellow jackets, consider eating inside (if you don't have a screened-in patio). Another possibility is to put out traps, although they help only somewhat; the wasps will still make a beeline for the food and drink. There's little you can do other than ducking out of their way as much as possible. Swatting at them will only make them mad.

Yellow jackets like to fly into open soda cans, attracted by the syrupy liquid. More than one person has been stung in the throat after drinking from a soda can with an unexpected inhabitant. If yellow jackets are likely to visit your cookout, pour the soda into cups. It won't stop the wasps from swarming around your cola, but at least you'll be able to see them.

Fending Off the Bad Bugs

Grilling is not the most precise of cookery methods. You can never be exactly sure when a food will be done, because the timing depends on humidity, wind, air temperature, how many coals you use, how cold the food is, how hot the coals are, and so on. This is why it is very important to remember that the cooking times in this book (or any other grilling book) are simply guidelines. Never rely on time alone to make sure a food is cooked through.

Since you want your guests to remember your Fourth of July picnic for all the fun they had, and not for the fact that they lived in the bathroom for 5 days afterward, it pays to handle and cook foods properly. Here's the scoop on food safety:

Don't Get Burned!

Juices from raw meat and poultry can drip onto other foods in your shopping cart. To prevent this, immediately drop the package of meat or poultry into one of the plastic bags supplied in the meat department.

Keep It Clean

➤ Store meats and poultry in the refrigerator away from other foods, and put a paper towel under the package to absorb any leaking juices.

➤ Never put cooked food on a platter that held raw food. If you use a paring knife to cut into a chicken breast that turns out to still be pink, wash the knife in hot soapy water before using it to cut into the chicken again.

➤ If you marinate raw meat, poultry, or fish, and want to also serve the marinade as a sauce, either set some aside before you add the rest to the meat, or in a saucepan bring the marinade to a boil for a full minute before reusing it. Don't count on the vinegar or other acid to kill germs; at most, it'll just slow them down. You can use the marinade or sauce to baste the meat during cooking, but stop basting at least 5 minutes before you expect the food to be done, so the outside gets hot enough to kill bacteria.

➤ Wash all produce thoroughly. That especially applies to berries, lettuce, and other items you're likely to eat raw, unless you buy already trimmed and washed vegetables in a bag.

Keep It Cold (or Hot)

➤ Keep meats, poultry, or seafood in the refrigerator until it's time to put them on the grill.

➤ Defrost foods in the refrigerator, under cold water that you change every 30 minutes, or in the microwave. Because microwave defrosting warms up foods, don't defrost foods that way unless you plan to cook them immediately.

➤ Once you grill foods, serve them immediately, or refrigerate them. Cooked foods, including meats, salads, coleslaw, and the like, should not sit out longer than one hour on a fairly warm day. (Dry foods, such as breads or cookies, are OK for longer periods.)

Cook It Through

You bring the nicely browned chicken to the table, only to discover it's still pink inside. The next time, you try to compensate by adding another 5 minutes to the grilling time, and wind up with stringy chicken that your guests politely chew, and chew, and chew.

How you tell whether a food is done without being cooked to death depends, not surprisingly, on the type of food. Wiggling a drumstick works great with a whole chicken, but not too well with chicken breasts.

After some practice, you'll get better at telling when a food is most likely done. Meats, fish, and poultry tend to firm up and lose that "squishy" feel

Hot Tip

When are foods considered cooked through? Here are the minimum temperatures:

Beef steaks, lamb chops	145°F
Pork, kebabs, ground beef	160°F
Poultry (dark meat)	180°F
Poultry (breast)	170°F

when they're cooked through. Clams and similar shellfish advertise their doneness by opening their shells. Foods like shrimp turn color. For more on judging when individual foods are cooked through, see Chapters 11 through 14.

To take the guesswork out of the process, use an instant-read thermometer. Many grills, especially gas grills, come with a thermometer. Note that you do *not* stick an instant thermometer into the food while it cooks—it can break. Instead, you put it in the cooked food, and wait about a minute or until the needle stops moving. One trick to using an instant-read thermometer is that the tip needs to go far enough into the food to get an accurate reading. Here's how to use it in different foods:

➤ Steaks, chops, chicken breasts: Insert the probe through the *side* of the meat so the tip reaches the center.

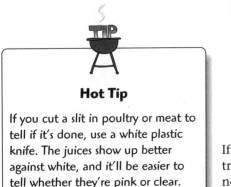

Hot Tip

If you cut a slit in poultry or meat to tell if it's done, use a white plastic knife. The juices show up better against white, and it'll be easier to tell whether they're pink or clear.

➤ Roasts, turkey breast: Insert the thermometer so the tip is in the thickest part of the meat but not touching fat or bone. The bone conducts heat, so can provide a false reading.

➤ Whole chickens or other poultry: Insert the probe into the thickest part of the thigh, but be careful that it isn't touching the bone.

If you don't have a thermometer handy or if you don't trust what it's telling you—and food thermometers are not always 100 percent reliable, especially if you've dropped them—cut a slit in the food or pierce it with the tip of knife. The meat does lose some juices that way, so resist the temptation to poke it every other minute, and only start testing when it's been on the grill for the minimum time listed in the recipe.

The juices should run clear for any ground meat and for chicken. Pork can still have a tinge of pink. Beef and lamb (not ground) can have a fair amount of pink in the juice.

If you still can't tell, cut into the meat to see whether the center is pink or not.

So What Are These Awful Bugs, Anyway?

So is it truly necessary to get that cautious with your food? The short answer is, yes. Here's why:

E. coli

The reason the medium-rare burger is, alas, a thing of the past. Short for *Eschericia coli*, this bacterium is found in our guts and the guts of animals, including beef cattle. In its normal form, *E. coli* helps synthesize vitamins and keep "bad" bugs at bay. However, some mutated forms, especially a variety called *E. coli* O157:H7, can be harmful. Fortunately, *E. coli* O157:H7 is fairly rare. Unfortunately, when it does hit, it can be deadly, especially to children. It has popped up in other foods, including raw milk, lettuce, and unpasteurized apple cider, but it's associated mostly with ground beef.

So why can you eat your steak, but not your hamburger, medium rare?

Ground meats always pose a greater risk than whole cuts. That's because *E. coli*, a contaminant that's often spread from the animal's intestines to its meat during slaughtering, is generally found on the surface of the meat. When the beef is ground, those surface bacteria get mixed throughout the meat.

Unlike some other bugs that have to be present in large numbers to make you sick, apparently it takes only a small amount of *E. coli* to "get" you. This is why you should ignore well-meaning food writers who advise that you lessen the risk (and presumably make rare or medium rare burgers "safer") by buying very fresh meat, keeping it cold, and grinding it yourself. No way! Besides the fact that your kitchen equipment probably isn't as clean as that in restaurants and supermarkets and your refrigerator isn't as cold, these writers are confusing *E. coli* with bugs like salmonella, which multiply rapidly in unclean or warm environments, and that must be present in large numbers to make you sick.

The good news is that the food industry has developed a simple test for *E. coli*, which is in the pilot phase. Maybe soon they'll be able to certify beef *E. coli*–free, and we can go back to enjoying juicy pink burgers. But until then, the only way to eliminate the risk of *E. coli* is to cook meat all the way through. Period.

Campylobacter jejuni

Good old "campy" is the leading cause of bacterial diarrheal illness in the United States. Federal health experts blame it for 2 to 4 million cases of illness per year. Raw chicken is a common source of this bug. It tends to especially hit kids under 5 and young adults ages 15 to 29. It usually lasts a week to 10 days, and while it's rarely fatal, it induces plenty of misery. To prevent poisoning, handle raw meat and poultry carefully. Wash your hands, cutting boards, and utensils in hot, soapy water, and don't let poultry juices drip onto other foods. Cook poultry all the way through.

Salmonella

This large family of bacteria causes 2 to 4 million cases of foodborne illness every year in the United States. Salmonella bacteria aren't picky about where they live—you'll find them in animals, water, soil, insects, cutting boards, animal feces, raw meats, dairy products, raw poultry, raw seafood, and raw eggs. The most common sources of poisoning, though, are poultry and eggs. Salmonella poisoning is highly unpleasant, but usually goes away after a couple of days. However, it can seriously sicken and even kill infants, older people, or those who have a weakened immune system. To avoid salmonella, keep foods cold, keep your kitchen, utensils, and grilling area clean, and thoroughly cook foods, especially poultry, before eating them.

Don't Get Burned!

Don't mix anything red or dark—such as paprika, spices, spaghetti sauce, Worcestershire, or barbecue sauce—into ground beef, turkey, or other meats before grilling them. It will be very hard to see when they are no longer pink in the middle.

Botulism

This one usually throws a scare into people, since the illness can often be fatal. Fortunately, this illness, caused when the spores of *Clostridium botulinum* produce potent toxins, is fairly rare. Although the spores can thrive in any nonacidic food, botulism often is associated with canned foods because it thrives in airless environments, and with vegetables such as potatoes and garlic that come into contact with the soil. From a griller's standpoint, there are two chief areas to watch out for: homemade flavored oils (see Chapter 4), and potatoes, either baked (or grilled) in foil, or in potato salad.

Hetero What?

If you follow nutrition news at all, you've probably read about cancer-causing substances formed when meats are cooked at high temperatures. Because scientists are allergic to short words, these substances are called heterocyclic amines, or HCAs, and polycyclic aromatic hydrocarbons, or PAHs.

The bad news is that grilling, with its intense heat, definitely creates these nasty substances. The good news is that cancer researchers rank HCAs and PAHs way down on the list of things we need to worry about. Eating too much red meat, for example, is still considered a much bigger cancer risk than how you cook it. In fact, the evidence is only suggestive that HCAs might pose a cancer threat to humans. The evidence for PCAs is a bit stronger, but they're found in a lot of other places besides the food we eat, and our bodies usually excrete them within days.

Still, if you eat a lot of grilled foods, you might want to know how to reduce any risks.

First, the HCAs. When you cook protein foods, but especially muscle meats (that's meat, poultry, and fish) over high heat, natural chemicals in the meat react to form these substances. Studies have shown that frequently eating well-done meats cooked at high temperatures might be linked to colorectal, pancreatic, breast, and stomach cancer.

So how can you cut the risk and still enjoy meat on the grill? There are several ways:

➤ Marinate the meat. Researchers at Lawrence Livermore National Laboratories found that soaking chicken breast even briefly in a cider vinegar-oil marinade before grilling it drastically cut the amounts of HCAs produced. It's important to note that, as of this writing, they had not tested this on other meats, and could not say for sure whether the same would hold true. But marinating certainly can't hurt, and it may help.

Tasty Tidbit

So what did those researchers marinate the chicken in to reduce those dangerous chemicals? A tasty mixture of cider vinegar, lemon juice, olive oil, garlic, brown sugar, mustard, and salt. They pointed out, though, that there was nothing magical about the marinade they used. Soaking the chicken in any marinade showed similar results.

➤ Microwave the meat. Partially cooking the meat first in the microwave seems to drain off HCAs in the juices. You can then finish cooking it on the grill. Don't microwave the meat until the grill is heating up and nearly ready to go. Zap it for about 2 minutes, and drain off any juices that collect. Bacteria can multiply rapidly in partially cooked meats, so you need to get it onto the grill right away.

➤ Eat meats medium-rare when it's feasible. Since foodborne bacteria pose a much bigger and more immediate threat than any slightly increased risk of cancer down the road, it would be very foolish to eat your chicken, pork, or hamburger medium-rare. But if you're eating steak or lamb chops, don't overcook them.

Now, about those PAHs. They're formed when meat juices drip onto the coals, creating that wonderfully flavorful smoke. Unfortunately, the smoke contains these cancer-causing substances, which then cling to the meat. Fortunately, your body usually excretes PAHs within days.

Probably the best way to limit exposure to PAHs is to cook lean, well-trimmed meats on the grill over medium-hot coals. This will reduce the amount of fat dripping into the coals, and thus the amount of smoke.

The Least You Need to Know

➤ Grills can be dangerous; take care in setting up and using them, and don't leave them unattended.

➤ Keep things clean to avoid cross-contamination, and keep hot foods hot and cold foods cold.

➤ Check carefully that foods are cooked through to safe temperatures.

➤ Grilling produces potentially cancer-causing chemicals in food—but the risk is nothing to get all lathered up about.

Chapter 8

It's Your Party

In This Chapter

➤ Planning a successful party

➤ How much food to buy

➤ Timing your cooking on the grill

Thanks to the wonders of modern science, we now can answer the burning question that has confronted every griller since time immemorial: Does it really rain more on Memorial Day?

Yes.

In much of the United States, May is normally a pretty rainy month anyway. And recently some researchers discovered that—at least in the cities of the Northeast—it does rain more on the weekends than you normally would expect it to, statistically speaking. (And Memorial Day, of course, is the end of a long weekend.)

Their theory is that emissions from all those rush-hour auto exhausts build up all week long and "seed" the clouds, which let loose when the traffic lightens over a weekend.

So drag out the umbrella and don a slicker for your Memorial Day party, and be prepared to splash around and sing "Grillin' in the Rain."

Ironically, May, in all its soggy glory, is National Barbecue Month.

You can party outdoors anytime, of course, whether you're celebrating Mother's Day, Memorial Day, the Fourth of July, your son's graduation, or your daughter's wedding— or nothing at all. And no matter what time of year it is, always have a backup plan in case it rains.

Tasty Tidbit

When we throw parties, outdoor cookouts rank at the top of the list. Surveys show that when people entertain, 42 percent host an outdoor cookout, while only about 37 percent prefer dinner or cocktail parties.

The advantage to outdoor cookouts is that you're right where the party is. Instead of being closeted in the kitchen while your guests nosh appetizers, you can grab a beer or lemonade and joke with your guests while you flip the salmon steaks.

One disadvantage is that grilled foods usually have to be cooked "to order." Unless you're serving it as part of a salad or sandwich, you really can't grill that juicy steak 3 hours ahead of time and reheat it before serving.

You're also confined to one cooking method, at least in the final stages. Unlike a dinner party, where you can warm the bread in the oven while you heat the spinach on the stovetop, an outdoor cookout pretty much means cooking on the grill, period (although you may have access to a side burner on a gas grill). If you are the sort of person who buckles under pressure, or if you expect things to be particularly chaotic at the party (it's your son's sixth birthday), you can get around this limitation in several ways:

➤ Prepare a main course that takes longer to cook. Grill-roasting a chicken over indirect heat, for example, will take close to an hour, freeing up some time for last-minute preparations elsewhere.

➤ Make sure all the side dishes, desserts, and appetizers are foods that can be prepared ahead of time.

➤ Enlist a second person to help in meal preparation (always a good idea anyway).

You also can go the other way and celebrate this difference by cooking the entire meal on the grill, from the appetizers through the dessert. In fact, after you have done most of your grilling and the coals are cooling down, it is even possible to do some baking (although we wouldn't recommend, say, baking a cake from scratch on the grill). As long as you've gone to the trouble to light the grill, why not get as much cooking out of it as possible?

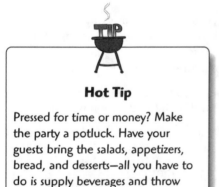

Hot Tip

Pressed for time or money? Make the party a potluck. Have your guests bring the salads, appetizers, bread, and desserts—all you have to do is supply beverages and throw something on the grill.

You can only cook everything on the grill, of course, if you have a large enough cooking surface to do so. If you have a hibachi, better stick with Plan A. And if you do plan to make a meal this way, you'd better be well organized.

In fact, outdoor parties always require that you have everything organized and ready before you light the coals. And by everything, we mean beverages, ice, salads, gelatin molds, bread, silverware, serving utensils, napkins—the whole enchilada.

The easiest way to do this is to make a very complete list, and check it twice. Put *everything* on that list: buy ice, check the cooler, start the coals, buy the flank steak, don't forget the potato salad, put out the napkins and lobster forks, husk the corn, find the barbecue tongs, soak the wood chips, warm the rolls.

A Grilling Timetable

There's no reason, of course, that you can't just toss a party together. Call a few friends, pick up some ground beef on the way home, and voilà, a party. These days, though, when nearly everybody works outside the home, a little planning goes a long way.

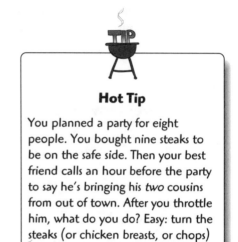

Hot Tip

You planned a party for eight people. You bought nine steaks to be on the safe side. Then your best friend calls an hour before the party to say he's bringing his *two* cousins from out of town. After you throttle him, what do you do? Easy: turn the steaks (or chicken breasts, or chops) into kebabs, fajitas, or sandwiches.

While you don't have to create something quite as precise as a train timetable, you should jot down how long everything is expected to take to cook, and juggle accordingly. If you're making brisket, you'll obviously need to stick around all day to keep an eye on it. If you're making pork chops, grill-baked potatoes, and grilled apples, the potatoes need to start first. Then you add the pork chops. Finally, as the coals begin to cool, you grill the fruit.

Several Days to a Week Before

Draw up a final menu and shopping list, and shop for nonperishable foods, beverages, and paper supplies.

Make sure you're not low on charcoal or propane, and buy it if you are.

Make sure you have enough chairs and table space. If you don't, ask some of the guests if they can bring a lawn chair or two. (If you really need more chairs, you may have to rent them, which should be done sooner than this.)

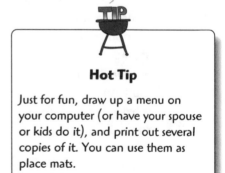

Hot Tip

Just for fun, draw up a menu on your computer (or have your spouse or kids do it), and print out several copies of it. You can use them as place mats.

A Day or Two Before

Make sure the picnic furniture is clean. Scrub it down if necessary. Make sure your grilling tools are clean as well, and that the kids aren't raising toads in the ice cooler.

The day before the party, make any marinades, rubs, and sauces you'll be using. Refrigerate them if necessary.

Make a shopping list for the perishable foods, and buy them. For the amounts you'll need, consult the table. (If you're grilling shellfish, it's best to buy it the day of the party.)

Make the dessert (if it's a non-grilled one).

Table: How Much Food to Buy

These are averages, of course. If you're entertaining the twentysomething males on the softball team, they'll undoubtedly eat more than the fiftysomething women from your reading club. For most parties, though, you'll find that the light eaters and heavy eaters tend to average out, and these quantities should work fine. These amounts are for main courses. For appetizer servings, cut the amounts down by a third to a half, depending on the type of food.

Weights are for the food *as purchased,* including bone and/or skin. In other words, you would buy a 3-pound chicken to feed 6 people ($^1/_2$ pound per person). The amounts are based on "real life" servings, not necessarily the 3 ounces of lean meat or poultry recommended by nutritionists. Most people will probably eat more than that in a party setting.

When in doubt, buy a little more than you think you'll need. Eating chicken every day for a week beats running out of food.

All Red Meats (beef, pork, lamb, veal, buffalo, venison)

Boneless roasts or steaks	4 to 6 oz.
Bone-in roasts	6 to 8 oz.
Chops (loin or shoulder)	1 to 2 chops
Cutlets (scallopine) or sandwich steaks	4 to 6 oz.
Ground meats	4 to 6 oz.
Sausages	1 med. to large link, or 3 oz. bulk

Beef or Bison

Individual steaks	1 steak, or
(ribeye, Porterhouse, etc.)	$^1/_2$ large steak
Short ribs	6 to 8 oz.

Pork

Spareribs	$^3/_4$ to 1 pound
Whole pig	$1^1/_4$ to $1^1/_2$ pounds

Lamb

Leg or shoulder (bone-in)	6 to 8 ounces
Rack, rib or crown roast	2 ribs
Chops (rib)	2 chops

Poultry

Chicken or turkey, whole	$1/2$ lb.
Chicken or turkey, boneless parts	$1/4$ lb.
Turkey, parts (bone-in)	$1/2$ lb.
Chicken, parts (bone-in)	1 to 2 pieces, or 6 to 8 oz.
Duck or goose, whole	1 lb.
Duck, boneless breast half	$1/2$ to 1
Cornish hens	$1/2$ to 1 bird
Squab, partridge	1 bird
Quail	2 birds

Fish and Shellfish

Fish, whole (gutted, with head)	$3/4$ lb.
Fish, whole (headless)	$1/2$ lb.
Fish, fillets	6 to 8 oz.
Fish, steaks	1 each, or 6 to 8 oz.
Clams, large, in shell	6 to 8
Clams, steamers	16 to 18
Mussels	8 to 10
Oysters, on the half shell	6 to 8
Oysters, shucked	6 to 8, or $1/4$ pint
Crab, soft shell	2 each
Crab, meat only (crab cakes)	$1/4$ lb.
Shrimp, in shell	6 to 8 ounces
Shrimp, peeled	4 to 6 ounces
Squid, whole or in pieces	$1/4$ lb.
Scallops (no shell)	$1/4$ lb.
Lobster, whole	1 to 2 lbs.
Lobster, cooked tail	1 each, or 5 to 6 ounces

Side Dishes

Rolls or buns	1 or 2
Deli salads (potato or pasta salad, coleslaw, baked beans, etc.)	4 to 6 oz.
Green salad	2 to 3 oz.

Several Hours to a Day Before

Make any nongrilled desserts and side dishes (except, of course, for highly perishable ones like tossed salads). Refrigerate.

Trim all meats and vegetables you'll be grilling. Cover and refrigerate.

Just Before the Party

Have all the paper goods—cups, plates, forks, knives—ready to go. Spread out the tablecloth if you're using one.

Check the grilling area. Are the tools, oils, grill screen, and everything else you need handy?

Make the tossed salad if you're serving one. Cover it lightly with a damp (*not* wet) paper towel and refrigerate it.

Anywhere from 30 Minutes to an Hour and a Half Before You Plan to Serve Food

Light the grill. How much time you allow depends, of course, on what you're cooking. Take the estimated cooking time of the food and add 30 minutes for charcoal, 15 minutes for gas. Allow some extra time if it's cold, very humid, or windy.

Hot Tip

If you have herbs in your garden, snip some sprigs, especially if they're in flower, and put them into vases of water for herb bouquets. They make casual, charming table decorations.

When the Food Is Nearly Finished Grilling

Have your spouse, kids, or some of the party guests set the table and bring out all the side dishes and condiments.

After the Party

Make sure the grill vents are closed, and the lid on, so the coals will die down.

Clean up. Remove full garbage bags and transfer them to covered trash cans so you don't get critters sniffing around your patio. Make sure the area around the grill is cleaned of meat juices, oil, and so on.

The Wine (Well, Beverage) List

The most popular "outdoorsy" beverages are no doubt beer, iced tea, soft drinks, and lemonade. For non-beer alcoholic beverages, consider wine cocktails or punches, such as mimosas (champagne and orange juice) or sangria (red wine and fruit punch). Both are festive, go well with a variety of foods, and can be made low in alcohol.

If you do want to serve wine, you can either go traditional, pairing the proper wines with each course, or serve a more "picknicky," light, sipping-style wine with some fruit. For example, if the main course is a whole salmon grilled over oak, you could pair it with an oaky Chardonnay to play up the wood, or just serve a lighter wine with more fruit for the whole menu (for example, a Fume Blanc with tropical fruit undertones).

For more heavily smoked foods, a wine with a lot of fruit and a fair amount of sweetness, such as a German Riesling, is often just the ticket. If you feel out of your depth, ask your wine merchant for recommendations.

Some Suggested Menus

We like the idea of cooking your entire meal—or at least, just about all of it—on the grill. Here are some menus that do just that.

Picnic in the Park

> ➤ Focaccia
> ➤ Jerk Strip Steaks
> ➤ Grilled Garlic Potato Skins
> ➤ Mixed Greens Topped with Grilled Vegetables
> ➤ Campfire-Style S'Mores

Backyard Family Barbecue

> ➤ Tortellini Vegetable Salad
> ➤ Carolina-Style Slow Smoked Pulled Pork, or Chicken Pieces with Molasses Barbecue Sauce
> ➤ Blueberry-Apple Cobbler on the Grill
> ➤ Beer, iced tea, and fruit punch

Fourth of July Celebration

> ➤ Five-Minute Mussels
> ➤ Very Simply Salmon
> ➤ Grilled Tomatoes and Green Onions
> ➤ Apricots Topped with Raspberries and Raspberry Sherbet

Don't Get Burned!

At a party, it's easy to get distracted and forget how long foods have been sitting out. Except for "dry" foods such as breads (plain) or cookies, cooked or raw dishes should not stand at room temperature for longer than an hour. On a really hot day, bring foods out just long enough for everyone to serve themselves. Then return the foods to the refrigerator or cooler.

Pacific Rim–Style Dinner Party

➤ Chicken Yakitori

➤ Salmon Steaks with Asian Marinade

➤ Asparagus and Mushrooms with Sage Brushing Sauce

➤ Wine-Brushed Pears

➤ A Riesling or a light, fruity red wine

Just Appetizers

➤ Turkey Sausage on a Stick

➤ Five-Minute Mussels

➤ Focaccia

➤ Walnut-Stuffed White Mushrooms

➤ Grilled Antipasti

➤ A light red wine, such as Chianti

Shore Grill Dinner 1

➤ Soft-Shell Crabs on the Grill

➤ Coastal Shrimp in Beer

➤ Mixed Greens Topped with Grilled Vegetables

➤ Warm Apple Cinnamon Slices with Cheddar Cheese

➤ Beer, of course

Shore Grill Dinner 2

➤ Crab Cakes

➤ Down Maine Clambake, or Whole Maine Lobsters

➤ New Potatoes with Garlic and Cilantro

➤ Grilled Angel Food Cake and Pineapple

➤ A good, smooth ale

Grilling Party for Kids

➤ Buffalo Cheese and Tomato Sauce Pizza, or Cheeseburgers Deluxe

➤ Fruit Kebabs

The Least You Need to Know

➤ The key to any successful party, even a spur-of-the-moment one, is setting a timetable and following it.

➤ It's possible, and even desirable, to cook the whole dinner, from appetizers through dessert, on the grill.

➤ For outdoor parties, keep it simple. Grilling requires concentration; cleanup and preparation should require less.

Chapter 9

Chew the Fat—Not

In This Chapter

➤ The essentials of healthful eating

➤ How to trim the fat in your party without sacrificing fun or flavor

➤ Which recipes in this book are low in fat and/or vegetarian

Traditional etiquette holds that the guests who are on diets, have sensitive colons, are not eating meat, or are eating only foods that begin with "Y" not bother the host or hostess with their peculiarities (one exception is a genuine food allergy). A good guest should instead politely eat what's served—or at least those parts of the dinner that he or she can and will eat—and politely push the rest around the plate.

But traditional etiquette derives from the days when people didn't endlessly discuss food preferences, the best-seller lists weren't dominated by diet and vegetarian books, and people generally didn't outlive their arteries. These days, it's not unusual for a host to plan a party knowing that one guest is a vegetarian, another has diabetes, one has lost 150 pounds on a lowfat, high-protein diet, and still another has been put on a near-zero-fat regimen by his cardiologist. For that matter, it's not unusual for the host to be following dietary restrictions as well.

And etiquette or not, you want your guests to enjoy the party and think kindly of you as a host. Fortunately, accommodating a variety of eating styles is not at all difficult to do these days.

Pyramid Power

Of course, even without specific dietary restrictions, we should all be eating more healthfully anyway. Unless you've been on a desert island for the past decade, you've probably seen the U.S. Department of Agriculture's Eating Right Pyramid. It emphasizes that we should be eating mostly grains, fruits, and vegetables, and small amounts of meat or poultry—3 ounces is about the size of a deck of cards—with the fat trimmed off.

But hey, you say, it's just one cookout, and I've been craving a big ol' steak for weeks.

The good news is that it's your diet over time, not in one evening, that counts. Even better news is that, with only a small amount of extra attention, it is possible to put together a menu that will satisfy just about anyone.

As just one example, you could cook up your steaks, thinly slice them, and serve them with grill-warmed tortillas, salsa, lettuce, sliced avocados, grilled onions, and sliced tomatoes. In other words, tacos *al carbon*, as they say in Spanish.

You can satisfy your steak craving by skipping the tortillas and everything else and just piling the meat on your plate. Your fat-watching guests can put a small amount of meat and a lot of lettuce and tomato in a tortilla. Your vegetarian guests can skip the meat altogether and stuff the tortillas with the veggies.

Hot Tip

Should you trim the fat from meats and remove the skin from poultry before or after you grill? We vote for *after*. Grilling produces dry heat, and the fat or skin helps baste the meat, keeping it moist. This method adds very little additional fat, as long as you do trim the meat or remove the poultry skin before serving.

Other Guest-Pleasing, No-Fuss Strategies

The real key to successful entertaining is variety. If you serve a lot of different foods, and make sure that at least several of them are lowfat and/or meatless, everyone should be able to find something to eat. You don't have to kill yourself to do this: You can buy all kinds of salads and other prepared foods at the supermarket or local deli. Even if you choose to cook everything yourself, what's the big deal about slapping a couple of peppers on the grill?

Here are some more tips:

➤ Trim the fat from meats and remove the skin from poultry. Serve reduced-fat—or better, fat-free—dairy products such as milk, yogurt, and sour cream.

➤ When you're choosing deli salads for side dishes, keep in mind that salads with oil-and-vinegar type dressings (or, no dressing at all) tend to be lower in fat than those with creamy dressings, if only because creamy dressings are thicker and cling better to the vegetables. Some possibilities: coleslaw (with a vinaigrette-type dressing), cucumber salad, three bean salad, fruit salad, gelatin molds.

➤ If you're making your own salads, use reduced-fat or nonfat dressings. Or, cut the high-fat mayonnaise or other dressing with some nonfat yogurt or sour cream.

In most cases, you can also use less than the amount of dressing called for. That's especially true if you're using your mom's ancient recipe for potato salad, which probably calls for twice the dressing you actually need to moisten and flavor the salad. Oh, those devil-may-care 1950s . . .

Don't Get Burned!

Watch the condiments. If you're trying to eat foods lower in fat, don't sabotage the effort by pouring on the salad dressing, mayonnaise, or other high-fat extras.

➤ Serve high-fat sauces and condiments on the side. Pass the tartar sauce for the fish or ranch dressing for the green salad or chocolate sauce for the grilled fruit at the table so guests can help, or not help, themselves to it.

➤ One area where people seem to be especially calorie-conscious is beverages. Always make sure you have sparkling water, unsweetened ice tea, and/or diet sodas on hand.

➤ Think fruits and vegetables. If you're not grilling vegetables, put out a relish tray of raw cut-up veggies. Vegetables in jars, such as roasted peppers and artichoke hearts, can come in handy, too. Greens in a bag make it ever so easy to serve a tossed salad. Grill some fruit for dessert—ice cream strictly optional.

➤ Think starch. Rice salad, pasta salad with a light dressing, lowfat crackers, pretzels, grilled polenta (slices of cooked cornmeal), corn tortillas, plenty of bread—all of these are filling yet low in fat.

➤ Watch the dips. If you're putting out chips or pretzels, serve fat-free bean dip and salsa in addition to, or instead of, the creamy dips. You can also buy lowfat creamy dips. Reduced-fat ranch dressing makes a good dip. Mix chives and other herbs into nonfat sour cream for a quick, nutritious dip.

➤ Serve two kinds of whatever it is, as long as it's not too much effort. Grill some pork brats for those who want the traditional flavor and turkey brats for those watching their fat intake. Or beef burgers for the traditionalists and veggie burgers for the vegetarians on your list. Or, just grill a lower-fat cut, such as turkey breast or pork tenderloin, for everybody.

Table: Lean Meat and Poultry Cuts

These numbers apply to meats trimmed of all visible fat and poultry without the skin. The servings are 3 ounces, cooked weight. All have less than 10 grams of total fat and 3 grams of saturated fat.

Meat	Saturated fat	Total fat
Turkey breast	0.2 g	0.6 g
Bison (buffalo)	0.8 g	2 g
Chicken breast	0.9 g	3 g
Turkey leg	1.3 g	3.2 g
Pork tenderloin	1.4 g	4.1 g
Beef eye of round	1.5 g	4.2 g
Beef top round	1.9 g	4.2 g
Chicken drumstick	1.3 g	4.8 g
Beef round tip	2.1 g	5.9 g
Beef top sirloin	2.4 g	6.1 g
Pork top loin	2.3 g	6.6 g
Pork center loin	2.5 g	6.9 g
Lamb sirloin	2.8 g	7.8 g
Chicken thigh	2.6 g	9.3 g

Tasty Tidbit

While the number of dedicated vegetarians is still a small segment of the population, restaurateurs report there's a lot of interest in meatless dining. Walk into nearly any sit-down restaurant these days, and you'll find several meatless selections on the menu.

➤ Serve the lower-fat version of whatever it is: mayonnaise, crackers, chips, cheese, potato salad. It's getting hard to find a food these days that does not have a reduced-fat or even fat-free version.

➤ You often can simply eliminate the oil in a marinade, especially one made with a mellower acid such as wine or orange juice, rather than lemon juice or vinegar. You nearly always can reduce it by at least a fourth. Or replace it with reduced-fat mayonnaise, buttermilk, or yogurt. These are also good choices for homemade salad dressings, where the fat actually matters more (most of the oil in marinades is drained off anyway).

➤ If some of your guests are vegetarians, be on the alert for animal products that are easy to overlook. If they're just eating vegetarian for health reasons, they probably won't care if there's a trace of fish in something, but if you're entertaining a convention of animal welfare activists, better hold the Worcestershire (it's made with fish) and gelatin (beef hooves). If your guests are vegans (vegetarians who eat no animal products whatsoever), don't make cheese pizza for the main course.

Fats 101

So what's all this stuff about saturated, polyunsaturated, and monounsaturated fats? And what about trans fats?

Carbon and hydrogen chains and how they're arranged determine which kind of fatty acid predominates. (Nearly all foods have all three kinds of fat, in varying proportions.) But you don't really want to know that. So here's the short course:

Saturated fats, which are hard at room temperature, have been shown to be a risk factor for heart disease. The biggest sources in the U.S. diet are meats, high-fat dairy products, and chicken skin.

Polyunsaturated fats are liquid at room temperature, and are generally considered OK as long as you take it easy on them. (They tend to lower both "bad" and "good" cholesterol, and in extremely high amounts could increase the risk of cancer.) The biggest sources are salad dressings, vegetable oils (such as soybean and corn), and nuts.

Monounsaturated fats have been shown to lower "bad" cholesterol while leaving "good" cholesterol alone, so some researchers theorize that these fats not only are not harmful, but may be beneficial. Two of the richest sources are olive oil and canola oil.

Trans fats occur naturally, but most of these fats in our diet come from vegetable oils that have been hydrogenated to make them hard at room temperature. Margarine, shortenings, and baked goods made with them are major sources. Researchers are discovering that trans fats act much like saturated fats in raising cholesterol.

Lowfat and Vegetarian Recipes in the Book

Putting together a healthful menu is easy; just choose dishes from the following lists.

The following dishes are easy on the fat and saturated fat. Those followed by a "V" in parentheses are vegetarian as well.

Appetizers

Five-Minute Mussels

Focaccia

Grilled Garlic Potato Skins (V)

Grilled Antipasti (easy on the olives; V, minus the ham)

Smoked Shrimp with Chili-Orange Mopping Sauce

Main Dishes

Pork Tenderloin in Flour Tortillas

Cantonese-Style Sweet and Sour Chicken Breasts

Grill-Roasted Turkey Breast (skin removed)

Swordfish in Buttermilk Marinade

Tarragon-Scented Striped Bass

Halibut Steaks au Poivre

Orange Roughy with Salsa

Minted Flounder on Lime Slices

Red Snapper Margarita

Scrod with Grilled Apple Slices

Soft-Shell Crabs on the Grill (minus the butter on the side)

Whole Maine Lobsters (minus the butter)

"Poor Man's Lobster" (Monkfish) with Grapefruit Relish

Coastal Shrimp in Beer

Prawns with Honey Brushing Sauce

Down Maine Clambake (minus the butter on side)

Individual Smoked Whitefish

Vegetables and Grains

Asparagus and Mushrooms with Sage Brushing Sauce (V)

Mixed Grilled Vegetables in a Pita Pocket (V, main course)

New Potatoes with Garlic and Cilantro (V)

Mixed Green Salad Topped with Grilled Vegetables (V)

Grilled Tomatoes and Green Onions (V)

Baby Artichokes with Rosemary (V)

Baked Potato with Vidalia Onions (V; could be main course)

Desserts

Glazed Mixed Fruit Grill (V)

Apricots Topped with Raspberries and Raspberry Sherbet (V)

Grilled Angel Food Cake and Pineapple (V)

Vegetarian But Not Necessarily Low in Fat

Buffalo Cheese and Tomato Sauce Pizza (serve to 4, as main course)

Tortellini Vegetable Salad (with nonmeat-filled pasta; skip the salami)

The Least You Need to Know

➤ These days, it pays to be savvy about various dietary preferences.

➤ Serving a variety of foods is the easiest way to please everyone, including yourself.

➤ Emphasizing seafood, vegetables, fruits, and starches is an easy way to make menus more healthful.

Part 3
Ladies and Gentlemen,
Start Your Grills

So now you've got the fire going . . . here's how to put it to good use. In this section, you'll learn everything you need to know about marinades, rubs, and sauces. We share the secrets of selecting, preparing, and cooking meats, poultry, seafood, and vegetables and grains for the grill. And just in case you should have some leftovers—or are smart enough to create "leftovers"—we share tips for turning grilled foods into fabulous second-day soups, salads, sandwiches, and stir-fries.

Chapter 10

There's the Rub

In This Chapter

➤ The basics of marinades

➤ The basics of rubs

➤ The basics of finishing or table sauces

Let's face it, grilling and barbecuing techniques are pretty basic. You barbecue meat or seafood in Raleigh the same way you cook it in St. Louis or New Orleans or Houston or Seattle. What sets these cities apart in how they define "barbecue" is not cooking techniques, but how they flavor the meat.

One cook may use a rub; another uses a marinade. One puts ketchup in the sauce; another would blanch at the very idea. In Raleigh, they like their sauce with real bite; in St. Louis, they like it sweet; in New Orleans, they like it with butter; in Seattle, they often like it with a bit of ginger, soy sauce, or juniper berries, and in Houston, they like the sauce on the side or not at all.

Historically, rubs and marinades played a large role both in tenderizing meats and in preserving them. When you're eating a very old goat, it doesn't take long to discover that marinating it in yogurt might help a little. And in the days before refrigeration, folks relied on the preservative properties of alcohol, vinegar, and spices such as garlic, rosemary, juniper, and chiles—along with smoking or drying—to keep their meats longer.

Marinades and Pastes

A marinade is a mixture that contains an acid (wine, vinegar, citrus juice) and, usually, oil and seasonings. Its purpose is to penetrate at least the outermost layers of the meat.

Hot Tip

In a hurry? Most bottled salad dressings, especially the oil-and-vinegar types, make perfectly decent marinades. Just dump about a cup of salad dressing over the meat, and you're all set.

The acid in the liquid tenderizes the meat by breaking down its proteins. The oil bathes it in moisture. And the herbs or other seasonings flavor it. Marinades are defined as liquids, though they may be pretty thick (as yogurt marinades often are). When they are thick enough to cling to the meat, we define them as pastes.

Although they can be used with any meat, poultry, fish, or even vegetables (such as mushrooms or tofu), marinades frequently are used for leaner cuts such as chicken breast or skirt steak, to add both flavor and moisture.

Examples of classic dishes from around the world that are usually marinated (some grilled, some not) include German sauerbraten, Chinese cha shao (seasoned, barbecued or roasted pork) and Peking duck, Japanese yakitori (chicken and chicken liver kebabs), Korean bulgogi (barbecued beef), Turkish shish kebab, American fajitas, and Greek souvlaki (lamb kebabs) and gyros (a mixture of lamb and beef cooked on a spit that is also found in the Middle East).

Because marinades usually contain acid, you should not marinate foods in aluminum or cast-iron pans, or any other reactive metal. The acid will discolor the pan and pick up "off" flavors from the metal. Marinate foods in glass, ceramic, or stainless steel.

First, mix the marinade ingredients. Put the food in a container. Pour the marinade over it. Turn the food to make sure all parts of it are coated with the marinade. Then loosely cover the food and refrigerate it. At least once or twice during the marinating time (and three or four times if you're marinating it for several hours), turn the meat to make sure it gets coated with the liquid.

Hot Tip

Gallon-size self-sealing plastic bags make marinating a snap. Just put the marinade and food in the bag, zip it tightly shut, and shake and press the bag to mix up the marinade ingredients and coat the meat completely with the liquid. Do put the bag in a bowl before refrigerating it, though, in case of leaks.

Marinades can only penetrate about the first inch of the meat's surface, so a thick cut will still need to be cooked with care so it's tender. Marinating meat for a longer period than suggested does not make it more tender, nor does it make the marinade penetrate any further. On the contrary, it can turn the surface of the meat mushy, and overpower the flavor.

Because spices and oils are at their best warm, marinades have more potency at room temperature. But you don't want to create a colony of bacteria, either. You can marinate foods up to 1 hour at cool room temperature, but for any longer than that, refrigerate them.

Any acidic foodstuff can be used in a marinade. These include yogurt, buttermilk, vinegar, wine, fruit juice, even cola soft drinks.

To make a simple marinade, mix $1/3$ cup wine vinegar (white or red) or lemon juice with $2/3$ cup of olive oil, a couple of cloves of garlic (peel and smash them with the side of a knife) or some sliced onion, and whatever fresh or dried herbs and spices you like. For an Asian-style marinade, use rice vinegar or sherry instead of the wine vinegar, a couple of pieces of ginger, a tablespoon of soy sauce, and peanut or canola oil.

You also can skip the vinegar and use equal parts of wine and oil. Or, use orange juice and oil. Do not add salt to a marinade or use cooking wine, which contains a lot of salt. Salt can toughen foods if added prematurely—and besides, your guests will want to salt their food to taste at the table.

An hour or two in a marinade is a long enough bath for most foods. Fish marinates for less time; if you overmarinate it, the fish will "cook" in the acid. However, large cuts of meat that are to be slow-cooked may call for several hours of marinating, even as long as overnight.

Pastes are a cross between marinades and rubs. They are wet, like marinades, but chunkier and thicker, either because they contain less liquid or the liquid ingredient is thick (such as sour cream or yogurt). Classic pastes include the various fiery Thai chile pastes; the equally fiery north African berbere (made with chiles and spices); the Italian basil pesto (which means—surprise—"paste"); the blend of lemongrass, sugar, shallots, and fish sauce used to season grilled meats in Vietnam; the curried sauce that flavors and tenderizes Indonesian satay; the yogurt-spice mixture used to marinate tandoor-grilled chicken in India, and the mustard-spice blend slathered on pork in the Carolinas.

Because they're thick, pastes have to worked into the meat. They work very well for foods with a lot of crevices, such as whole poultry. The only effective way to apply a paste is to dip your hands in the mixture and rub it over the meat, making sure you get every nook and cranny. Put the meat in a glass, ceramic, or stainless-steel container, loosely cover it, and let it marinate for the recommended amount of time. Because paste adheres to the surface, you don't need to turn the meat.

If the paste is very thick, you'll want to scrape some of it off and pat the meat dry before grilling it.

Don't Get Burned!

It's tempting to make flavored oils at home. The problem is that garlic and other herbs or vegetables can contain traces of the spore that causes botulism. And smothering them in oil creates the airless environment botulism loves. Commercial processors add acid or other preservatives to their oil. It's safest not to mess with homemade flavored oils, but if you must, refrigerate the oil and use it within 2 weeks.

Hot Tip

A mini–food chopper can make chopping herbs, garlic, and other ingredients, as well as making pastes, a snap. Regular food processors are too big to handle these small jobs, and few cooks own a mortar and pestle.

Rubs

When you marinate meat, you drain it before cooking, leaving traces of the marinade behind. Rubs, on the other hand, stay on the meat as it cooks, lending their bold, toasted-spice, crusty personalities to the finished dish.

Think of Jamaican jerk chicken, Western barbecued beef, Cajun blackened redfish (OK, so it's not cooked on a grill), and French steak au poivre. Their fame lies in the rub.

What's What

Jerk refers to a seasoning mixture traditionally used to flavor slow-cooked pork in Jamaica. Its ingredients vary, but it always contains Jamaican pimento, or allspice. Other common ingredients include chiles, ginger, thyme, and garlic. Jerk is either used dry as a rub, or in a marinade. It's most commonly used on pork and chicken, but is also excellent with beef or fish.

Although it may have a few moist ingredients (such as fresh garlic or a dab of oil), a rub is basically a dry mixture of spices. A typical rub will contain at least four or five different seasonings, usually something hot and something sweet. Besides flavoring the meat and, depending on the spices, tenderizing it a little, the rub forms an oily crust on the surface of the meat when it cooks, helping to seal in juices. Unlike marinades, rubs often contain salt and sometimes contain sugar as well.

You can easily make your own rubs, or buy a nice spice mixture for an instant rub. Lemon pepper, chili powder, curry powder, Chinese five spice—all can be used as rubs. Just crack up a bunch of peppercorns, press it into your steak and, voilà, steak au poivre. Or go the Cajun route by combining garlic, onion, thyme, red pepper, celery salt, and a bit of basil. Dried or finely grated fresh citrus peel is also very nice in rubs.

What's What

In normal cooking terminology, *dust* is a verb meaning to very lightly coat a food with flour or any other fine powder. We've borrowed the term to mean a very fine, powdery rub.

Because rubs are dry, they don't always cling well to the meat. Coarser rubs, such as cracked peppercorns, can be pressed firmly into the meat. For finer rubs, you may want to lightly brush the food with a bit of olive oil first. Use your fingers to press the rub into the meat. Put the meat on a plate, cover it loosely with plastic wrap, and refrigerate it for the recommended length of time.

Rubbed meats are either served plain, as in Texas-style beef, or with a finishing sauce, as in spareribs or Carolina pulled pork.

Basting and Finishing Sauces, and Condiments

If you've ever eaten Carolina pulled pork or New Orleans barbecued shrimp, you know the importance of a great finishing sauce. In fact, you could argue pretty convincingly that the New Orleans shrimp sauce, a rich mix of butter and spices, could easily finish you.

Marinades and rubs are nothing to basting and finishing sauces. Rib joints guard their barbecue sauce recipes under lock and key. The finishing sauces and condiments offer the real culinary road map of the continent: the shot of bourbon in Kentucky, the pico de gallo in Texas, the yellow mustard that defines a ballpark hot dog anywhere in the United States, that sprinkling of cinnamon and cumin in New Mexico, the malt vinegar in eastern Canada, the tartar sauce on Great Lakes smoked whitefish, the whisper of maple syrup in New England, the dash of soy or sprinkling of lemongrass in California.

Finishing sauces often are added to the food after grilling and before serving. That's the case with the Carolina sauce, in which a mixture of vinegar, salt, and red chiles is tossed lightly with the shredded pork. It's also the case with New Orleans' famous shrimp, which are tossed with melted butter, hot pepper, and herbs. Sometimes the sauces are served as a dip on the side, which is generally true with ribs anywhere and beef in the West. The ribs usually are basted with the sauce during cooking as well.

"Barbecue" sauce, as most of the country knows it, is usually a blend of ketchup, vinegar, sugar in one form or another, and whatever else the creator feels like putting in it. Worcestershire sauce is a pretty standard ingredient. Barbecue sauce contains the ingredients you want in a basting sauce: acid for a bit of tenderness, spices for flavor, and sugar, which caramelizes on the grill to give foods that irresistible smoky sweetness.

Tasty Tidbit

One survey by the Barbecue Industry Association ranked U.S. metropolitan areas by how much barbecue sauce their residents consume. Here are the winners. (We're not sure why "the Carolinas" were defined as a metro area, but nonetheless . . .)

1. New York City
2. Los Angeles
3. Chicago
4. The Carolinas
5. St. Louis

Don't Get Burned!

To prevent cross-contamination of foods, never reuse a marinade or barbecue sauce in which you've soaked raw meat, poultry, or fish without first reheating it to a full boil. Once it has been boiled, it's safe to use as a basting or table sauce. Also, toss any sauce you've used to brush raw meat on the grill.

Sugar does burn easily, though, so you should baste foods with barbecue sauce only during the last 5 to 10 minutes of the cooking time. It's usually best not to marinate foods in barbecue sauce, but if you have, you should turn the food very frequently as you cook it.

If your supermarket has a limited selection of barbecue sauces, don't despair. You can always get some interesting sauces, many with distinctive regional flair, by mail order. You don't really have to make your own sauce. But it is a good way to get a sauce that's truly to your taste. (And who knows, it may make you famous as well.)

Start with about a cup of ketchup, $1/4$ cup of vinegar, and $1/4$ cup of brown sugar or molasses. Heat the mixture until the sugar melts, then add seasonings until you get the flavor you like. Possibilities include Worcestershire, whiskey, smoke flavoring, soy sauce, mustard, cayenne, cumin, chili powder—well, your imagination is the only limit here.

Barbecue sauces keep very well. Pour the sauce into a sterilized glass jar (you can sterilize it in boiling water or just run it through the dishwasher), cover it tightly, and refrigerate for up to a month.

The Least You Need to Know

➤ Marinades and pastes are liquids that are used to tenderize, moisten, and flavor foods.

➤ Rubs are dry spice rubs that are used to flavor foods and help seal in their juices on the grill.

➤ Basting and finishing sauces are used mostly for flavor and to caramelize foods, and vary widely by the region and the cook's whim.

Chapter 11

The Meat of the Matter

In This Chapter

➤ Selecting the right cuts of meat for grilling

➤ Grilling steaks and burgers

➤ Slow-cooking ribs or brisket

➤ Pork, lamb, and veal on the grill

➤ Flavors that go well with red meats

When it comes to choosing the best red meats to grill, the rules are simple. If you can broil it, you can grill it. If you can roast it or pan-fry it, you can grill it over indirect heat or, possibly, direct heat if you marinate it first. If you'd normally cook it in liquid, it's too tough for regular grilling, but with some care, you may be able to slow-cook it in a smoker.

Steaks and Burgers

No matter how much you may try to eat healthfully, we'd wager that when we say "beef on the grill," your mind probably jumps to steak. Not one of those lean 3-ounce nutritionist-approved steaks, either, but a thick, well-marbled prime rib-eye or Porterhouse, crusty on the outside and still oozing juices on the inside.

Or maybe your imagination runs more to a thick, juicy hamburger, with all the fixings, on a grill-toasted bun.

As for which red meats Americans love to grill, there's really no contest. Every survey shows that it's steaks and burgers.

Well, we're here to help you broaden your horizons, at least when it comes to cooking red meat on the grill. At the same time, we have no intention of ignoring steaks and burgers. After all, they're favorites for a reason.

A Juicy Steak, Texas Style

Just about everybody would agree that when it comes to beef, nobody knows how to grow it or cook it like a Texan—well, maybe a Coloradoan or Oklahoman here or there, but Texas is bigger, so they win. When we wanted advice on cooking a perfect steak, we consulted a Texan (actually, he lives in the Midwest now, but once a Texan always a Texan). Here's how he describes the process:

"Cooking it right is a matter of knowing your grill. You need to find the hot spot. Every grill—indoor, outdoor, gas, coal, campfire—has one. The trick is to sear the steak for 45 seconds on a side on the hot spot; the theory being that searing the steak seals in the juice. Anything that will caramelize—barbecue sauce, marinade, whatever—will also help.

"Once the meat is seared, move it to the medium heat spot of the grill and cook it 90 seconds on a side. One rotation is rare; two rotations, medium rare; three rotations is generally considered burnt (what Yankees call 'medium'). Anything beyond that doesn't bear thinking about. With a really good piece of meat, you can knock the first rotation down to 45 to 60 seconds on a side and serve it up what I call very rare, and what the French, in an interesting display of colorblindness, call bleu.

What's What

Rare (130 to 135°F) refers to meat that is still mostly red inside and feels soft. *Medium-rare* meat (145°F) is still quite pink in the center, but warm. *Medium* (155°F) is pinkish in the center. *Medium well* (160°F) is brown throughout, with perhaps a trace of pink. *Well done* (165°F) is completely brown throughout.

"Unfortunately, nowadays, the only way to order a steak in a restaurant is to ask for it 'as rare as your lawyers will allow you to cook it.'"

Alas, we need to point out here that our lawyers would no doubt insist that we tell you to follow the USDA meat safety guidelines and cook steak to at least 145°F (that's what the government calls medium rare and what our Texan friend would call shoe leather). So we offer the above primarily as a historical curiosity.

Here's a roundup of beef steaks that are great for the grill. We have to admit we were surprised to learn that a cut from the chuck—that's the pot roast part of the steer—ranks right under the filet mignon in tenderness. As a bonus, it's usually a lot cheaper than T-bones and strip steaks.

Table 1: The Most Tender Steaks

Tenderloin (also known as filet mignon)

Top blade steak (boneless chuck or charbroil steak)

T-bone

Strip steak (top loin, New York strip, Kansas City)

Rib-eye steak (Delmonico, Spencer)

Top sirloin steak

Source: Texas A&M University

Non-Texan cooking experts describe a somewhat different method for steaks. Sear them over hot charcoal for 2 minutes per side, then finish cooking over medium heat.

To sear meats on a gas grill, turn all the burners to high and preheat the grill to 500 to 550°F. Place the meat on the cooking grate. Close the lid and sear the steak for 2 minutes per side if it's an inch thick and 4 minutes if it's 1^1/$_2$ to 2 inches thick. Then turn the steak and grill it over medium heat, turning it halfway during the cooking time.

The Perfect (and Safe) Hamburger

Alas, the threat of E. coli has banished the juicy, medium-rare hamburger. To be safe, ground beef (and any other ground meat) should be cooked to 160°F, or until there's no longer any pink in the middle. Here are some tips to help make these well-cooked hamburgers both safe and edible:

➤ If fat content is not a major concern, use ground chuck rather than ground round or sirloin. It has a higher fat content, and will stay moister when cooked to medium well.

➤ Completely defrost ground beef before shaping it into patties. Otherwise, it may cook on the outside and still be underdone on the inside.

Don't Get Burned!

Get that spatula away from that burger! Flattening a burger with the spatula just presses out juices, drying out the meat.

➤ Thoroughly wash your hands and any surfaces or utensils the raw meat has touched with hot, soapy water.

➤ Grill the burgers over medium hot coals. If the coals are too hot, the meat will cook quickly on the outside and be burnt and dry by the time the inside is cooked through.

➤ Make the patties about ¹/₂ inch thick. Any thicker, and they will burn on the outside before the inside is cooked.

➤ Grill ¹/₂-inch-thick patties 11 to 13 minutes, or until there is no longer any pink in the center (160°F). Turn them once during cooking.

➤ Do not mix red or dark-colored spices or liquids (ketchup, paprika, barbecue sauce, soy or teriyaki sauce, etc.) into the meat before cooking, since it can mask pink meat. However, it's not a bad idea to baste the burgers with sauce during the last 5 minutes of cooking; it can help keep them moist.

➤ Do not put the cooked burgers on the same platter that held the raw burgers, unless you have washed it thoroughly first.

Hot Tip

For a juicy, flavorful burger, add a little ground pork to the beef. In some parts, they call this a "sooo-ee" burger.

Table 2: To Marinate or Not to Marinate: Meats on the Grill

Beef
Marinate, season, or just grill as is
Sirloin or top sirloin steak
T-bone steak
Top loin steak
Porterhouse steak
Beef tenderloin (filet mignon)
Rib steak
Rib-eye steak
Marinate first
Flank steak
Skirt steak
Top round steak
Tip steak

Marinate or rub and slow-cook (either over indirect heat, or in a smoker)
Short ribs
Back ribs
Brisket (must use a smoker)

Bison, Veal, Pork, and Lamb

Marinate, season, or just grill as is
Bison rib-eye, New York, or strip steaks
Veal cutlets (scaloppine)
Lamb rib chops
Lamb riblets
Pork or lamb loin chops
Pork tenderloin
Marinate or rub and slow-cook
Veal leg
Veal breast
Veal shoulder
Leg of lamb or leg of lamb roast

Fajitas

Skirt steak is a stringy cut, but it has a lot of flavor. It's the preferred cut for fajitas, although a lot of folks use flank steak these days. Traditionally soaked in lime and chiles, it's marinated in just about anything these days (yes, even in Texas). Cook flank steak quickly over direct heat; medium rare is best. It should be sliced very thinly and served in warmed tortillas, accompanied by pico de gallo (fresh tomato salsa) and guacamole.

Ribs and Brisket: Take Your Time

When you say "barbecue," a high percentage of people think "ribs." All ribs should be marinated and grilled over indirect heat, or cooked even more slowly in a smoker. Both beef and pork ribs are done when the thickest portion reaches an internal temperature of 160 to 165°F, or when you can easily tear the meat from the bone.

Tasty Tidbit

Fajita is the diminutive form of *faja,* or Spanish for "girdle." On a steer, the girdle (just behind the front legs) is where skirt steak comes from. So "chicken fajitas" is a contradiction in terms. Fajitas probably were invented by Mexican and African-American cowboys on the King Ranch, a massive spread that eats up a good portion of southwestern Texas. The ranch owners got the best cuts of meat; the hired hands got the tough stuff, which they turned into a great dish by marinating it, grilling it, and slicing it real thin.

Spareribs

This very popular cut comes from the pig's underbelly or side. Spareribs have a high percentage of fat, which helps keep them moist on the grill, and a rich flavor. They have the least meat of the rib cuts, though. They can be grilled over indirect heat, and usually are marinated or rubbed.

Baby Back Ribs (Loin Ribs)

Baby back ribs, which can be either pork or beef, come from the blade and center section of the loin. They have less meat than spareribs, but are very flavorful.

Country-style "ribs," which come in both pork and beef varieties, also come from the loin. They're very meaty and are usually eaten with a fork and knife. You can get them with or without the bones. Our suggestion is to go for the bones—they add flavor.

Short ribs, flanken ribs, or cross-cut ribs come from the beef chuck. These are not particularly tender, so they are best marinated and slow-cooked.

Lamb riblets are less popular, but delicious. They're small and don't have much meat, but are very tender. Unlike most ribs, they can be marinated and grilled over direct heat.

A Beautiful Brisket

Austin humorist Cactus Pryor is reported to have said, "It's common knowledge among the clergy that God invented brisket for Texans."

The brisket is about the toughest cut of beef you can find. Normally, it's not edible unless it's cooked for hours in liquid—and some might argue it's not edible even then. However, Texans are famous for barbecuing it to perfection. You cannot rush brisket. It requires long hours of cooking in a smoker—figure on a good hour or more a pound—to get tender. Barbecue it fat-side up. About halfway through the cooking time, wrap the brisket in foil to keep it from drying out too much. It's done when the inside reaches 160°F.

Pork Chops, Tenderloin, and Roast

We love pork tenderloin on the grill. As meats go, it's actually a very virtuous cut, rating just below chicken breast in saturated fat and total fat. And as long as you don't overcook it, it's also quite a delicious piece of meat.

The tenderloin, a strip from the center of the loin, usually weighs about ³/₄ to 1 pound; tenderloins often come two to a package. They're very good rubbed with a mixture of finely minced garlic, black pepper, and rosemary or sage. Or, give them an Asian touch with hoisin sauce, ginger, and garlic.

To keep it from toughening, cook the tenderloin over direct heat for a fairly short amount of time, usually about 18 to 25 minutes. It should get nicely crusted on the outside and be cooked through in the center but still very juicy.

Pork chops are delicious on the grill, and should be cooked like steaks, without the searing. Unlike steaks, they should not be served medium rare; cook them to 160°F.

Boneless rolled pork loin roasts also are excellent on the grill. Cook them over indirect heat.

Carolina pulled pork is made with pork butt, a roast that can be hard to find sometimes, at least outside of the Carolinas. Some folks cook the pork shoulder. This is another smoke-it-all-day affair (for a recipe, see page 247.)

Lamb

Lamb chops are superb on the grill, over direct heat. It's OK to cook them to medium rare (145°F).

Lamb sirloin roast or a leg half can be cooked over indirect heat. So can a whole leg, although slow-cooking in a smoker is probably the better way to go.

Veal

Although we mention it in the list above, veal is not a favorite for grilling. It's very lean and dries out quickly. Veal cutlets can be cooked quickly over direct heat. Roasting cuts can be cooked over indirect heat, but marinate them and serve them with some sort of sauce.

Flavors That Go Well with Meats

Vibrant, strong flavors go wonderfully with red meats, especially beef and lamb. Try orange or tangerine, onion, garlic, rosemary, cumin, cinnamon, red wine, beer, tomatoes, soy sauce, chiles, or black pepper—just for starters. Red wine or red wine vinegar marinades are a natural.

For smoking woods, hickory, pecan, oak, and mesquite all go very nicely with beef or lamb. Mesquite is really too heavy for pork, though, so try pecan, corn cobs, or a fruit wood such as apple.

The Least You Need to Know

➤ Steaks, burgers, chops, and pork tenderloin should be cooked quickly over direct heat.

➤ Roasts and ribs should be marinated and cooked over indirect heat.

➤ Match red meats with deep, vibrant flavors.

Chapter 12

Birds of a Feather

> ### In This Chapter
>
> ➤ Basic poultry preparation and grilling techniques
>
> ➤ Types of poultry, and how best to cook them
>
> ➤ Flavors that go well with poultry

Turkeys are a native American fowl. In fact, Ben Franklin wanted to make the turkey our national bird. The bald eagle, he complained to one correspondent, "is a bird of bad moral character," and not nearly as respectable as the turkey, "a true original native of America."

Actually, given Ben Franklin's reputation as a man of pleasure, we're tempted to suspect his real problem with the bald eagle was that it didn't taste as good as the turkey.

Then again, if the turkey were our national bird it would probably be a crime to grill it. And turkey—as well as all other fowl—is superb on the grill.

Poultry on the Grill

Chicken breast is one of the most popular cuts for grilling. It's lean, not too expensive, and cooks quickly. Its leanness also works against it, though. If you're not careful, chicken breast can turn to shoe leather on the grill. Here's how to keep it moist (the same tips apply to turkey breast, by the way):

Hot Tip

When you grill whole poultry or the wings by themselves, cut off the tips of the wings. They burn easily. Store them in freezer bags and use them to make chicken stock. (To do that, just cover with water, toss in some pieces of carrot, celery, and onion, and simmer for 1 to 2 hours.)

➤ Grill it in its skin. The fat will help baste the meat. You can still get rid of nearly all the fat by removing the skin before serving.

➤ Marinate skinless, boneless breasts in a liquid that contains oil, or simply brush lightly with olive oil before grilling.

➤ Don't overcook it. Chicken breast is done when it reaches 170°F. It will feel firm, and when you pierce it, the juices will run clear.

Check poultry for doneness by wiggling a drumstick (it should move freely), piercing the skin (the juices should run clear), or inserting an instant-read thermometer in the thickest part of the bird but not touching bone (it should read 170°F for the breast, 180°F for dark meat).

Don't worry if the meat near the bone looks bloody, if the chicken is otherwise cooked through. This is caused by the red hemoglobin seeping out of the bones, and is especially common in young chickens. It's harmless.

Poultry generally does not need long marinating: 1 to 2 hours should be enough in most cases.

When you cook poultry with the skin over direct heat, set it a bit off center on the grid, rather than directly over the hot coals, so the fat dripping from the skin does not cause flare-ups.

If you smoke poultry for longer than 2 hours, the skin will be tough. Remove it before serving.

Should you wash poultry before using it? This gets rid of surface bacteria on the bird, but also tends to splatter said bacteria around the sink area. If you do rinse poultry, be sure to carefully clean up the sink and surrounding area with hot, soapy water.

Slip herbs under the skin for more flavor. Place the whole chicken or turkey breast side up on a clean surface, with the cavity facing you. Gently ease up the skin on one side of the breastbone, trying not to tear the skin, to form a pocket. Using your fingers, carefully enlarge the pocket until your fingers (or whole hand, depending on the size of the bird) are inside. Don't force the skin away where it's attached to the breastbone or bottom of the drumstick. Repeat on the other side of the breastbone. Rub spices, garlic, and/or herbs between the chicken meat and the loosened skin. As the bird grills, fat from the skin will combine with the flavorings to baste the bird and produce a delicious dish.

Don't salt poultry before cooking; that draws out its juices.

Cutting slits into chicken or turkey legs will help the marinade or paste penetrate deeper in the meat. If you're not marinating the bird, never pierce or cut slits in it before grilling; the chicken will lose juices and dry out.

To butterfly poultry, use poultry shears or a boning knife to remove the backbone. Then press on the bird to flatten it. You'll hear a few joints crack (hopefully they're the bird's, not yours). Butterflied poultry cooks more quickly and evenly. You'll only need to butterfly poultry when there's no one else around who can do it—after all, that's what butchers are for. Don't be afraid to ask your butcher to cut an order to your liking.

Hot Tip

When you grill or rotisserie a whole chicken or turkey, tuck or tie the legs and wings close to the body. This helps keep them from burning before the interior of the bird is done.

Ditto for boning chicken breast. If you have a recipe for grilling boneless breasts and all you have is bone-in breasts in the fridge, just make the recipe with the bone-in breasts and extend the cooking time a bit. Life really is too short to bone a chicken breast unless you're getting paid to do it.

Never thaw poultry, especially whole birds, at room temperature. Instead, remove it from the freezer to the refrigerator. In a pinch, you also can thaw poultry, still wrapped, in a sinkful of cold water, replenishing the water frequently. Smaller chicken pieces, such as boneless breasts and thighs, can be thawed in the microwave as long as you cook them immediately. Never defrost whole poultry in the microwave.

So, What About That Thanksgiving Turkey?

Won't your friends and family be impressed when you've cooked your holiday turkey on the grill? Can a brisket be far behind?

Of course, what you don't have to reveal to your friends is that cooking large pieces of poultry on the grill requires more time and patience than skill. Besides yielding a totally luscious bird, cooking turkey on the grill frees up your oven for the side dishes. And as anyone who's juggled a holiday menu knows, that's no minor consideration.

Here's how to do grill a 12- to 14-pound turkey (enough to feed 8 to 10 people, with leftovers), step by step:

1. The No. 1 important step: Make sure your grill is large enough to hold the turkey you have in mind! A tabletop model won't cut it here. The average grill has a large enough cooking grid to accommodate a 12- to 14-pound turkey, but you also need to make sure the lid is deep enough to cover the grill with no gaps. If in doubt, take a measuring tape to the store. (If nothing else, it will amuse your fellow shoppers.)

2. If the turkey is frozen, you'll have to thaw it first. Remove it from the freezer to the refrigerator a good 2¹/₂ days before you plan to cook it. A 12- to 14-pounder shouldn't take more than 2 days to thaw, but the extra half day is "insurance" in case your refrigerator runs a bit colder than normal.

3. If you like, you can marinate the turkey for a couple of hours in a mixture of white wine, a little olive oil, and herbs of your choice. This is just for flavor, and not necessary for tenderness; the fat from the skin will baste the turkey nicely.

4. Remove the neck and giblets from the body cavities (usually there will be two bags, one in the neck cavity and one in the tail end). Rinse the turkey inside and out, and pat it dry.

5. Place the turkey on a roasting rack in a heavy-duty foil roasting pan. Tuck the legs and wings in to streamline the turkey's shape as much as possible. For best results, fold down the flap of neck skin to cover the cavity, and tie the legs together with cotton string or twine. If the turkey has a metal piece holding the legs in place, leave it in place (that is, if you can get the giblets out without removing it). If you like, you can stick a couple of garlic cloves, some lemon or orange slices, or bay leaves in the cavity. Brush the outside of the bird with a little melted butter or olive oil.

6. Prepare your charcoal or gas grill for indirect heat. Refrigerate the turkey while the coals heat.

7. Place the turkey, in its roasting pan, on the center of the cooking grid over the drip pan (or in a gas grill, the burner(s) that's off). Grill for 11 to 13 minutes per pound, or until a thermometer inserted into the thickest part of the thigh reads 180°F. The drumsticks should move easily when wiggled. The total cooking time will be about 2¹/₄ to 3 hours. Adjust the time upward if you're grilling in a snowstorm.

8. If you are using a charcoal grill, you will have to replenish the charcoal every now and then. Check the coals every 45 minutes, and add more lit coals as necessary.

9. Let the turkey stand for 15 minutes, then carve it.

You can cook a turkey breast or breast roast the same way. Grill it to an internal temperature of 170°F. You also can cook turkey legs over indirect heat, to a temperature of 180°F.

Types of Poultry, and How to Prepare and Grill Them

Regardless of type, most whole birds should be cooked over indirect heat, and should stand for 15 minutes before carving, so the juices have a chance to settle.

Broiler/fryer

Young chickens weighing about 2 to 3$\frac{1}{2}$ pounds, these are mildly flavored, tender, and a bit fatty. Whole broiler/fryers and large pieces are cooked indirectly. Figure on 45 minutes to an hour for a whole bird. Cut-up pieces (drumsticks, thighs, breast halves) can be cooked over direct heat.

Free-Range Chicken

A broiler-fryer that's been raised in the yard, rather than in cages. Most free-range birds also are raised without the use of feed additives, hormones, and so on. Aficionados (who include us) say they have a slightly richer flavor than conventionally raised chicken. They tend to be smaller, averaging 1$\frac{1}{2}$ to 3$\frac{1}{2}$ pounds. Unless they're butterflied or cut into serving pieces, they should be cooked over indirect heat.

Chicken Wings

Brush them lightly with sauce and cook briefly over direct heat. Because you cannot really remove the skin without removing much of the meat, wings do tend to be high in fat—which is probably why they're so popular. Do snip off the wing tips before grilling so they won't burn.

What's What

The most famous chicken wing dish is undoubtedly *Buffalo wings,* named for the city in New York where they originated. To make them, you snip the wings in two (making a mini-"drumstick" and a wing portion), marinate them in a spicy red pepper rub, and grill. If your calorie and fat allotment allow, you can drizzle them with a mixture of butter, wine vinegar, and Tabasco before serving. Buffalo wings are traditionally served with celery sticks, and a blue cheese dip.

Capon

The traditional roasting chicken, a capon is a male bird that has been castrated to make it fatter. An average bird weighs in at about 6 to 8 pounds. It has a bit more fat than a broiler/fryer. You should grill-roast capon whole, over indirect heat.

Cornish Hen

These small (16- to 20-ounce), fairly lean birds have a mild flavor. If they're butterflied, they can be cooked over direct heat; otherwise, cook them by the indirect method.

Duck and Goose

These birds are so fatty that it's best not to cook them over direct heat; you'll have nothing but one flare-up after another. However, they're both great cooked over indirect heat or, even better, slow-cooked in a smoker.

Boneless duck breast is great on the grill. Unfortunately, it's also rather hard to find outside of gourmet markets and some meat markets. You can buy it mail order (see Appendix C: Resources). Duck breast has a rich, full-bodied meat that needs little dressing up. Cook it with the skin on direct heat, but off to the side a bit so it's not right over the coals. It will cause flare-ups.

Because of different processing methods, duck is less subject to salmonella than chicken is. Thus, duck breast often is served with some pink in the middle.

Both duck and goose are dark meat poultry, and often are served with red wine.

Quail

Tiny birds that usually weigh in at about 3 to 6 ounces. Plan on two per serving. They are small enough to be cooked over direct heat. Quail have lean, dark meat that's a bit on the chewy side, and benefit from being marinated for an hour or two. You'll find fresh or frozen quail in some Asian markets (they're popular in Vietnamese cooking), gourmet food stores, and some larger supermarkets.

Squab

Somewhat larger than quail but rarely bigger than Cornish hens, squab are actually . . . well, pigeons. We hasten to add that these are not the cooing intruders that poop all over your windowsill, but young, domesticated pigeons that have never flown, making them nice and plump and tender. Squab usually weigh under a pound, and can be grilled like Cornish hens. They're available frozen, and occasionally fresh, in some gourmet markets.

Ground Turkey or Chicken

Depending on whether it's just the breast meat or has the skin ground in as well, ground turkey can be very lean, or as fatty as ground beef. Grill it the same way you grill lean ground beef, being very careful not to overcook it. Brushing turkey breast burgers with a little olive oil helps keep them moist.

Turkey or Chicken Sausages

Generally lower in saturated fat, and usually total fat, than their all-beef or pork cousins, turkey and chicken sausages come in all sorts of flavors these days, from Italian to bratwurst to California-style with garlic and sun-dried tomatoes. Grill them as you would any sausage, but be extra careful not to overcook them since they can be leaner than their porky counterparts.

Actually, regardless of the type of sausage, we find it often works best to simmer the sausages first, then just heat them through on the grill.

Flavors That Go Well with Poultry

Both rich and delicate, poultry is a good foil for nearly any flavor you match it with. That's why the "poultry herbs" include just about all of them: basil, rosemary, dill, oregano, garlic, marjoram, lavender, cilantro, sage, and tarragon. Citrus, especially lemon, is also a good friend to chicken and turkey, as is nearly any white wine. Among the sweet spices, ginger, nutmeg, and allspice are great paired with poultry.

Duck, goose, and dark-meat chicken are rich and hearty enough to go with a "deeper" range of flavors, such as sherry, soy, Chinese fermented black beans, thyme, or red wine.

Fruit is fabulous with all poultry. Try Cornish hens or duck with grilled plums for a memorable feast. Cranberry sauce, of course, is a natural with turkey.

Smoke chicken over pecan or fruit woods. Duck or goose is assertive enough to stand up to hickory and possibly even mesquite.

Hot Tip

Chinese-style tea-smoked duck or chicken is delicious. Mix $1/2$ cup loose black tea with 1 cup brown sugar, and place it in the center of a double thickness of aluminum foil. Fold up the edges of the foil slightly. Place the tea packet right on the coals in your smoker. Or, put it on the coals or heat diffusers in a regular grill, cooking the poultry by the indirect method.

The Least You Need to Know

➤ Chicken breasts and other small or thin pieces should be cooked directly over the coals.

➤ Whole poultry is best cooked over indirect heat.

➤ There are very few seasonings that *don't* go with poultry.

Chapter 13

The Angle on Fish

In This Chapter

➤ The basics of fish preparation and grilling

➤ The basics of shellfish preparation and grilling

➤ Flavors that go well with fish and shellfish

You may never have enjoyed the memorable pleasure of catching a rainbow trout, or walleye, or salmon, and cooking it over a fire that very same afternoon. Or of digging up clams, and roasting them in a pit in the bracing salt air. But even if you don't fish, you have access to very fresh fish and shellfish, thanks to the wonders of modern transportation. A snapper that was merrily swimming around the Gulf Coast a couple of days ago can be jetted into Chicago in time for today's fish delivery, and be on your plate tonight.

Farm-raising of fish has made a difference as well. It has its drawbacks (as anyone who's tasted farm-raised salmon side by side with its wild cousin can attest), but it has made really fresh salmon, trout, mussels, and other delicacies readily available across the country.

Surveys show that Americans still don't grill fish much. We think that's a real shame. There's no better way to cook a good piece of fish or shellfish. Grilling allows seafood to keep its native flavors, while acquiring an intriguing hint of char. And don't even get us started on the wonders of smoked salmon, or mussels, or shrimp, or trout . . .

Freshness Is Everything

Because fish and shellfish are highly perishable and begin to deteriorate soon after they're caught, it's essential to make sure you get the freshest piece of seafood possible.

Choosing a good fish market is the first step. First, the place should smell briny, but clean. While occasional smells are unavoidable, you definitely want to avoid anyplace that makes you want to hold your nose when you walk in. If there are strong fishy smells, it means the market's storage and/or cleanup practices aren't up to par. And that probably extends to the fish as well.

Second, the market should have a high turnover. If the shrimp and salmon look like they've been sitting in the case for awhile, they have.

What's What

When a whole fish is *dressed,* that doesn't mean it's wearing clothes. It does mean that the fish has been scaled, gutted, and is ready to cook.

Third, the folks behind the counter should exhibit some knowledge. If you ask where the shrimp is from and whether it's been frozen before, they should know. If you ask them for a good substitute for halibut on the grill, they should know that too.

Fourth, but not necessarily last, the cooked fish and shellfish should be segregated from the raw stuff. And, signs should clearly label fish as fresh, or as previously frozen (or as supermarkets like to say, "thawed for your convenience").

Buying It

So, you've found a good market. How do you judge the freshness of an individual piece of fish? Let us tell you the ways:

➤ With rare exceptions (walleye being the most notable), whole fish should have clear, not cloudy eyes. It should look pink or faintly red, not brown, around the gills.

➤ Fish fillets and steaks, as well as scallops and shrimp, should look moist and shiny, not dull or milky. If you're on friendly terms with the fishmonger, ask to touch and smell the fish. It should smell faintly briny or somewhat nutty and sweet, never like ammonia. When you touch a fish fillet or steak, the flesh should be elastic enough to spring back.

➤ The tail on a live lobster should curl under its body, and it should wave its antenna and look fairly interested.

➤ Crabs should move when you poke them.

➤ Mollusks such as oysters, clams, and mussels should have tightly closed shells. Occasionally mussels will open their shells slightly, but should snap them smartly shut when you tap the shell with a fingernail or rap it lightly on the counter. Discard any shellfish whose shells won't close. They're dead, and deteriorating rapidly.

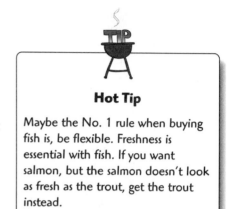

Hot Tip

Maybe the No. 1 rule when buying fish is, be flexible. Freshness is essential with fish. If you want salmon, but the salmon doesn't look as fresh as the trout, get the trout instead.

If you buy frozen fish, be absolutely certain that it is frozen solid. Ideally, frozen fish should be in an undamaged, moisture-and vapor-proof wrapping. It should have no odor. If you detect any aroma, notice any drying, white spots, deterioration, or spotting—or even suspect that the fish has been thawed and refrozen—do not buy it.

Fish Forms

Whole fish can be small, such as trout, or large, such as salmon. Small fish can be cooked over direct heat; large fish can be cooked over direct or indirect heat, depending on how thick it is and whether it's stuffed.

Fillets are cut lengthwise from the side of the fish, and are usually boneless. They should go skin side down on the grill, and are not turned unless they're at least an inch thick.

Steaks are cut crosswise. Salmon, swordfish, mahi mahi, and other fairly firm fish are sold this way. It's safe to assume that any fish sold as steaks can be grilled.

Kebobs. These are 1- to 1½-inch cubes cut from the steaks. You can cut kebabs from the fillets, but they'll be thinner pieces that may need to be threaded in 2 or 3 places on the skewers.

Storing and Thawing It

Fresh fish is very perishable; use it within 2 days of buying it. Use shellfish within one day. Frozen, raw fish will keep for 1 to 6 months. Plan to use frozen fish with a high fat content, such as salmon, within a month or two.

Never refreeze fish. It ruins the texture. You can store cooked fish in the refrigerator and use it within 2 days.

If you cannot cook the fish within a day or two, you'll have to freeze it. (This is assuming that it was fresh, not frozen, to begin with.) Plenty of fish markets and experienced anglers suggest placing fish fillets and steaks or live or cooked shellfish in a self-sealing freezer bag. Fill the bag with water, zip it shut, and put it in the freezer. (You can also pack the fillets in rinsed out milk cartons filled with water.) For whole fish or crab, they recommend that you freeze it for 48 hours, remove it from the freezer, dip it in water to form a glaze, then put it in a plastic bag and return it to the freezer. Both the water-in-the-bag method and the glazing method help prevent freezer burn.

Thaw fish in its wrapper in the refrigerator for 5 to 24 hours. Never thaw fish at room temperature. If necessary, you can thaw the fish quickly by placing it, still tightly wrapped, in cold water. It will take about 1 hour per pound to thaw it by this method; refresh the water every 30 minutes. Frozen fish can also be thawed in the microwave on 10 percent power for 10 to 15 seconds. Repeat the cycles until the fish is nearly thawed. Let it stand for another minute or two, then cook it immediately.

Hot Tip

Have a second pair of tweezers (you know, not the ones you use to pluck your eyebrows or nose hairs) reserved for kitchen use. They're indispensable for picking those bones out of fillets that the fish market missed.

Great Catches on the Grill

As long as it's been cleaned, fish needs little preparation before cooking. Just rinse it under cold running water and pat it dry. If you're cooking fillets, remove any bones you find with tweezers. (For steaks, it's easier to remove the bones after cooking. You can marinate it if you like; white wine and olive oil marinades are good with fish.)

If the fish is not marinated, brush it very lightly with olive oil or canola oil before cooking it. Keep it refrigerated until the coals are ready.

Except for large, whole fish, nearly all fish and shellfish cook quickly, over direct heat. Another exception is smoked fish, which, of course, you slow-cook in a smoker. You can cook thin fillets of fish that are still frozen, as long as you allow a little extra time.

Besides the fact that fish skin is much easier to remove after the fish is cooked than when the fish is raw, it adds flavor, so leave it on during grilling. It does tend to stick to the cooking grid, though, so make sure both the skin and the grid are well-oiled.

Keep fish refrigerated until it's time to put it on the grill. This not only helps keep it safe, but slows the cooking time so the fish will absorb more flavor from the smoke and aromatics. Don't salt fish or shellfish before cooking, which will toughen it.

Firm-textured fish are great on the grill; they don't fall apart, and can be used for kebabs. They include such favorites as catfish, grouper, ono, shark, swordfish, and tuna.

Fishy Flavors

Because you really should buy the freshest fish (and hopefully, one that also happens to be on sale), here's a chart showing how fish can be substituted for each other. The fish in each column can be substituted for one another. Note that this chart is based on flavor only; you may have to adjust cooking methods or times when you substitute fish.

Mild, sweet: Sea bass, striped bass, grouper, snapper, halibut, mahi mahi, ocean perch, freshwater perch, catfish (farm-raised), cod, scrod, flounder, haddock, pollack, orange roughy, ono, sole

Medium-mild, distinct: Tuna (all kinds), pompano, salmon (farm-raised), shark, swordfish, rainbow and brook trout, walleye, whitefish

Oily, distinctive flavor: Bluefish, mackerel, lake trout, salmon (wild)

Thin, delicate fillets, such as sole, whitefish, or cod, can be cooked on the grill. Rather than laying them directly on the grid, lay some orange, lemon, or lime slices, sliced peppers or onions, or sprigs of tarragon or other herbs on the grid, then lay the fish atop them (oil it first). Cover the grill, and do not turn the fish during cooking. Delicate fish can also be cooked in an oiled grill basket, on a nonstick grill screen, or on a double thickness of oiled aluminum foil into which you've poked a bunch of holes.

Fish also is an excellent choice for smoking. Whitefish, trout, salmon, shrimp, and mussels are very good smoked.

The classic cooking rule for fish is 10 minutes per inch of thickness, regardless of the type of fish or cooking method. Ninety percent of the time, it works like a charm. Fish is done when it turns opaque (but not dry) and flakes when prodded with a fork. Or, use a thermometer; fish must cook to an internal temperature of at least 145°F.

What's What

What, exactly, do we mean by *flake?* If you look at a fish fillet, you'll see that it's in sections, marked by faint lines in the flesh. When you prod cooked fish gently with a fork, these sections will begin to separate into pieces that look like large flakes. The same test works for most fish steaks, although they'll flake lengthwise instead of horizontally. However, the fish should not fall into pieces when you prod it; if it does, it's overcooked.

Marvelous Mollusks

If you like oysters raw on the half-shell, you'd better learn to shuck them, or order them out in restaurants. But if you want to cook your mollusks—whether you're talking mussels, oysters, or clams—on the grill, the good news is that there's no reason to pry open the shells and risk losing a thumb. Just put them on the grill, and when they get hot enough, the shells will pop open. Nothing could be easier.

What's What

Just so this doesn't come as a shock, shellfish is called that because it has shells. Shellfish are divided into *mollusks* such as clams and mussels, which live inside hard shells, and *crustaceans*, which include shrimp, lobster, crayfish and similar critters who wear their skeletons on the outside.

Mollusks and small crustaceans such as shrimp should be cooked on a grill screen so they don't fall between the wires of the cooking grid. And unlike most foods, they're cooked over red-hot (glowing) coals. This heats them through quickly without turning them to rubber. Be very careful not to overcook shellfish; you want them to stay plump and juicy.

Mussels: These days, nearly all mussels are farm-raised and very clean. Just lightly scrub them, snip any "beards" (seaweed) hanging from the shells, and they're ready.

Hot Tip

Although any kind of clams will cook on the grill, we suggest using the smaller varieties, such as cherrystones, for grilling. They're generally more tender than the larger clams. Clams are available on both the West Coast and the East Coast.

Clams: When they're harvested, most clams clamp their shells shut, trapping sand and other stuff inside. This can make them gritty. To purge them of sand and other impurities, put the clams in salt water ($1/3$ cup of salt to a gallon of water) to which you've added a handful of cornmeal. Leave them for an hour. Drain off the water and debris, scrub the clams under cold water, and they're all set for the grill.

Scallops: Fortunately, these mollusks are nearly always shelled before they come to market. They require no preparation, other than an optional marinade, before cooking. You can grill bay scallops, but they are so small they have to be grilled quickly and on a grill screen. The sea scallops (about the size of a jumbo marshmallow) work best on the grill. If fresh ones are not available, frozen scallops are acceptable.

Oysters: You can thread shucked oysters on skewers (they're really good alternated with pieces of soft-cooked bacon) and cook them, kebab style, over direct heat.

Crispy Crustaceans

Crustaceans do need a certain amount of preparation before cooking, but if you're smart, you'll have the fishmonger do it. Note that crustaceans sold live, such as lobsters and crabs, must be cooked within hours of being killed and cleaned. So if you have the fishmonger clean them, buy them the same day you plan to grill them.

Lobsters: For quicker cooking, ask the fishmonger to butterfly the lobsters for you. If you cannot buy them the same day you'll be cooking them, you will have to buy them whole (that is, live) and refrigerate them. You can try butterflying them yourself: Put the lobster on its back, and with a very sharp knife, make a deep slit from thorax to tail, and cut the lobster in half lengthwise without cutting through the topshell. Open and press the lobster flat, and remove and discard the stomach and the white intestinal vein. The green tomalley (liver) and roe can be left in place.

If all this is too much for you, serve lobster tails or grill them whole after killing them (plunge a knife through the lobster right below the head). You can buy them frozen.

More to the point is how you *eat* a whole lobster. Pick the cooked lobster up in one hand and with the other hand, twist off the claws, one at a time. Pick up the lobster cracker (a tool that resembles a nutcracker) in your right hand, insert one of the lobster claws into it, and press down hard until the shell breaks. Break the lobster claw-shell in several places. Remove as much of the shell as possible with your fingers and eat the meat from both claws.

Next, pick up the whole lobster, holding the tail in one hand and the body/head section in the other, and bend the lobster up in the middle so it cracks in half; you'll have one section in each hand. Lay the tail section down and hold the body/head section belly side up. Stick your thumb between the meat and the shell and lift, using your fingers to pull the meat out of the shell. Break off the tiny claw-legs connected to the meat you've removed and reserve them for a moment. Then remove the second, softer undershell, called the belly shell.

Next, discard the black vein that runs the length of the body meat. You should also discard the small sac at the base of the lobster's head called the sand sac. Everything else—including the tomalley (green-colored liver)—is safe to eat. You may even find some coral-colored roe (eggs), if your lobster is female. Both the tomalley and the roe are delicious.

Finally, pick up the tail section. Bend the tail back and break the flippers off the end. Insert a lobster fork into the hole you've made and gently push the tail meat out the other end. Remove the black vein that runs the length of the tail and discard. To eat the small claw legs, put the open end of each into your mouth, and suck out the meat as if using a straw.

Or, with a sharp knife or scissors, cut away the translucent membrane from the tail meat, then use the knife to pry the lobster meat from the shell.

Shrimp: They can be shelled before or after cooking. To shell shrimp, tear open the shell on the inside of the curve (where the legs are), then peel off the rest of the shell. Although it is perfectly safe to eat the shrimp without removing the black sand vein located along the curved back, it is usually preferable to remove it for aesthetic purposes. Make a shallow cut down the back of the peeled shrimp and wash the black vein out under cold running tap water. Or, slip the tip of a small knife underneath it and pull it out. If you wish to cook the shrimp in their shells, split the shell down the back and remove the vein without removing the shell.

Soft-Shell Crabs

Although they look pretty passive in the fish case, crabs are sold live (unless they're already cooked). Have the friendly fishmonger clean them for you, and plan to grill them the same day you buy them. Soft-shell crabs are superb on the grill; just brush them with butter, and cook. You eat the shell right along with the meat.

If you grill hard-shell crabs, you follow basically the same procedure, with variations of course, that you do for getting the meat out of a lobster: crack, pick, and pry.

Flavors That Go Well with Fish and Shellfish

Citrus (lemon, lime, orange, tangerine, and sometimes grapefruit) was born to go with fish of any kind. The same holds true for dill and tarragon. Cilantro, fennel, and basil also are "fish-friendly."

Woods and aromatics: Try looking around your garden. Dried lilac twigs, soaked for 30 minutes, drained and scattered on the hot coals, delicately flavor fish. Alder is a time-honored smoking wood for fish, especially Northwest salmon. Be careful of hickory, mesquite, or other strong-flavored woods, which can overpower delicate fish. Stronger fish such as mackerel or salmon, however, can stand up to bold flavors.

The Least You Need to Know

➤ The fresher the fish or shellfish, the better.

➤ Handle and cook fish gently.

➤ Never refreeze fish.

➤ Never cook mussels, clams, or oysters whose shells stay open before cooking, or serve those that aren't open after cooking.

➤ "Ten minutes per inch" is a good cooking rule for fish.

Chapter 14

Fruits, Vegetables, and Grains

In This Chapter

➤ Grilling methods that work well with vegetables and fruits

➤ Which fruits and vegetables grill well, and how to prepare them

➤ Grain foods that can be grilled, and how to prepare them

➤ Flavors that go well with vegetables and grains

Grilling is usually associated with meat. That's probably a natural side effect of culinary evolution. Our forebears needed to build pits for cooking animals. They did roast the occasional root vegetable as well, but tended to eat a lot of their veggies raw and their fruits raw or dried.

With the modern grill, it's silly not to cook vegetables and fruits this way. Many of them taste downright luscious on the grill, and it's simply a matter of putting your equipment and fuel to good use. While you're grilling six hamburgers, why not brown some potato skins as well?

Most vegetables and fruits need to be cut or sliced before they go on the grill. That also means they have to be cooked on a grill screen, or threaded on skewers.

If you're cooking a roast or whole chicken over indirect heat, toss some vegetables on the grill as well, during the last 15 to 20 minutes of the meat's cooking time. Simply put them on a double thickness of foil, add a tablespoon or two of water, and seal up the foil into a loose package. The vegetables should get tender-crisp in 15 to 30 minutes, depending on the type of vegetable.

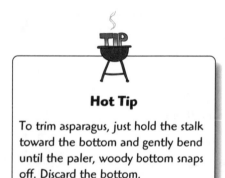

Vegetables

These vegetables are especially suited for grilling.

Artichokes

You'll need to use either fresh baby artichokes—the kind that can be eaten whole, with just a little trimming—frozen artichoke hearts, or marinated artichokes from a jar. Drain them well before grilling. They're great seasoned with rosemary, parsley, and/or basil; garlic, and a squeeze of lemon.

Asparagus

This one's easy. Just trim the woody bottoms from the stalks, brush the stalks lightly with oil, and grill until they begin to brown.

Beets

Because they're so dense, beets can be tricky. You can wrap them in foil and cook them right in the embers, like potatoes. But it's probably easier to boil them until they're fork-tender but still firm. Drain them, peel them, cut them in half, brush them lightly with oil, and char on the grill. If you like, soak them in an orange juice-based marinade for an hour first. They have a high sugar content and can burn easily, so keep an eye on them.

Carrots

They're very good grilled, but really need to boiled briefly first, or cooked by the foil-packet method. Brush them lightly with butter or oil, and sprinkle with mint or tarragon.

Corn

The classic way to grill corn is as whole ears. Old-time recipes will tell you to first use roasting ears—whatever that means. You're likely to have one or two varieties of sweet corn to choose from—whatever your store or farmers market is selling that day. Just about all the sweet corn sold these days is the sugar-enhanced stuff that can burn easily on the grill.

Pull down the husks of each ear, but do not pull them off. Remove as much of the silk as possible. Replace the husks, and tie the top. Soak the ears of corn in a tub of cold water for at least 30 minutes, and preferably an hour or so. Then put on the grill over medium-hot coals. Cover, and grill for at least a half hour.

However, for the sake of convenience and excellent flavor, we find it works a bit better to husk the ears, cut them into three pieces each, and just grill directly for about 6 minutes, turning them 2 or 3 times, until slightly charred. You don't need to soak the corn when you use this method, though you should lightly brush it with butter or oil.

Eggplant

Small eggplants just need to be trimmed.

Trim off the cap of the eggplant and cut it length-wise into $1/4$ to $1/2$-inch-thick slices. Grill directly over the coals, turning at least 2 or 3 times, until lightly charred and tender. This can take a good 20 minutes.

Garlic

Grill-roasted garlic is a real treat. Peel off the outermost papery skin, but leave the inner skin intact. Leave the head of garlic whole; don't separate the cloves. Brush it lightly with olive oil, then wrap it loosely in foil. (This keeps it from charring and turning acrid.) Cook over direct heat for about 30 minutes, or indirect heat for about 45 minutes, or until the garlic softens enough that you can squeeze it out of its skin, like toothpaste.

Hot Tip

Some eggplants, especially the larger, seedier ones, tend to be bitter. To avoid this, slice the eggplant, salt the slices on both sides, and let the eggplant drain in a colander for 20 to 30 minutes. Rinse, then pat dry. This draws out the bitter juices.

Mushrooms

They're great on the grill. An especially good grilling mushroom is the *portobello*. Brush the whole or sliced caps with oil, sprinkle with marjoram or rosemary, and grill until browned and tender, about 4 minutes for smaller caps, 10 minutes for very large ones. Smaller mushrooms can be grilled the same way.

What's What

Its fancy name aside, the *portobello* (also called *portabella*) is essentially just a large *cremino,* or brown domesticated mushroom. You can buy whole mushrooms or the sliced caps in the produce department. Portobellos have a very chewy, some might say meaty, texture and deep flavor that make them a good meat alternative. They're good on pizzas, in sandwiches, or as an appetizer, grilled and sprinkled lightly with herbs.

Onions

It's best to cut them into thick rings or wedges. Brush lightly with olive oil, and cook over direct heat (but not the hottest part of the grill) for about 10 minutes, or until lightly charred and tender. Green onions (scallions) are really good grilled; just trim, brush with oil, and grill for about 5 minutes.

Peas

For obvious reasons, you can't grill regular old round peas on the grill, even with a screen. Snow peas and snap peas, though, can be lightly grilled, either directly for a minute or two, or in foil packets for a few minutes. Cook them just until they turn bright green.

Peppers

To roast peppers, leave them whole. Place them on the grill over medium-hot or glowing-hot coals. When the pepper is charred and blistered, rotate it a quarter turn (or turn it over if it's a fairly flat pepper) and roast that side. Continue until the pepper is charred all over. While it's still hot, place it in a heavy-duty self-sealing plastic bag for 5 minutes to steam. Then, remove from bag, and pull and scrape the skin off under cold running water. Cut off the stem, cut the pepper in half lengthwise, and remove the core and seeds. Serve immediately, refrigerate for up a week, or put the peppers in freezer bags, seal tightly, and freeze.

Potatoes

Potatoes can be wrapped in foil, pierced in several places, and cooked either on the grid over indirect heat or right in the coals (charcoal grill only). They'll take anywhere from 45 minutes to $1^{1}/_{2}$ hours to cook. Serve immediately, or refrigerate.

Summer Squash

Zucchini and yellow squash are very good on the grill. Just slice them lengthwise, brush them with some olive oil, sprinkle with a few herbs, and grill for a couple of minutes on each side.

Sweet Potatoes

Sweet potatoes can be wrapped in foil and cooked in the embers, like regular potatoes, for about 1 to 1½ hours, depending on their size. Or, boil or microwave the sweet potatoes until tender but still firm, cut them in half lengthwise, brush with a bit of butter or oil, and grill, cut side down, until charred. Sprinkle them with candied ginger.

Tomatoes

Cherry tomatoes are a longtime standard on kebabs. Or, cut larger tomatoes in half lengthwise, salt lightly if desired, brush with oil, and grill, cut side down. Tomatoes should be grilled only briefly so they don't get too soft.

Winter Squash

Winter squash can be cooked over indirect heat, just like you would bake it in the oven. Pierce it in several places, and cook until fork-tender.

Vegetables You Can't Grill

Lettuce, spinach, cabbage, cucumbers, radishes, celery. They'll either shrivel, or grilling will bring out their bitterness. Save them for the salad. Oh, and olives. Theoretically you could probably grill them, but why would you? And forget avocados; they'd turn to mush.

Fruits

One of the simplest, best-tasting desserts of all is grilled fruit, plain or sprinkled with a bit of sugar. A hint of smokiness beautifully enhances the sweetness of bananas, kiwifruit, melon, oranges—you name it. For a taste-tempting selection of fruit-based desserts, see Chapter 23.

Do remember that because of its sugar content, fruit burns easily. Be sure to keep an eye on it while it cooks.

Apples

They're very nice on the grill, either as a dessert, or as a side to savory foods such as fish or pork. Core and slice them, brush lightly with butter, and grill just until tender and beginning to brown.

Bananas

They were born for the grill. They discolor, so they should be peeled and sliced lengthwise shortly before grilling. Sprinkling them with a little lemon or lime juice will help keep them from turning too brown. Brush them with a bit of melted butter, sprinkle lightly with cinnamon, nutmeg, or allspice, and grill, cut side down, until they just begin to caramelize. Grilled bananas are out of this world with vanilla ice cream or frozen yogurt.

Cantaloupe

Remove the peel and seeds and cut it into wedges or slices. Brush with a little oil, sprinkle lightly with brown sugar, and grill just until warmed through.

Citrus Fruits

They make a great foil for fish, pork, and poultry. Lemons and limes can be sliced and put under fish, or used as a flavoring agent in the drip pan. Grapefruit makes a tangy relish for fish. Directly grilling lemons and limes could make them acrid, but orange sections or slices are great sprinkled with sugar and briefly warmed on the grill.

Tasty Tidbit

Did you know that a medium kiwifruit has more vitamin C than an orange? In fact, the jewel-green fruits also are excellent sources of fiber, potassium, and vitamin E. All this, and they're good-looking, too. Don't put them in a gelatin mold, though; a substance in the kiwi inhibits jelling.

Kiwifruit

This one's easy. Cut it in half crosswise, brush lightly with oil or butter, and grill, cut side down, just until toasted a bit. Your guests can scoop the fruit out with spoons to eat it.

Mangoes

Marvelous. Cut lengthwise through the fruit on all four sides, cutting as close to the pit as possible. You'll want large, lengthwise slices. It may be easiest to leave the skin on until after they're cooked. Brush the mango slices lightly with butter and grill, cut side down, just until they begin to lightly brown.

Papayas

Perfect. Prepare them like cantaloupe.

Peaches or Nectarines

Fabulous when brushed with a bit of melted butter and/or melted peach jam. Peaches should be peeled first. You'll have to cut up the fruit just before grilling it, since it can discolor.

Pears

They're great. Prepare them like apples.

Pineapple

Here's another fruit that was born to be grilled. Grill thick pineapple rings (preferably fresh) just until lightly browned. Sprinkle with a bit of rum and/or brown sugar if you prefer.

Legumes and Grains on the Grill

No, you probably don't want to cook beans on the grill—although placing a pan of already baked beans over charcoal can infuse them with a pleasing smokiness. But tofu grills beautifully. So do breads and polenta (cooked cornmeal). You can even brown cake on the grill. Pair it with grilled fruit for a superb finish to your meal.

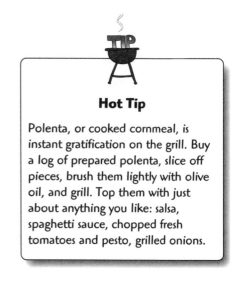

Hot Tip

Polenta, or cooked cornmeal, is instant gratification on the grill. Buy a log of prepared polenta, slice off pieces, brush them lightly with olive oil, and grill. Top them with just about anything you like: salsa, spaghetti sauce, chopped fresh tomatoes and pesto, grilled onions.

Breads

The heat on a grill is a bit too variable to successfully bake most breads from scratch. You can bake a pizza crust, though (see page 220), and warm up tortillas and other breads of every description.

Cake

No, you can't bake it on the grill, of course. But you can slice a dense cake such as pound cake, brush it lightly with butter, and lightly toast it on the grill. Superb! For more information and for recipes incorporating grilled cake, see Chapter 23.

Tofu

Also known as soybean curd, this is actually more of a protein food than a vegetable. Firm tofu, with the liquid squeezed out of it, is very good on the grill. Squeeze out the liquid by cutting the tofu into $1/2$-inch thick slices; place between paper towels, and gently but firmly press on the tofu.

Tofu takes well to any marinade, and will absorb flavors like a sponge. Just marinate it in your favorite barbecue sauce (or in a mixture of soy sauce and molasses), pat dry, and grill on an oiled grill screen until it is golden and crusty.

Flavors That Go Well with Vegetables and Grains

You normally don't have to marinate fruits and vegetables, although you can if you want to add some flavor. In general, sweet herbs and spices go with sweet vegetables, and salty or sweet-salty sauces are nice with more bitter vegetables. Try ginger, hoisin sauce, or barbecue sauce. Rosemary goes with an incredible array of vegetables and fruits. So does basil.

For smoking, pick fruit woods for sweet vegetables: apple or pear for sweet potatoes, and so on. Pecan goes beautifully with all vegetables. Be careful about using strong flavors such as hickory or mesquite with starchy foods such as potatoes, or with tofu; they can absorb quite a bit of smoke, becoming unpleasantly bitter.

The Least You Need to Know

➤ Vegetables and fruits can be cooked or warmed very successfully on the grill.

➤ Fruits burn easily on the grill, so keep an eye on them.

➤ You can't bake breads, other than pizza crust, from scratch on the grill, but you can warm them.

Chapter 15

A Second Life

Phoenix-o-matic

In This Chapter

➤ Properly storing grilled leftovers

➤ Heating them up

➤ Soups, sandwiches, salads, and other dishes to use up grilled favorites

---

You will, of course, have no leftovers from your grilling parties. Everyone will gobble down every last bit of food and praise you for cooking it so beautifully. On the off chance, however, that you do have a scrap of tuna, chicken, or potato left, we want to point out that grilled foods taste wonderful in a vast variety of "recycled" soups, salads, and sandwiches.

We've put together a list of ideas for using up grilled leftovers. These are not recipes, but merely ideas. How you use them depends entirely on what you've grilled, how much you have left, and whatever ingredients you can scrounge up.

Storing Leftovers

Foods must be refrigerated promptly. If the barbecued chicken has been sitting out on your patio for 4 hours, toss it. Foods should be refrigerated, in shallow containers, within 1 hour of when they finished cooking. Cover them with plastic wrap so they don't dry out.

Grilled foods should be used within a few days. They may be frozen, although not for as long as raw foods. See Chapter 4 for specifics on storing foods.

Hot Tip

Whenever you grill, try to cook more than you'll need. "Planned left-overs" make future meals much easier. This also means thinking ahead when you're thawing meats; take out not only the steaks for tonight's meal, but the chicken breasts you'll grill for tomorrow's dinner.

Don't Get Burned!

The microwave can turn meats into rubber if you overcook them. Start off at 80 percent power and short cycles (a minute or two), and repeat until the food is heated through. If your microwave does not have a rotating surface inside, turn the plate a quarter turn between cycles.

Heating Them Up

The cardinal food safety rule—keep hot foods hot and cold foods cold—applies to cooked leftovers as much as it does to raw foods. You can slice that grilled steak cold from the refrigerator for a nice sandwich, but if you're going to heat it, heat it all the way through. While cooking does kill bacteria, foods pick up bacteria from the air, your knife, and even the plate you put them on. Bacteria love to thrive in that zone between 40 and 140°F.

One of the easiest ways to reheat leftovers is in the microwave. But it also poses a danger, because the microwave tends to cook foods from the outside in, meaning that chicken breast can look steaming hot on the outside and still be cool or warm in the center. The most efficient way to reheat in the microwave is to cut food into slices or other small pieces, arrange it on a plate with the thickest portions facing out, and cover the plate loosely with waxed paper.

If you're using meats in soups or stir-fries, just add them to the dish and stir until they're heated through.

Creative "Recycling"

So, here are some ideas for fabulous soups and casseroles, salads, and sandwiches made with various grilled foods.

How you use leftovers depends on how they're seasoned. You don't really want to add chicken flavored with basil and rosemary to a Chinese-style dish.

Poultry

➤ *Chicken noodle soup.* Heat up a large can of chicken broth. Toss in some grilled, diced chicken, some cooked spaghetti, and some sliced scallions and/or herbs. To make an even richer soup, toss any wing tips (raw) that you've saved into the boiling broth.

➤ *Chicken salad.* Cut the chicken into small cubes. Toss it with some chopped raw celery and onion, and cubed apples or pears, or halved grapes. Moisten with mayonnaise, French dressing, or another dressing of your choice. Serve in sandwiches or on a bed of lettuce.

➤ *Chicken Caesar.* Chop up some Romaine lettuce (or buy a bag or two already chopped). Cut the cooked chicken into strips. Mix the lettuce with some Caesar salad dressing. Add the chicken and a generous handful of grated fresh Parmesan cheese. Toss well. Top with seasoned croutons. If you like, you can finely chop a drained anchovy fillet or two and add it to the salad, or just wipe it around the bowl for subtle flavoring.

➤ *Chicken slaw.* Shredded, cold grilled poultry of any kind can be added to broccoli slaw or cabbage slaw. Add a handful of raisins and some coleslaw dressing, and toss.

➤ *Poultry-grain salad.* Chop the chicken or turkey and add it to stuffing (made from scratch or a mix), a grain salad, or tabbouleh (a bulgur salad of middle eastern origin— delicious).

➤ *Turkey deli sandwich.* Thinly slice grilled turkey, chicken, or duck. Put on toasted egg bread (such as challah) that has been spread with cream cheese and cranberry sauce.

➤ *Instant burritos.* Thinly slice the chicken and roll it up in warmed tortillas with refried beans and a light sprinkling of cheese. Serve with salsa.

Don't Get Burned!

Chicken should not be overcooked on the grill as it will get dry and tasteless. When the chicken begins to look done, cut into one piece and check the center. The chicken is done when all traces of pink are gone, but the juices still flow freely.

Tasty Tidbit

Caesar salad is not named for the man of "Et tu, Brute" fame—at least not directly. The Romaine lettuce salad, dressed with a garlic vinaigrette and tossed with grated Parmesan, is named after Italian chef Caesar Cardini, who supposedly created it in 1924 at his restaurant in Tijuana, Mexico.

Beef

➤ *Philly-style sandwich.* Thinly slice grilled steak. Reheat it and pile it on a length of French bread, with grilled onions and melted American cheese.

➤ *Beef and peppers.* An awesome combo. Thinly slice the beef and grilled red or green peppers, and pile between slices of French or Italian bread. Season with a bit of Italian dressing.

➤ *Tacos al carbon.* Spread guacamole thinly over a flour tortilla. Thinly slice grilled beef and roasted chiles, and arrange them evenly on the tortilla. Wrap up tightly, and cut crosswise in half.

➤ *Roast beef sandwich, deli style.* Put thinly sliced grilled beef on dark rye rolls with good pickles and a generous smear of grated horseradish.

➤ Chop up the meat and put it in chili.

➤ Cut the beef into cubes and add it to beef or vegetable stew (homemade or canned).

Pork

➤ *Pork and fruit salad.* Cold, seasoned pork is good sliced and served with apple wedges, sliced pears, or pineapple chunks.

➤ *Midwest-style sandwich.* Slice pork thinly and put between slices of whole-grain bread, with grainy brown mustard and thinly sliced red onions.

➤ *Quick stir-fry.* Cut pork into slices and add to a stir-fry with broccoli and hoisin or oyster sauce (to keep from overcooking the meat, add it to the stir-fry during the last minute or two, just to warm through).

➤ *Asian-inspired salad.* Cut cold pork into slices. Make a salad by arranging the pork on a plate with canned, drained mandarin oranges (or fresh orange or tangerine segments) and canned, drained water chestnuts. Drizzle with an orange, poppyseed, or sesame dressing, and sprinkle with chopped green onions.

➤ *Pork 'n beans.* Cut it into small cubes, and add to baked beans, either homemade or out of a can.

➤ *Pork fried rice.* Cut it into small cubes, and add it to fried rice or lo mein. (No need to make them yourself, either—just add the pork to your Chinese takeout favorites.)

Sausage or Ground Meats (any kind)

➤ *Skillet casserole.* Cut one or two baking potatoes into small cubes (you can peel or not, as you like) and cook in a bit of oil until nicely browned. Crumble the meat and add it to the potatoes, along with some chopped onion and whatever seasonings you like. Cook until the onion is tender and the meat is heated through. For an even quicker version of this dish, use frozen hash browns instead of fresh potatoes.

➤ Or, crumble the meat and add it to chili or spaghetti sauce.

➤ Sausage is good with beans of any kind.

Lamb

➤ *Lamb and bean salad.* Dice up lamb and add it to a can or two of drained cannelini or other white beans, along with chopped tomatoes (preferably grilled), chopped fresh sage, olive oil, and salt and pepper. This dish is good cold or hot.

➤ *Lamb tacos.* Roll the meat up in tortillas with grilled onions, tomatoes, and a bit of salsa.

➤ *Mediterranean rice salad.* Add lamb to cooked rice and some chopped artichokes (if you have them), and dress with a mixture of wine vinegar, olive oil, and mint.

➤ *Gyros-style sandwich.* Place slices of grilled lamb and grilled onions or roasted garlic in pita pockets. Add a dab of yogurt.

Fish and Shellfish

➤ *Tuna salad niçoise.* Arrange grilled cold tuna, separated into chunks, with green beans and potatoes on a plate. Drizzle with a white wine vinaigrette and a sprinkling of tarragon.

➤ *Scandinavian-inspired sandwiches.* Separate grilled fish (any kind, but salmon or tuna is especially good) into chunks, and put into pita bread pockets with cucumber salad, some mayonnaise or yogurt, and a sprinkling of dill.

➤ *Seafood pasta.* Add scallops, cut in half; fish (any kind), separated into chunks, or crab, chopped, to angel hair pasta with Alfredo sauce.

Hot Tip

A nice marinara sauce (bottled or homemade) makes a great base for leftover grilled foods. Chop up grilled clams or mussels and toss them in. Or, add grilled, crumbled beef, turkey, or sausage to the sauce. For a meatless sauce, toss in grilled, chopped artichokes or tomatoes.

➤ *Bagel spread.* Flake grilled salmon and mix with softened cream cheese and a sprinkling of chopped chives or dill to make a great topping for bagels.

➤ *Fish cakes.* Leftover crab, salmon, or tuna can be made into patties. To avoid making the already-cooked fish dry and mealy, mix it with mashed potatoes and some olive oil to moisten, and cook it gently, just until heated through.

➤ *Tropical shrimp salad.* Chop up grilled shrimp, moisten with a mayonnaise-style salad dressing, and serve in a sandwich or on a bed of lettuce. This is great with papaya or mango slices.

➤ *Greek-style shrimp.* Heat chopped onions in a little olive oil. Stir in chopped fresh or canned tomatoes (grilled tomatoes are great if you have them), a little red wine, some chopped fresh parsley, and a sprinkling of dried oregano. Cook over medium-high heat until the tomato sauce thickens slightly. Add chopped grilled shrimp and cook just until heated through. Sprinkle with crumbled feta cheese, and serve with plenty of Greek or Italian bread. This is also good with any white fish.

Vegetables

➤ *Mushroom sandwich.* Grilled portobello mushrooms can be sliced and put in a sandwich with roasted peppers, grilled or thinly sliced raw onions, and a little mayonnaise or extra-virgin olive oil.

➤ *Almost beef Stroganoff.* Cook onions in a little oil, add grilled beef and grilled mushrooms, a little mustard, and a touch of nonfat sour cream. If the mixture is too dry, add a little beef broth. Serve with noodles. For a vegetarian version, just skip the beef.

➤ *Veggies Parmesan.* Season grilled summer squash or eggplant, tomatoes, and onions with fresh rosemary, basil, or oregano, some olive oil, and salt and pepper. Sprinkle with Parmesan cheese and bake in an oven at 350°F until heated through, about 10 to 15 minutes. The same vegetables make a great topping for a pizza crust; top them with mozzarella and Parmesan. Or, chop all the vegetables up and use as a sauce for pasta.

➤ *Asian-style sweet potatoes.* Grilled sweet potatoes are great reheated and splashed with a bit of soy sauce, sesame oil, and sesame seeds. Top with chopped green onions if you like.

➤ *Grilled tomato sauce.* Just mash grilled tomatoes with some minced garlic (or roasted garlic), chopped fresh basil, and salt and pepper. This sauce is good hot or cold on pasta or polenta.

➤ *Sweet potato puree.* Peel and mash grilled sweet potatoes, put in an airtight container, and freeze. Thaw, and use as an ingredient in sweet potato pie or quickbreads.

➤ *Post-holiday sandwich.* Slice grilled sweet potatoes and layer them with sliced turkey and cranberry chutney between slices of white or millet bread.

➤ *Cold asparagus.* Grilled asparagus is great in a pasta salad. Or serve as is (cold), drizzled with a mixture of mayonnaise and orange juice.

➤ *Vegetarian gravy.* Heat grilled onions and/or mushrooms in a skillet with a little butter or oil. Sprinkle lightly with flour, then stir in a bit of vegetable broth. Cook until thickened. Use as a topping for noodles, toast, rice, or baked potatoes.

➤ *Nouveau mashed potatoes.* Grill-baked potatoes can be mashed with a bit of light sour cream or yogurt, salt and pepper, and reheated in a microwave.

The Least You Need to Know

➤ Store cooked leftovers promptly

➤ Cooked foods should either be served still cold, or reheated completely through

➤ Grilled leftovers can be used in all kinds of dishes, from chili to sandwiches

Part 4
Hot Stuff: The Recipes

Now that you know every last thing about grilling, it's time to dig in.

*We've rated recipes as easy, intermediate, and advanced. **Easy** recipes require little more than mixing ingredients, marinating a meat, and grilling it. **Intermediate** recipes require some basic cooking skills in addition to grilling, or require a bit more grilling effort, such as cooking over indirect heat. **Advanced** recipes require more than basic skills, such as kneading bread.*

Each recipe also includes an "At the Ready" notation. This tells you what you will need to have on hand near the grill either just before, during, or after cooking. Although you'll of course need to have serving plates, salads, beverages, silverware, and other obvious items ready, "At the Ready" includes only those tools or ingredients used in the actual recipe.

All recipes are based on these assumptions:

> ➤ *You'll be preparing a charcoal grill by piling up the coals, igniting them, spreading them out as they glow, then letting them burn to ash (medium hot), unless otherwise instructed.*

> ➤ *If you have a gas grill, you'll be preheating it to high, then cooking over medium heat. (What constitutes "medium" may vary from grill to grill. On some grills, you'll set all the burners to medium, or 350 to 375°F; on others, you may need to turn one or more burners off to get the grill down to that temperature.)*

> ➤ *Unless otherwise stated, you will be cooking the food 4 to 6 inches above the coals. (Nonadjustable cooking grids are always at that height, so you're all set.)*

> ➤ *For smoked recipes, you are using a water smoker, rather than a wood smoker or a regular grill.*

Chapter 16

Here's the Rub

In This Chapter

➤ Cajun Spice Rub

➤ Two-Mushroom Dust

➤ Tennessee Whiskey Barbecue Sauce

➤ Herb Marinade for Fish

➤ Orange or Tangerine Marinade for Poultry or Pork

➤ Ginger Marinade for Chicken or Pork

➤ Red Wine Marinade for Meat

➤ Rosemary Brushing Marinade for Lamb

➤ Cranberry Raisin Ketchup

➤ Pineapple Salsa

➤ Tartar Sauce

It's the rub, marinade, or sauce that lifts a plain old hunk of grilled meat out of the ordinary. Although we've included suggested uses for these marinades and seasonings, feel free to experiment with different foods.

These rubs will spice up a variety of meats, poultry, fish, or vegetables. Use your hands to work them thoroughly into every nook and cranny of the food. If the rub mixture doesn't want to stick, lightly brush or rub the food with oil before rubbing in the spice mixture.

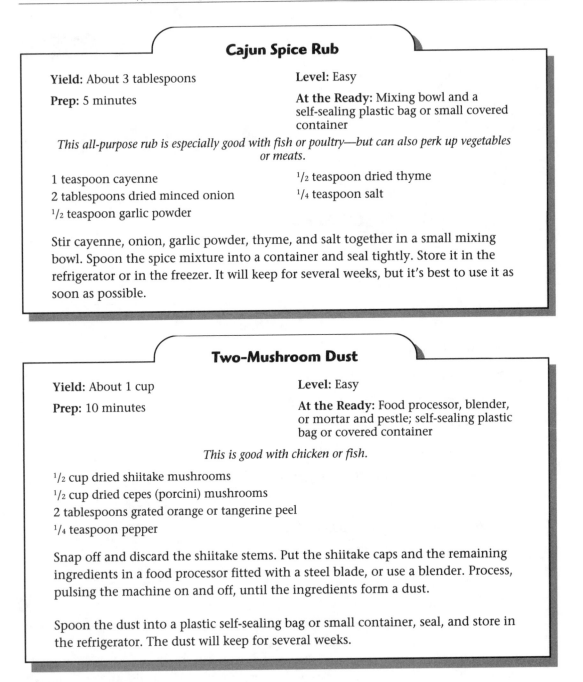

Cajun Spice Rub

Yield: About 3 tablespoons

Prep: 5 minutes

Level: Easy

At the Ready: Mixing bowl and a self-sealing plastic bag or small covered container

This all-purpose rub is especially good with fish or poultry—but can also perk up vegetables or meats.

1 teaspoon cayenne
2 tablespoons dried minced onion
1/2 teaspoon garlic powder

1/2 teaspoon dried thyme
1/4 teaspoon salt

Stir cayenne, onion, garlic powder, thyme, and salt together in a small mixing bowl. Spoon the spice mixture into a container and seal tightly. Store it in the refrigerator or in the freezer. It will keep for several weeks, but it's best to use it as soon as possible.

Two-Mushroom Dust

Yield: About 1 cup

Prep: 10 minutes

Level: Easy

At the Ready: Food processor, blender, or mortar and pestle; self-sealing plastic bag or covered container

This is good with chicken or fish.

1/2 cup dried shiitake mushrooms
1/2 cup dried cepes (porcini) mushrooms
2 tablespoons grated orange or tangerine peel
1/4 teaspoon pepper

Snap off and discard the shiitake stems. Put the shiitake caps and the remaining ingredients in a food processor fitted with a steel blade, or use a blender. Process, pulsing the machine on and off, until the ingredients form a dust.

Spoon the dust into a plastic self-sealing bag or small container, seal, and store in the refrigerator. The dust will keep for several weeks.

What's What

Shiitakes are a full-bodied, flavorful mushroom. Originally they were cultivated in Japan but now are grown in several places throughout the United States. Dried shiitakes are available all year in large supermarkets and in Asian food stores. Richly flavored *cepes*, also called Boletus or porcini mushrooms, are a bit harder to find, but can be found in many gourmet markets, some supermarkets, and some natural-food stores.

Tennessee Whiskey Barbecue Sauce

Yield: About 3 cups

Cooking Time: 20 minutes

Level: Intermediate

At the Ready: Saucepan, wooden spoon, covered container

This sauce (and all similar sauces) should be brushed on the food late in the cooking process, and/or served on the side. If you like your food a bit more charred, though, you can "break the rules" and brush the meat before grilling. Just be sure to watch the food carefully and turn it frequently, since the sugar in the sauce burns easily.

3 tablespoons vegetable oil
4 cloves garlic, minced
1 medium onion, minced
3/4 cup ketchup
2 ripe tomatoes, minced
1/4 cup cider or red vinegar

1/4 cup brown sugar
2 to 3 tablespoons Tennessee whiskey, or to taste
1/2 cup water
Dash of Tabasco sauce, or to taste
1 tablespoon chili powder
2 teaspoons ground cumin

Heat the oil in a saucepan over medium heat. Add the garlic and onion and cook about 5 minutes, until tender, stirring occasionally. Stir in the ketchup, tomatoes, vinegar, brown sugar, whiskey, water, Tabasco, chili powder, and cumin. Reduce the heat to a simmer and continue cooking, uncovered, for 15 minutes, stirring occasionally. The sauce will thicken.

Remove the sauce from the heat and let it cool. Taste and adjust the seasonings. Pour the sauce into a container, cover tightly, and refrigerate until needed. The sauce will keep for up to a week.

Hot Tip

Use a marinade when you want to add a bit of zest to a food without overpowering its natural flavors. These acidic mixtures keep well, and can be made as long as a week in advance.

Herb Marinade for Fish

Yield: About 1²/₃ cups

Prep: 15 minutes

Level: Easy

At the Ready: Bowl, whisk, plastic self-sealing bag or covered container

1 cup vegetable oil or olive oil
²/₃ cup lime juice
2 cloves garlic, smashed

1 teaspoon crumbled dry thyme
1 teaspoon crumbled dry marjoram
¹/₄ teaspoon freshly ground black pepper

To make the marinade, whisk the olive oil together with the juice in a glass bowl. Whisk in the garlic, herbs, and pepper. Taste and adjust the seasonings if necessary. Pour into a covered container or self-sealing plastic bag and refrigerate for up to a week.

Hot Tip

For the best flavor, use freshly squeezed citrus juices. Pasteurized or frozen juices are acceptable; use bottled juices only as a last resort. You can substitute lemon or orange juice in this marinade.

Orange or Tangerine Marinade
for Poultry or Pork

Yield: 1³/₄ cups

Prep: 15 minutes

Level: Easy

At the Ready: Mixing bowl, whisk, self-sealing bag or covered container

1 cup cider vinegar

¹/₂ cup orange or tangerine juice

¹/₄ cup vegetable oil

1 tablespoon dark brown sugar

1 teaspoon paprika

1 clove garlic, smashed

In a small bowl, mix together the cider vinegar, orange juice, oil, brown sugar, paprika, and garlic. Pour the marinade into a self-sealing plastic bag or a container, seal or cover tightly, and store in the refrigerator for up to a week.

Don't Get Burned!

If you want to use the remaining marinade as a brushing sauce, it must be brought to a boil first.

Ginger Marinade for
Chicken or Pork

Yield: 1 scant cup

Prep: 5 minutes

Level: Easy

At the Ready: Mixing bowl, whisk, self-sealing plastic bag or covered container, ginger grater or paring knife

¹/₂ cup rice vinegar

¹/₄ cup vegetable oil

1 tablespoon grated or finely minced fresh ginger

2 cloves garlic, peeled and smashed

2 tablespoons soy sauce

¹/₂ teaspoon five-spice powder

continues

continued

In a small mixing bowl, whisk together the vinegar, oil, ginger, garlic, soy sauce, and five-spice powder. Place the marinade in a self-sealing bag or a container. Seal or cover tightly, and refrigerate it until you're ready to use it. Use it within a day or two. This recipe can easily be doubled.

Hot Tip

Five-spice, a mixture of cinnamon, cloves, fennel, star anise, and Sichuan peppercorns, is available in many supermarkets and Asian food stores.

Red Wine Marinade for Meat

Yield: About 1¹/₂ cups

Cooking Time: 5 minutes

Level: Easy

At the Ready: Small saucepan, bowl, whisk, a plastic self-sealing bag

1 cup dry red wine
¹/₄ cup red wine vinegar
2 tablespoons grainy mustard
¹/₄ cup vegetable oil, canola blend oil, or olive oil

3 cloves garlic, peeled and smashed
2 tablespoons sugar
2 tablespoons chopped fresh basil, or 1 tablespoon dried basil
¹/₄ teaspoon black pepper or crushed red pepper

In a small saucepan, whisk together the wine, vinegar, mustard, oil, garlic, sugar, basil, and pepper. Bring the marinade to a boil over medium heat. Reduce the heat to a simmer and continue cooking for 2 minutes, stirring occasionally. Let cool.

Do not use the marinade until it has cooled completely, as the warmth may encourage bacterial growth in uncooked meat. Store the marinade in a covered container or in a self-sealing plastic bag until ready to use. The marinade will keep in the refrigerator for several days, but it is best to use it soon.

Rosemary Brushing Marinade for Lamb

Yield: About ³/₄ cup

Prep: 10 minutes

Level: Easy

At the Ready: Food processor or blender, mixing bowl, whisk, and a self-sealing plastic bag or small covered container

4 cloves garlic, peeled
1 small red onion, peeled, cut in half
¹/₄ cup olive oil
¹/₄ cup red wine

3 tablespoons fresh lemon juice
1 tablespoon fresh rosemary, chopped, or 1¹/₂ teaspoons dried rosemary
2 tablespoons fresh oregano, chopped, or 1¹/₂ teaspoons dried oregano
¹/₄ teaspoon fresh ground black pepper

Using a food processor fitted with a steel blade, process the garlic and onion a few seconds until slushy. Add the oil, wine, lemon juice, rosemary, oregano, and pepper, and combine.

Pour the marinade into a self-sealing bag or a container. Seal or cover tightly, and refrigerate. Use within a couple of days.

Hot Tip

Thick and piquant, ketchups, salsas, and tartar sauce add flair to grilled meats, poultry, or fish. They go best with foods that have not been heavily spiced.

Cranberry Raisin Ketchup

Yield: 1¹/₂ cups

Cooking Time: 15 to 20 minutes

Level: Intermediate

At the Ready: Medium saucepan, wooden spoon, a fine-meshed sieve, and a covered container

This ketchup makes an excellent condiment for chicken, turkey, and pork.

2 pounds fresh cranberries, washed, picked over, and shriveled ones discarded

³/₄ cup red wine vinegar

1 cup packed dark brown sugar

¹/₂ cup dark raisins

1 tablespoon ground cinnamon

¹/₂ teaspoon salt

¹/₄ teaspoon ground allspice

¹/₄ teaspoon ground cloves

In a heavy, medium-size saucepan, cook the cranberries over medium heat until they pop, about 4 to 6 minutes. Remove from the heat. Press the cranberries through a sieve. Then return the pulp to a clean pan. Mix in the vinegar, brown sugar, raisins, cinnamon, salt, allspice, and cloves.

Simmer the mixture on medium-low heat for about 15 minutes, stirring often, until the sauce thickens. Taste, and adjust the seasonings. Cool.

Pour the ketchup into a container, cover tightly, and refrigerate until ready to serve, or up to 1 week. Stir the ketchup before serving.

Hot Tip

Buy cranberries when they are in season and freeze them for later use. For an easier recipe, substitute 2 cans of jellied cranberries (16 ounces each) for the fresh cranberries, and reduce the amount of brown sugar to ¹/₄ cup. If using canned berries, you do not have to pass the mixture through a sieve.

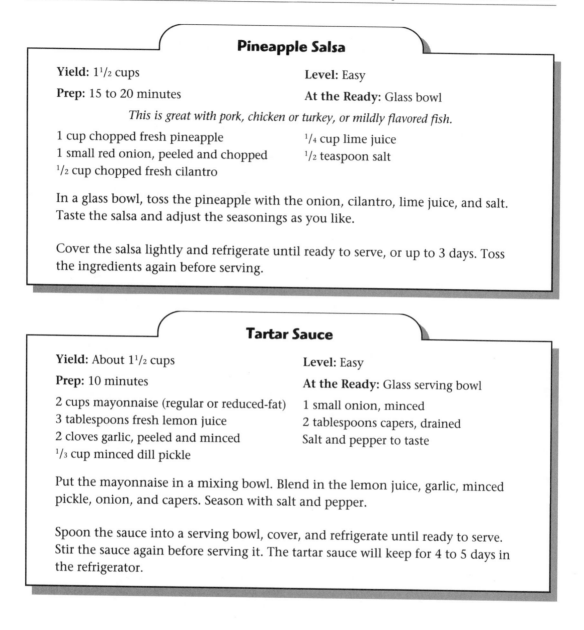

Pineapple Salsa

Yield: 1¹/₂ cups   **Level:** Easy

Prep: 15 to 20 minutes   **At the Ready:** Glass bowl

This is great with pork, chicken or turkey, or mildly flavored fish.

1 cup chopped fresh pineapple

1 small red onion, peeled and chopped

¹/₂ cup chopped fresh cilantro

¹/₄ cup lime juice

¹/₂ teaspoon salt

In a glass bowl, toss the pineapple with the onion, cilantro, lime juice, and salt. Taste the salsa and adjust the seasonings as you like.

Cover the salsa lightly and refrigerate until ready to serve, or up to 3 days. Toss the ingredients again before serving.

Tartar Sauce

Yield: About 1¹/₂ cups   **Level:** Easy

Prep: 10 minutes   **At the Ready:** Glass serving bowl

2 cups mayonnaise (regular or reduced-fat)

3 tablespoons fresh lemon juice

2 cloves garlic, peeled and minced

¹/₃ cup minced dill pickle

1 small onion, minced

2 tablespoons capers, drained

Salt and pepper to taste

Put the mayonnaise in a mixing bowl. Blend in the lemon juice, garlic, minced pickle, onion, and capers. Season with salt and pepper.

Spoon the sauce into a serving bowl, cover, and refrigerate until ready to serve. Stir the sauce again before serving it. The tartar sauce will keep for 4 to 5 days in the refrigerator.

The Least You Need to Know

➤ Marinades work best when you want the natural flavors of the food to shine through.

➤ Sweet barbecue sauces normally are brushed on foods near the end of the grilling time.

➤ Condiments such as ketchups or salsas go best with grilled foods that are not heavily spiced.

Chapter 17

Appetizers

In This Chapter

➤ Turkey Sausage on a Stick

➤ Five-Minute Mussels

➤ Glazed Polish Sausage

➤ Spicy Chicken Dogs

➤ Sweet and Sour Lamb Ribs

➤ Greek Cheese with Garlic Pita Chips

➤ Garlic Pita Chips

➤ Focaccia

➤ Walnut-Stuffed White Mushrooms

➤ Grilled Garlic Potato Skins

➤ Crostini

➤ Grilled Antipasti

Making appetizers on the grill means you can stay outside with your guests. It also means your guests will have something to nibble as they smell the enticing aromas of the main course wafting around your yard.

If you want to serve a hot appetizer, you certainly should plan on grilling it. Otherwise, you'll wind up running back and forth between the stove or oven and your grill. Most of the following dishes can be cooked quickly on the grill and served to guests to keep them occupied while you go on to grill the main course. The coals will stay medium hot for quite a while.

Of course, there's also no reason you can't just serve a variety of these delicious morsels for a party—and forget the main course. Just round out the menu with a good salad and some wonderful bread.

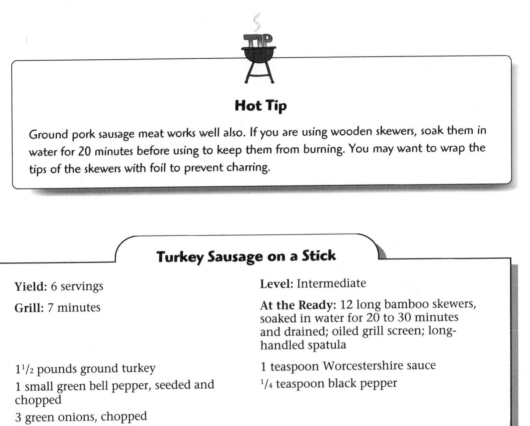

Hot Tip

Ground pork sausage meat works well also. If you are using wooden skewers, soak them in water for 20 minutes before using to keep them from burning. You may want to wrap the tips of the skewers with foil to prevent charring.

Turkey Sausage on a Stick

Yield: 6 servings

Grill: 7 minutes

Level: Intermediate

At the Ready: 12 long bamboo skewers, soaked in water for 20 to 30 minutes and drained; oiled grill screen; long-handled spatula

1¹/₂ pounds ground turkey

1 small green bell pepper, seeded and chopped

3 green onions, chopped

1 teaspoon Worcestershire sauce

¹/₄ teaspoon black pepper

Soak the wooden skewers in water for 20 minutes, then drain.

Combine the turkey, bell pepper, onions, Worcestershire sauce, and black pepper in a bowl.

Using clean hands, take about ¹/₄ cup of the turkey mixture and mold it around the top third of a skewer to make a sausage shape about 4 inches long. Repeat until all of the meat has been used.

Prepare the grill for direct heat. Oil or spray the grill screen. When the coals are medium hot, set the skewers on the screen, then on the cooking grid, 4 to 6 inches from the heat. Grill the sausages, uncovered, for 7 minutes, or until cooked through. Using a long-handled spatula, turn the skewers every 2 to 3 minutes.

Put the cooked sausages on a serving dish and serve immediately. These are delicious served with mustard and pickles.

Five-Minute Mussels

Yield: 6 servings   **Level:** Easy

Grill: 5 minutes   **At the Ready:** Grill screen

Note that these should be cooked over hot, not medium-hot, coals.

3 cups chopped fresh tomatoes	$1/4$ teaspoon pepper
2 tablespoons capers, drained	2 tablespoons red wine vinegar
$1/2$ teaspoon salt	3 dozen mussels, scrubbed and debearded (see Chapter 13 for instructions on cleaning mussels)

Toss the tomatoes, capers, salt, pepper, and vinegar in a bowl. Cover and refrigerate until ready to serve.

Prepare the grill for direct heat. Oil or spray the grill screen. When the coals are glowing hot, set the mussels on the grid, 4 to 6 inches from the heat. Grill the mussels, covered, for 5 minutes. When you uncover the grill the mussels should be opened. If not, cover and grill a few minutes longer until the shells open. Discard any mussels that don't open even after additional cooking.

Put the mussels on individual plates and spoon the chopped tomato mixture on top. Serve hot.

Glazed Polish Sausage

Yield: 8 servings   **Level:** Easy

Grill: 12 minutes   **At the Ready:** Small sharp knife, oil for brushing, grill screen

1 cup orange marmalade	2 tablespoons Dijon mustard
1 tablespoon water	2 pounds smoked Polish sausage

continues

continued

Combine the orange marmalade and water in a small saucepan. Heat the mixture over medium for a few minutes, stirring often, until the marmalade thins and is hot. Remove the marmalade from the heat and stir in the mustard.

Prick the sausages with a fork and brush them with the sauce. Prepare the grill for direct heat. Lightly oil or spray the cooking grid. When the coals are medium hot, set the sausages on the grid. Grill them, uncovered, for about 12 minutes, turning them every 3 minutes, until they're nicely browned and cooked through.

Remove the sausages from the grill to a wooden board and cut on the diagonal into serving-size pieces. Serve hot.

Spicy Chicken Dogs

Yield: 8 servings

Grill: About 8 to 10 minutes

Level: Easy

At the Ready: Long-handled fork, oil or nonstick cooking spray, basting brush

$^3/_4$ cup ketchup

1 cup chopped tomatoes (fresh or canned)

1 can (16 ounces) crushed tomatoes

2 tablespoons grainy mustard

2 tablespoons chili powder

$^1/_3$ cup firmly packed light brown sugar

3 cloves garlic, minced

1 can ($4^1/_2$ ounces) chopped green chiles

2 pounds chicken or turkey hot dogs, pricked with a fork (See Hot Tip on the next page)

Mix the ketchup, chopped and crushed tomatoes, mustard, chili powder, brown sugar, garlic, and chiles in a saucepan. Bring the mixture to a boil over medium heat. Reduce the heat to a simmer and continue cooking for 5 minutes. Remove the sauce from the heat and allow to cool. When completely cooled, brush the hot dogs with the sauce.

Prepare the grill for direct heat. When the coals are medium hot, set the hot dogs on the oiled grill screen about 4 to 6 inches from heat source, covered. Cook for about 8 to 10 minutes, turning the hot dogs as they char on each side. The meat will be cooked and brown. Remove the hot dogs and cut into 1-inch pieces.

Reheat the reserved sauce. Place the hot dogs in a deep bowl, and mix in sauce. Serve with toothpicks.

Hot Tip

You can either use regular hot dogs cut into pieces, or cocktail franks left whole. The sauce can be prepared early in the day.

Sweet and Sour Lamb Ribs

Yield: 6 to 8 servings

Grill: 45 minutes

Level: Intermediate

At the Ready: Oil or nonstick cooking spray, grill screen, brush, long-handled fork

These are good as either an appetizer or a main course for 4 to 6 people. If you're serving them as an appetizer, you may want to cook them ahead of time, then reheat them in a 300°F oven.

Sweet and Sour Sauce

1 medium onion, minced

³/₄ cup grape jelly

³/₄ cup chili sauce

1 cup light beer

2 cloves garlic, minced

¹/₄ teaspoon pepper

5¹/₂ pounds lamb ribs, cut in individual ribs

In a saucepan, combine the onion, jelly, chili sauce, beer, garlic, and pepper. Bring the mixture to a boil over medium heat. Reduce the heat to a simmer and stir occasionally until all the ingredients are blended, about 3 to 4 minutes. Cool.

Trim the excess fat from the ribs, wash them, and pat dry with paper toweling. Pour the marinade in a glass bowl. Add the ribs, and turn to coat them all over with the marinade. Cover. Refrigerate for 2 hours, turning the ribs once or twice.

Drain the ribs, reserving the marinade. Prepare the grill for indirect heat. Oil or spray the cooking grid. When the coals are medium hot, set the ribs on the oiled grid, about 4 to 6 inches from the heat source. Cover and adjust the vents. Grill the ribs 40 to 50 minutes, or until done to taste, turning every 10 to 15 minutes. If you're using a charcoal grill, replenish the briquets as necessary. Brush the ribs

continues

continued

with marinade about 10 to 15 minutes before you expect them to be done. The ribs will char. Remove the ribs to a serving platter, and serve hot. Be sure to give diners lots of napkins.

Hot Tip

For those who like extra sauce, you can serve these ribs with their marinade—but be sure to reheat it to a full boil first.

Greek Cheese with Garlic Pita Chips

Yield: 8 servings

Grill: 2 to 5 minutes

Level: Easy

At the Ready: Oil or nonstick cooking spray, long-handled spatula, grill screen, brush

1 cup milk
1 egg, lightly beaten
1 1/2 cups fine bread crumbs

1 pound Greek saganaki cheese, cut into eight 1/2-inch pieces
3 tablespoons brandy, preferably Metaxa
Garlic Pita Chips (recipe follows)

In a shallow bowl mix together the milk and egg. Set the bread crumbs on a plate. Roll the cheese slices in the milk mixture and then in the bread crumbs. Place the cheese on a dish and refrigerate, covered, for at least 1 hour.

Prepare the grill for direct heat. Oil or spray a grill screen. When the coals are medium hot, set the cheese pieces on the grill screen, and set that on the cooking grid, about 4 to 6 inches from the heat. Grill the cheese, uncovered, about 2 minutes on each side, turning the pieces over with a long-handled spatula. The cheese should be lightly browned on the outside, and runny but not completely melted on the inside.

Set the cheese on individual plates and sprinkle with the brandy. Serve immediately with Garlic Pita Chips (recipe follows).

Garlic Pita Chips

Yield: 6 to 8 servings

Grill: 2 to 4 minutes

Level: Easy

At the Ready: Melted butter for brushing, brush, long-handled spatula, kitchen scissors

$^1/_3$ cup melted butter or margarine
1 tablespoon minced garlic

4 pita breads

Using a serrated knife, carefully cut crosswise through each pita to make 2 rounds. In a small bowl mix the melted, cooled butter with the garlic. Brush the pita rounds with the butter mixture.

Prepare the grill for direct heat. Oil or spray a grill screen. When the coals are medium hot, set the pita bread rounds on the grill screen, and set that on the cooking grid, about 4 to 6 inches from the heat. Grill, uncovered, about 1 to 2 minutes on each side. The bread will begin to color slightly. Do not overcook. Remove the pita rounds to a work area and using a pair of kitchen scissors, cut each round into 6 pieces. Serve the chips hot.

Don't Get Burned!

The pita chips heat quickly, so pay attention and do not leave to do something else while they grill.

Focaccia

Yield: 8 servings

Level: Easy

Grill: About 6 to 7 minutes

At the Ready: 3 baking tiles suitable for the grill, cookie sheet or grill screen, long-handled spatula, oil for brushing, basting brush

Focaccia is a pizza-style bread heated and served right from the grill. The toppings can be changed to your taste.

1 large onion, sliced thin

Olive oil

2 tablespoons butter

1 large tomato, sliced thin

1 plain, store-bought focaccia (already-baked pizza crust or Italian flatbread)

$1/4$ cup sliced pitted black olives

Cook the onion in the butter over medium heat for about 7 to 8 minutes, until soft and translucent but not browned. Remove from the heat and let cool slightly.

Brush the top of the focaccia lightly with oil. Arrange the tomato slices decoratively on top. Arrange the sauteed onion and olives over the tomatoes.

Prepare the grill for direct heat. When the coals are medium hot, set a cookie sheet or grill screen on the grill about 4 to 6 inches from the heat source, then set the tiles atop that. (Using a cookie sheet or grill screen makes it easier to remove the tiles from the grill, and also lowers the heat slightly so the focaccia is less likely to burn.) Preheat for at least 5 minutes. Put the focaccia on a pizza pan and then set it on the tiles. Cover. Grill for about 3 minutes, then turn the bread half way around. Cover and continue cooking for 3 minutes, or until the focaccia is hot. Watch that it doesn't char.

Set the focaccia on a serving table and cut it into serving-size pieces. This is good hot or warm.

Walnut-Stuffed White Mushrooms

Yield: 8 servings

Grill: About 3 to 5 minutes

Level: Intermediate

At the Ready: Oil or nonstick cooking spray, grill screen, brush, and long-handled spatula

24 large white mushrooms
3 tablespoons olive oil
1 small onion, minced
³/₄ cup chopped walnuts
1 stalk celery, minced

³/₄ cup fine bread crumbs
¹/₄ cup minced fresh parsley
2 teaspoons minced fresh sage
Additional olive oil for brushing

Clean the mushrooms with a damp paper towel. Remove the stems and finely chop them; leave the caps whole. Set aside.

Heat the oil in a frying pan. Add the chopped mushroom stems and onion and cook over medium heat for about 5 minutes, or until the onion is tender, stirring occasionally. Mix in walnuts, celery, bread crumbs, parsley, and sage. Remove from the heat.

Using a tablespoon, gently mound the stuffing into each mushroom cap. Brush the outside of each mushroom cap lightly with oil.

Prepare the grill for direct heat. Oil or spray a grill screen. When the coals are medium hot, set the mushrooms on an oiled grill screen on the grill about 4 to 6 inches from the heat. Cover and adjust the vents. Grill the mushrooms for 3 to 5 minutes, or until heated through but still firm to the touch.

Put the mushrooms on a plate and serve immediately.

Hot Tip

To keep mushrooms, which already are high in water, from getting waterlogged, clean them by wiping them with a damp paper towel.

Grilled Garlic Potato Skins

Yield: 8 servings

Level: Easy

Grill: About 4 to 6 minutes, plus 1 hour for baking or grilling potatoes

At the Ready: Aluminum foil, small sharp kitchen knife

6 large baking potatoes, skin on, scrubbed

Vegetable oil for brushing

2 teaspoons garlic powder

1 teaspoon ground cumin

1/2 teaspoon black pepper

Scrub the potatoes under cold running water. Prick them several times with the tip of a sharp knife. Wrap the potatoes in aluminum foil. Prepare the grill. When the coals are medium hot, carefully set the potatoes directly on the coals if you're using a charcoal grill, or on the rack if you're using gas. Cover the grill and cook the potatoes about 1 hour, or until they can be pierced easily with a fork, turning them 2 or 3 times during grilling. Or, bake the potatoes, minus the foil, in a preheated 425°F oven for about 1 hour. The potatoes are done when you can pierce them easily with a fork. Let cool. The potatoes can be grilled or baked the day before. Refrigerate them.

When the potatoes are cool enough to handle, cut in half lengthwise. Scoop out the potato, leaving 1/4 inch of potato lining the skins. Refrigerate the potato meat and reserve it for another recipe. Cut the potato skins again in half lengthwise. Brush the skins with oil and sprinkle with the garlic powder, cumin, and pepper.

Prepare the grill for direct heat. Oil or spray a grill screen. When the coals are medium hot, set the potato strips, skin side down, on the grill screen and then set that on the grid, about 4 to 6 inches from the heat. Cover and grill for about 3 to 4 minutes. Turn the potato skins over and continue grilling until they are hot and beginning to brown.

Using a long-handled spatula, remove the potato skins to a serving plate. Serve hot. These are good sprinkled lightly with cheese or served with dabs of sour cream.

Don't Get Burned!

When you wrap potatoes in foil to cook them, be sure to serve them while they're still hot or, if you don't plan to serve them until later, refrigerate them. This will reduce the risk of botulism.

Crostini

Yield: 8 servings

Grill: About 3 to 4 minutes

Level: Easy

At the Ready: Oil for brushing, grill screen, brush, long-handled spatula

This is an adaptation of a classic Italian dish. Here we use thin slices of provolone cheese and anchovy slices on Italian bread.

8 slices of fresh Italian or French bread, ¹/₂-inch thick

Olive oil for brushing

¹/₂ pound provolone cheese, sliced thin

1 can (2 ounces) anchovies, drained

Prepare the grill for direct heat. Oil or spray a grill screen. Brush the bread slices lightly with olive oil on both sides. When the coals are medium hot, put the grill screen on the grid about 4 to 6 inches from the heat. Put the bread on the grill screen and grill, uncovered, only a minute, or until lightly toasted. Working quickly, remove the bread from the screen. Turn the bread over and place 2 slices of cheese on top of each piece of bread, then set an anchovy atop that. Return the bread to the screen and grill a minute or until the bread is just lightly toasted on the bottom. The bread burns quickly so watch it closely, and do not leave the grill. In fact, you might want to make the crostini in two batches so you can watch it carefully. Serve hot.

Grilled Antipasti

Yield: 8 servings

Grill: 5 to 12 minutes

Level: Intermediate

At the Ready: Basting brush, oil for brushing, grill screen, long-handled spatula

Substitute seasonal vegetables of your choice for any of the vegetables in this recipe. You can prepare the vegetables ahead of time and refrigerate them until grilling time.

8 cloves elephant garlic, unpeeled, brushed with olive oil

8 brown Italian or white mushrooms, cleaned, stems removed

2 large yellow or red peppers, seeded and cut in $^1/_2$-inch circles

3 medium-small zucchini, cut lengthwise into thin slices

1 jar (6$^1/_2$ ounces) marinated artichoke hearts, drained

Olive oil

Lemon juice

Salt and pepper to taste

6 ounces thinly sliced deli-style ham

1 small ripe cantaloupe, seeded, cut in 1-inch slices

$^1/_2$ pound black olives

Wrap the oiled garlic cloves in aluminum foil and set aside. Prepare the mushrooms, peppers, zucchini, and artichokes. Brush the vegetables lightly with oil and sprinkle with lemon juice, salt, and pepper. Wrap a half slice of ham around each cantaloupe piece, leave cut side down and brush the ham with oil.

Prepare the grill for direct heat. Oil or spray a grill screen. When the coals are medium hot, set the grill screen on the cooking grid about 4 to 6 inches from the heat. Set the garlic on the screen first, cover the grill, adjust the vents, and let the garlic cook about 10 minutes, turning once. Remove the cover, and add the remaining vegetables and the wrapped cantaloupe to the grill screen. Grill the wrapped cantaloupe 1 or 2 minutes on each side, then remove to a platter. Grill the remaining vegetables 5 to 10 minutes, turning as necessary, until tender and beginning to brown. Remove the vegetables as they cook. The garlic will take about 20 minutes to become tender. Remove one clove with a spatula, remove the foil, and squeeze to see if it is tender, being careful not to burn your fingers as it will be very hot.

Put all the vegetables, the ham-wrapped cantaloupe, and the garlic cloves decoratively on a platter, along with the olives. Sprinkle with more olive oil and lemon juice. Serve hot with Italian bread.

What's What

Elephant garlic isn't actually garlic, but a relative of the leek. It looks like giant garlic, though. Its extra-large, white-skinned bulbs have a milder flavor than regular garlic.

The Least You Need to Know

➤ Cooking the appetizers on the grill allows you to stay outside with the guests.

➤ You can create a whole party menu of nothing but "appetizers."

Chapter 18

Meats

In This Chapter

➤ Skirt Steak with Grilled Peppers and Shallot Marinade Sauce

➤ Grilled Sliced Meat Loaf with Chopped Tomatoes

➤ Jerk Strip Steaks

➤ Flank Steak Strips on Salad Greens with Lemongrass Mopping Sauce

➤ Cheeseburger Deluxe

➤ Beer-Basted Short Ribs

➤ Pork Tenderloin in Flour Tortillas

➤ Pork Chops with Apple Slices

➤ Greek-Style Lamb Chops

➤ Lamb Rib Chops with Fresh Mint

➤ Lamb Burgers

➤ Shish Kebabs

Beef, pork, and lamb—these are the foods the grill was invented for. Here's a collection of recipes that showcase red meats at their best. They run the gamut of flavors and traditions, from classic American to Middle Eastern to Caribbean.

It's important to watch meats carefully, especially the leaner cuts. Overcooking will make them tough and stringy. On the other hand, undercooking meats—especially ground meats—can be unsafe. Steaks and chops benefit from searing: quickly browning the outside of the meat over hot coals to seal in the juices. Finish cooking them over medium-hot coals.

Skirt Steak with Grilled Peppers and Shallot Marinade Sauce

Yield: 6 servings

Grill: About 7 to 9 minutes

Level: Easy

At the Ready: Oil for brushing, brush, grill screen, and a long-handled spatula

This acidic marinade helps tenderize the beef skirt, a fairly tough but very flavorful cut.

$1/4$ cup light (reduced-sodium) soy sauce

3 shallots, peeled and minced

2 tablespoons light brown sugar

$1/4$ cup pineapple juice

$1/4$ cup cider vinegar

2 pounds beef skirt steak, trimmed and cut into 6 serving pieces

3 large green or red bell peppers, seeded and cut in rings

In a small saucepan, combine the soy sauce, shallots, brown sugar, pineapple juice, and vinegar. Bring the mixture to a boil over medium heat, stirring often. Remove the pan from the heat and cool.

Set the meat in a glass bowl and cover with the marinade. Cover lightly and marinate for 1 hour in the refrigerator, turning once. Drain.

Prepare the grill for direct heat. Oil or spray the cooking grid. When the coals are medium hot, set the steak on the oiled grid. Cover the grill and adjust the vents. Grill the steak for 4 minutes. Turn the steak over and put the peppers on the grill. Grill the peppers about 2 to 3 minutes on each side, until they begin to char and are tender. Continue grilling the steak for another 4 to 5 minutes, or until just cooked through. The time depends on the thickness of the steak; do not overcook. Serve the meat and peppers hot, with guacamole on the side.

Grilled Sliced Meat Loaf
with Chopped Tomatoes

Yield: 6 to 8 servings

Grill: About 6 minutes

Level: Intermediate

At the Ready: The cooked meat loaf, grill screen, oil for brushing, brush, and a long-handled spatula

2 tablespoons vegetable oil

2 cups sliced white or brown mushrooms

1 pound ground beef or veal

³/₄ pound lean ground pork

³/₄ cup fresh white or whole wheat bread crumbs

2 eggs

1 small onion, minced

1 cup peeled and chopped tomato

1 cup drained corn kernels

1¹/₂ teaspoons dried crumbled thyme

1 teaspoon ground cinnamon

¹/₂ teaspoon salt

¹/₂ teaspoon pepper

¹/₂ teaspoon allspice

3 large tomatoes, chopped

Heat the oil in a nonstick frying pan over medium heat. Add the mushrooms and cook, partially covered, about 5 minutes or until tender, stirring as necessary. Drain and cool. Put the mushrooms in a large mixing bowl. Blend in the meats, bread crumbs, eggs, onion, tomato, and corn. Add the spices and mix well. Mound the mixture into a 9-x-5-x-3-inch greased nonstick loaf pan. Preheat the oven to 325°F. Bake the meat loaf in the center of the oven for 1 hour or until the juices run clear. Cool completely. When you are ready to grill, cut the meat loaf into 1-inch-thick slices.

Prepare the grill for direct heat. Oil or spray a grill screen. When the coals are medium hot, set the grill screen on the cooking grid. Set the meat loaf slices on the screen. Grill, uncovered, for about 2 to 3 minutes on each side. The meat loaf should be heated through and beginning to brown. Remove the hot slices to a platter and sprinkle with the chopped tomatoes. For added flavor, you can brush one side of the meat loaf with a barbecue sauce during the last minute or two of grilling. Serve hot.

Hot Tip

This is a good way to use up leftover meat loaf. Make it a day or two in advance.

Jerk Strip Steaks

Yield: 6 servings

Grill: About 10 minute

Level: Easy

At the Ready: Food processor, blender, or mortar and pestle, brushing sauce, brush, and a long-handled fork

We call for jalapeño peppers in this marinade because they're easier to find in most supermarkets. To be more authentic, you can use one or two habanero peppers, the fruity, super-hot, bonnet-shaped beauties.

1 large onion, peeled and roughly chopped

3 jalapeño peppers, seeded and minced

³/₄ cup light (reduced-sodium) soy sauce

¹/₄ cup vegetable oil

¹/₄ cup dark brown sugar

1 teaspoon dried crumbled thyme

¹/₂ teaspoon black pepper

¹/₂ teaspoon ground allspice

¹/₂ teaspoon ground cinnamon

6 beef strip steaks, about 8 ounces each, trimmed of all fat

Put the onion, peppers, soy sauce, oil, sugar, thyme, pepper, allspice, and cinnamon in the container of a food processor fitted with a steel blade. Process for about 15 seconds to make a paste. Spoon the paste into a small bowl. Cover and set aside.

Rub the steaks with the jerk paste and place them on a glass plate. Cover lightly and refrigerate for 3 to 4 hours.

Prepare the grill for direct heat. When the coals are medium hot, set the steaks directly on the cooking grid. Cover the grill and adjust the vents. Grill the steaks 4 to 6 minutes on each side, or until they reach desired doneness. Serve the steaks hot on individual plates with grilled vegetables.

Flank Steak Strips on Salad Greens with Lemongrass Mopping Sauce

Yield: 6 servings

Grill: 7 to 10 minutes

Level: Easy

At the Ready: Mopping sauce, brush or barbecue mop, long-handled fork, cutting board, and the salad greens

Lemongrass Mopping Sauce

2 tablespoons vegetable oil

1/2 cup red wine vinegar

1/4 cup lime juice

1/4 cup lemon juice

1 1/2 tablespoons dried or fresh minced lemongrass, or grated lemon peel

1 teaspoon Worcestershire sauce

1 green onion, minced

3/4 cup crushed tomatoes, including juice

10 to 12 cups assorted salad greens, washed and dried

3 large tomatoes, sliced

1 red onion, sliced

3/4 cup Italian salad dressing

2 cups garlic-flavored croutons

2 pounds beef flank steak

In a saucepan combine the oil, vinegar, lime juice, lemon juice, lemongrass, Worcestershire sauce, onion, and tomatoes. Bring the mixture to a boil over medium heat, stirring often. Remove the pan from the heat. Let cool.

Arrange the salad greens, tomatoes, and onion slices on individual dinner plates. Cover and refrigerate until ready to serve.

Mop the steak with the cooled lemongrass mixture and place it in a glass container. Cover and refrigerate for 2 hours.

Prepare the grill for direct heat. When the coals are medium hot, set the steak on the cooking grid. Cover the grill and adjust the vents. Grill the steak 5 to 7 minutes on each side, depending on the thickness of the meat, turning once or twice. Mop the steak with the sauce as you turn it.

Remove the steak to a cutting board, and let it stand for 5 minutes.

While the steak stands, sprinkle the salads with salad dressing and the croutons.

Cut the meat across the grain into thin slices. Arrange the warm slices over the salad.

What's What

Lemongrass, used widely in Southeast Asian cooking, is a citrusy herb that looks a bit like a tough scallion. You use only the bottom part, and peel off the tough outer leaves. You can find it fresh in Asian markets and some supermarkets, or dried in the spice sections of many large supermarkets.

Cheeseburger Deluxe

Yield: 6 servings

Grill: About 10 minutes

Level: Easy

At the Ready: Grill screen, oil for brushing, brush, long-handled spatula, buns and "fixings"

2 pounds ground beef sirloin

1 small onion, peeled and minced

3 tablespoons barbecue sauce

$^1/_2$ pound blue cheese or sharp cheddar cheese, crumbled (for children or less adventurous appetites, use a slice of mild cheese)

6 hamburger buns, split and brushed with melted butter

Lettuce leaves

Sliced tomatoes

Thinly sliced red onions

Grainy mustard and ketchup

In a large bowl, mix the ground beef with the onion. Shape the meat mixture into 6 equal patties. Brush lightly with the barbecue sauce. Set the patties on a plate and refrigerate them until ready to grill.

Prepare the grill for direct heat. Oil or spray the cooking grid. When the coals are medium hot, set the hamburgers on the grid. Cover the grill and adjust the vents. Grill the hamburgers about 5 to 6 minutes on each side, or until they are completely cooked through, with no pink in the middle. While they cook, brush once on each side with barbecue sauce. If you are using Cheddar cheese, place it atop the burgers a minute or so before they're done.

Toast the open rolls on the grill (not directly over the coals) about 1 to 2 minutes, watching carefully as they burn easily.

Arrange a lettuce leaf and tomato slice on each bun. Set a burger on top and sprinkle with the blue cheese if using. Pass the sliced onions, mustard, and ketchup at the table. Serve hot.

Don't Get Burned!

This next recipe requires indirect heat and low heat. If you're using a charcoal grill, keep the heat low by using fewer coals, waiting until they are ashen, and adding only enough lit coals periodically to keep the fire going. These ribs are worth the effort.

Beer-Basted Short Ribs

Yield: 6 servings

Grill: 50 to 60 minutes

Level: Intermediate

At the Ready: Long-handled fork, basting sauce

Beer Basting Sauce

1 can (12 ounces) dark beer

$^{1}/_{2}$ cup packed dark brown sugar

$^{1}/_{2}$ cup cider vinegar

$^{1}/_{2}$ cup chili sauce

2 teaspoons chili powder

1 teaspoon cumin

$^{1}/_{4}$ teaspoon cayenne

4 pounds beef short ribs, cut 1 inch thick and trimmed of fat

In a saucepan combine the beer, brown sugar, vinegar, chili sauce, chili powder, cumin, and cayenne. Bring the sauce to a boil over medium heat, stirring often. Reduce the heat to a simmer and continue cooking for about 4 to 5 minutes. Let cool.

Remove 1 cup of the sauce for brushing the ribs at the grill. Brush the ribs with the remaining sauce and put them in a glass bowl. Cover and refrigerate for 2 hours.

continues

continued

Prepare the grill for indirect heat. When the coals are covered with a thick layer of ash, put the ribs on the grill. Cover the grill and adjust the vents. Grill the ribs 50 to 60 minutes or until cooked through, turning occasionally. You will probably need to add a few coals now and then, just enough to keep the heat going. (If you're using a gas grill, you want the temperature at between 225 and 250°F.) Brush the ribs with sauce as you turn them. Serve hot. These are good with grilled corn (see page 124), red chili beans, and coleslaw.

Pork Tenderloin in Flour Tortillas

Yield: 6 servings

Grill: About 18 minutes

Level: Easy

At the Ready: Long-handled spatula, oil or nonstick cooking spray, grill screen, meat or instant thermometer

3 cloves garlic, minced

$1/_4$ cup lime juice

1 tablespoon chili powder

2 teaspoons ground cumin

2 teaspoons ground coriander

2 teaspoons paprika

$1/_2$ teaspoon ground cinnamon

2 pounds pork tenderloin, washed and patted dry

6 flour tortillas

In a small bowl, combine the garlic, lime juice, chili powder, cumin, coriander, paprika, and cinnamon. Rub the pork loin all over with the spice mixture and place it in a glass dish. Cover the pork loosely with plastic wrap, and refrigerate. Marinate for 1 hour.

Prepare the grill for direct heat. Oil or spray the cooking grid. When the coals are medium hot, place the pork on the grid. Cover and adjust the vents. Grill for about 18 to 25 minutes, turning 2 or 3 times, or until cooked through (the pork should reach an internal temperature of 160°F).

Remove the pork to a slicing board and let it rest 5 minutes. Cut the pork into thin slices and serve on warm tortillas with fried onions, salsa, and black beans.

Hot Tip

Warm the tortillas, wrapped in foil, on the grill for 1 to 2 minutes on each side, or warm them individually on the grill for a few seconds on each side.

Pork Chops with Apple Slices

Yield: 6 servings

Grill: About 7 to 9 minutes

Level: Easy

At the Ready: Vegetable oil or non-stick cooking spray, melted butter for brushing apple slices, brush, grill screen, $1/2$ cup dried thyme, soaked in water 5 minutes and drained (optional aromatic)

1 cup orange juice
Dash Worcestershire sauce
6 center-cut pork chops, 1-inch thick
3 large Granny Smith apples, cored and sliced into rounds

Melted butter
$1/4$ cup sugar

Combine the orange juice and the Worcestershire sauce in a small bowl. Brush the pork chops with the sauce.

Prepare the grill for direct heat. Oil or spray the cooking grid. When the coals are medium hot, sprinkle the dried soaked thyme onto the coals if desired, and set the pork chops on the grid. Set the apples, brushed with butter, in a single layer on an oiled grill screen, then set it on the grid. Cover the grill and adjust the vents. Grill the pork chops about 4 minutes, turn, and continue grilling 4 to 5 minutes, or until cooked through. All signs of pink should be gone from the center, but do not overcook. Cook the apple slices a minute or two on each side, or until they soften and begin to brown; remove them from the grill while the pork continues cooking. Sprinkle them with the sugar. Set a pork chop on each plate along with some apple slices.

Greek-Style Lamb Chops

Yield: 6 servings

Grill: About 8 to 10 minutes

Level: Easy

At the Ready: Long-handled spatula, oil or nonstick cooking spray, grill screen, and a brush

If you like, you can use oregano rather than rosemary in this recipe.

12 lamb loin chops, about $4^1/2$ ounces to 5 ounces each, trimmed of fat

4 cloves garlic, peeled and minced

3 tablespoons minced fresh rosemary, or 1 tablespoon chopped dried rosemary

$^1/4$ cup olive oil

$^1/2$ teaspoon black pepper

2 lemons, cut in half

Arrange the lamb chops in a flat glass dish. In a small bowl, mix the garlic, rosemary, olive oil, and pepper together. Brush the chops on both sides with the mixture, and squeeze the lemon halves over them.

Prepare the grill for direct heat. Oil or spray the cooking grid. When the coals are medium hot, set the lamb chops on the grid. Cover the grill and adjust the vents. Grill the chops for 5 minutes. Turn them and continue grilling for 5 minutes, or until they are done to taste. Do not overcook. Remove the chops to individual plates and serve hot. These are good with potato skins or potatoes baked on the grill.

Lamb Rib Chops with Fresh Mint

Yield: 6 servings

Grill: About 8 to 10 minutes

Level: Easy

At the Ready: 1 cup dried mint, soaked in water 5 minutes and drained (optional aromatic); long-handled spatula or tongs; vegetable oil or nonstick cooking spray; and a basting brush

Serve these luscious chops with drained, grilled artichoke hearts and warm pita bread.

12 rib lamb chops

Olive oil

1 cup minced fresh mint, or $^1/2$ cup dried mint

Salt and pepper to taste

Brush the chops lightly with oil, sprinkle with the mint, and press so that the herb adheres to the lamb. Prepare the grill for direct heat. When the coals are medium hot, sprinkle the dried, soaked mint over them if desired. Set the chops on the grid. Cover the grill and adjust the vents. Grill the chops 4 to 5 minutes, turn them over and continue grilling for 4 or 5 minutes, or until done to taste. Remove the chops from the grill and sprinkle with salt and pepper. Set 2 chops on each plate and serve hot.

Lamb Burgers

Yield: 6 servings

Grill: About 8 to 10 minutes

Level: Intermediate

At the Ready: Oil or nonstick cooking spray, grill screen, basting brush, long-handled spatula, 3 to 4 handfuls of dried grapevine twigs, soaked in water 30 minutes and drained (optional)

Serve these in warmed pita bread with yogurt or crumbled feta cheese, and olives.

$1^3/_4$ to 2 pounds ground lamb
4 cloves garlic, peeled and minced
1 small onion, peeled and minced
1 egg white

1 tablespoon dried oregano
1 teaspoon ground coriander
$^1/_2$ teaspoon salt

Put the ground lamb in a mixing bowl. Mix in the garlic, onion, egg white, oregano, coriander, and salt.

Using clean hands, shape the lamb mixture into 6 equal patties. Place them on a platter. Cover and refrigerate until ready to grill.

Prepare the grill for direct heat. Oil or spray a grill screen. When the coals are medium hot, scatter the drained grapevines over the coals if desired. Set the burgers on the grill screen, then set it on the grid, about 4 to 6 inches from the heat. Cover and adjust the vents. Grill the burgers for 4 minutes. Turn them over and continue grilling until cooked through, about 4 to 5 minutes, depending on the thickness of the burger. All pink should be gone from the center, but do not overcook them or they'll dry out.

Remove the burgers from the grill, place on individual plates, and serve hot.

Shish Kebabs

Yield: 6 servings

Grill: 9 to 12 minutes

Level: Intermediate

At the Ready: 6 long oiled metal skewers, vegetable oil or nonstick cooking spray, grill rack, $^1/_2$ cup dried oregano soaked in water 5 minutes and drained (optional)

You can prepare the kebabs hours head of time and keep them covered and refrigerated until ready to grill.

$^1/_3$ cup olive oil

$^1/_3$ cup vegetable oil

1 cup balsamic vinegar

3 cloves garlic, peeled and minced

1 teaspoon dried and crumbled oregano

$^1/_2$ teaspoon ground coriander

$1^1/_2$ pounds lean leg of lamb or shoulder, trimmed of fat and cut into $1^1/_2$-inch cubes

6 small ripe plum tomatoes, cut in half lengthwise

2 green or red bell peppers, seeded and cut into 1-inch squares

1 large red onion, peeled, cut in half and separated into wedges or rings

In a bowl, whisk together the oils, vinegar, garlic, oregano, and coriander. Add the lamb, cover, and marinate 2 hours in the refrigerator, turning once or twice. Drain.

Thread the skewers, beginning with a piece of lamb and alternating the meat, tomatoes, peppers, and onion. Set the kebabs on a plate. Cover and refrigerate until you're ready to grill them.

Prepare the grill for direct heat. Oil or spray a cooking screen. When the coals are medium hot, sprinkle them with the dried soaked oregano if you like. Set the kebabs on the grill screen, then set that on the grid. Cover the grill and adjust the vents. Grill the kebabs about 9 to 12 minutes, or until cooked through, rotating them every 3 to 4 minutes. The lamb should no longer be pink in the center, but don't overcook it. Set a kebab on each dinner plate. Serve hot with noodles or rice.

The Least You Need to Know

➤ Meats take well to grilling.

➤ It's important to watch meats carefully so they're not overcooked or undercooked.

➤ Searing can help seal in the juices in steaks and chops.

Chapter 19

Poultry

In This Chapter

➤ Cantonese-Style Sweet and Sour Chicken Breasts

➤ Whole Grilled Chicken with Apricot Sauce

➤ Chicken Yakitori

➤ Chicken Pieces with Molasses Barbecue Sauce

➤ Paella

➤ Chicken Dogs with Caramelized Onions

➤ Pesto Chicken

➤ Grill-Roasted Turkey Breast

➤ Turkey Burgers with Dried Cranberries

➤ Yogurt-Marinated Turkey Legs

➤ Grilled Quail

"Poultry is for the cook what a canvas is for the painter," wrote the famous nineteenth-century food authority Jean Anthelme Brillat-Savarin. We couldn't agree more. The naturally delicate flavors of chicken, turkey, and quail allow you to use sauces, flavored woods, and herbs in creative ways to tempt the tastebuds.

In this assortment of recipes, we "paint" the birds with a variety of colorful flavors: the anise pungency of pesto, the sweetness of molasses, the tart-sweet flavor of apricots, the tang of sweet-and-sour sauce.

As a bonus, the white meat of turkey or chicken is naturally low in fat (when you remove the skin). If you're watching your fat or cholesterol, you'll be delighted with the Cantonese-Style Sweet and Sour Chicken Breasts, Grill-Roasted Turkey Breast, or Turkey Burgers with Dried Cranberries (use lean, all-white-meat ground turkey).

Don't forget, large pieces of poultry such as whole chicken, turkey, or Cornish hens; boneless turkey breasts, and turkey legs must be cooked over indirect heat so the center cooks through before the outside burns.

Cantonese-Style Sweet and Sour Chicken Breasts

Yield: 6 servings

Grill: About 10 minutes

Level: Intermediate

At the Ready: Long-handled spatula or tongs, vegetable oil, basting brush, and the cooked sauce

This Cantonese sauce also works well on grilled pork, turkey, or fish.

6 boneless, skinless chicken breast halves

Lemon juice to cover chicken

1 tablespoon peanut oil or canola blend oil

$^1/_4$ cup red wine vinegar

$^1/_4$ cup light brown sugar

$^1/_2$ cup ketchup

1 cup pineapple juice

2 tablespoons cornstarch mixed with 3 tablespoons water

1 large tomato, cut into thin wedges

1 large green bell pepper, seeded and cut into strips

Place the chicken breasts in a glass bowl. Cover the chicken with lemon juice and marinate, covered, in the refrigerator for 3 to 4 hours, turning once or twice. Drain.

While the chicken is marinating, heat the oil in a small saucepan over medium heat. Stir in the vinegar, brown sugar, ketchup, and pineapple juice. Mix the cornstarch with water and blend it into the sauce. Continue cooking until the sauce turns clear and thickens slightly, and remove from the heat. Remember to reheat the sauce before serving.

Prepare the tomato and green pepper, cover and refrigerate until ready to serve.

Prepare the grill for direct heat. Oil or spray the cooking grid. When the coals are medium hot, brush the chicken breasts lightly with oil and place them on the grid, 4 to 6 inches from the heat. Grill, uncovered, about 5 minutes. Turn, again brush with oil, and continue cooking about 7 to 9 minutes, or until the chicken is fork tender and the juices run clear. Do not overcook. Cut the chicken into slices, then set on individual plates. Add the tomato and green pepper to the reheated sauce and pour it over the chicken. Serve immediately. This is good with cooked white or brown rice.

Hot Tip

The sauce can be prepared early in the day, and the vegetables cut and refrigerated. When the chicken is cooked, working quickly, reheat the sauce and mix in the vegetables.

Whole Grilled Chicken with Apricot Sauce

Yield: 4 to 6 servings

Level: Intermediate

Grill: About 1 hour, or until thermometer inserted in thickest part of thigh registers 180°F

At the Ready: 3 to 4 cups hickory chips, soaked in water 30 minutes and drained, cutting board, long-handled tongs or spatula, and pot holders, meat or instant thermometer

1 whole chicken, about 3^1/$_4$ to 3^1/$_2$ pounds, washed and patted dry

2 tablespoons vegetable oil

^{3}/$_4$ cup dry white wine

Apricot Sauce

1 cup dried apricot halves

1 cup orange juice

^{1}/$_4$ cup chicken broth

3 tablespoons orange liqueur (or 3 additional tablespoons orange juice)

3 cloves garlic, peeled and minced

^{1}/$_4$ teaspoon black pepper

^{1}/$_3$ cup chopped fresh parsley

1 teaspoon ground cinnamon

2 tablespoons light brown sugar

^{1}/$_2$ cup canned cranberry sauce

continues

continued

Remove any visible fat from the chicken. Put the chicken in a large self-sealing plastic bag. In a bowl, mix together the oil, wine, garlic, pepper, and parsley. Pour the marinade over the chicken. Seal the bag securely. Turn the bag several times, coating the chicken with marinade. Place the bag in a large bowl and refrigerate for 3 hours. Drain the chicken.

Prepare the grill for indirect heat. When the coals are medium hot, sprinkle the soaked hickory chips over them. Place the chicken, breast side up, on the grid directly over the drip pan (or over the unlit burner on a gas grill). Cover the grill and adjust the vents. Grill the chicken for about 1 hour. If you're using a charcoal grill, check the coals after 30 minutes and replenish with lit coals as necessary.

To test for doneness, insert a thermometer into the thickest part of the thigh; it should read 180°F. Or, insert a knife into the deepest part of the thigh. If the juices run clear and the joints move easily, the chicken is done. Let stand for 10 minutes before serving.

While the chicken is grilling, prepare the sauce. Put the apricots in a pot, and add enough water to cover them. Bring to a boil, reduce the heat to a simmer, and continue cooking over medium heat until the apricots are tender, about 10 minutes. Transfer them with any remaining cooking liquid to a food processor or blender, and puree. Stir in the remaining ingredients.

Serve the hot chicken cut into serving pieces, with the sauce.

Chicken Yakitori

Yield: 6 servings

Grill: 10 to 12 minutes

Level: Intermediate

At the Ready: 12 short bamboo skewers, soaked in water at least 20 minutes and drained; vegetable oil or nonstick cooking spray, a grill screen, and a basting brush

4 boneless, skinless chicken breast halves, washed and patted dry, and cut into 1- or 1$^{1}/_{2}$-inch slices

12 chicken livers, cut in half

$^{3}/_{4}$ cup light (reduced-sodium) soy sauce

$^{1}/_{2}$ cup dry white wine

2 tablespoons sugar

1 clove garlic, smashed

1 teaspoon grated ginger, or a 1-inch piece of fresh ginger, smashed

$^{1}/_{4}$ teaspoon cayenne pepper

1 can (6$^{1}/_{2}$ ounces) whole water chestnuts, drained

4 small green bell peppers, cut into 1-inch pieces

Put the chicken and liver pieces in a large self-sealing plastic bag.

Mix the soy sauce, wine, sugar, garlic, ginger, and cayenne together. Pour the marinade over the chicken and liver. Turn the bag several times to coat the meats with the marinade. Set the bag in a large bowl. Marinate in the refrigerator for 2 hours. Drain.

Thread the skewers, alternating the chicken, livers, water chestnuts, and peppers.

Prepare the grill for direct heat. Oil or spray a grill screen. When the coals are medium hot, place the skewers on the grill screen, then set it on the cooking grid. Grill the kebabs, uncovered, for 10 to 12 minutes, turning about every 3 minutes. Serve with hot brown rice or fried rice.

Chicken Pieces with Molasses Barbecue Sauce

Yield: 4 to 6 servings

Grill: 25 to 30 minutes

Level: Intermediate

At the Ready: 3 to 4 cups mesquite or fruit wood chips or dried twigs, soaked in water 30 minutes and drained; vegetable oil or nonstick cooking spray; long-handled tongs

1 chicken, about 3 to 3^1/$_2$ pounds
Molasses Barbecue Sauce
2 tablespoons vegetable oil
1 onion, minced
1 cup crushed tomatoes, including liquid
1 cup ketchup
^{1}/$_3$ cup light brown sugar

^{1}/$_4$ cup cider vinegar
^{1}/$_4$ cup dark molasses
1 tablespoon grainy mustard
1 tablespoon chili sauce

Cut the chicken into serving pieces, wash, and pat dry.

To make the sauce, heat the oil in a saucepan over medium heat. Add the onion and cook until tender, about 4 to 5 minutes, stirring occasionally. Blend in tomatoes, ketchup, brown sugar, vinegar, molasses, mustard, and chili sauce. Bring sauce to a boil, then reduce the heat to a simmer and continue cooking for 5 to 7 minutes, stirring occasionally. Remove the sauce from the heat and reserve.

continues

continued

Brush the chicken pieces lightly with the sauce, using about half of it. Place the chicken pieces in the plastic bag or in a glass bowl, covered. Refrigerate for 2 hours.

Prepare the grill for direct heat. Oil or spray the cooking grid. When the coals are medium hot, scatter the drained mesquite chips over them. Set the chicken pieces on the grid. Cover the grill and adjust the vents. Grill the chicken about 25 minutes, or until it is fork tender and the juices run clear. The wings will cook in about 10 to 15 minutes, and the thighs and drumsticks will take about 20 to 25 minutes. Use tongs to turn the chicken pieces 3 or 4 times during cooking. Brush the chicken with the remaining sauce during the last 5 minutes of cooking.

Paella

Yield: 6 servings

Grill: 25 minutes

Level: Advanced

At the Ready: Olive oil for brushing, grill screen, tongs, basting brush, the cooked rice, and the cooked peas

2 cups long-grain or converted rice

3³/₄ cups water or reduced-sodium chicken broth

2 pinches saffron, or ³/₄ teaspoon turmeric

2 cups frozen green peas, cooked according to package directions

1 chicken, about 3 to 3¹/₂ pounds, cut into serving pieces

Paprika to taste

Salt and pepper to taste

1 pound spicy sausage, pricked with a fork in several places

1 large onion, cut into ¹/₂-inch slices

3 tomatoes, sliced

24 mussels, cleaned

12 large unshelled shrimp, washed

Prepare the rice according to the package directions, but substituting the chicken broth for the cooking water. Omit salt and add the saffron or turmeric to the chicken broth.

Meanwhile, cook the peas and set aside.

While the rice is cooking, brush the chicken with oil and sprinkle with paprika, salt, and pepper.

Prepare the grill for direct heat. Oil or spray the cooking grid, and a cooking screen. When the coals are medium hot, put the chicken on the grid.

Cover the grill and adjust the vents. Grill the chicken pieces about 15 to 25 minutes, turning them occasionally. The wings should cook in about 10 to 15 minutes and the legs and breast will take at least about 5 to 10 minutes longer. While the chicken is cooking, set the sausages on the grill rack and cook them about 10 to 15 minutes, turning occasionally. Remove the sausages when they are cooked and browned. Cut into pieces and set aside.

Near the end of the chicken's cooking time, place the grill screen on the grid, and place the onion slices, tomatoes, mussels, and shrimp on it. Grill the vegetables and seafood about 5 minutes, turning once, until the mussels are open, the shrimp is opaque, and the vegetables are tender. Discard any mussels that do not open during grilling.

Toss the sausage pieces and the vegetables with the hot cooked rice. Arrange the shrimp, mussels, and chicken on the rice. Serve hot.

What's What

Paella is a Spanish dish that has numerous variations, depending on the cook. There are many recipes for paella, some including both seafood and meat, others using only seafood and still others using only vegetables. For example, you can add more chicken and not use the shrimp, or use a pinch of turmeric in the rice in place of the saffron, or eliminate the sausage and maybe add some grilled shrimp. Make it your own recipe by using the foods that you prefer.

Chicken Dogs with Caramelized Onions

Yield: 6 servings

Grill: 10 minutes

Level: Easy

At the Ready: Tongs, mustard, pickles or relish, and the hot dog rolls

2 tablespoons vegetable oil

3 tablespoons butter

4 cloves garlic, peeled and minced

3 large red onions, peeled and sliced thin

$^1/_4$ cup light brown sugar

$^1/_2$ teaspoon salt

$^1/_4$ teaspoon black pepper

6 chicken or turkey dogs, pricked in several places with the tip of a small knife or fork

6 split hot dog rolls, insides brushed lightly with melted butter

In a large nonstick frying pan, heat the oil and butter over medium heat. Add the garlic and onions. Cook the vegetables, stirring occasionally, for about 5 minutes, or until the onions are soft and golden. Stir in the brown sugar, salt, and pepper.

Continue cooking about 5 minutes, stirring as necessary. Set aside. Reheat before serving.

Prepare the grill for direct heat. When the coals are medium hot, set the hot dogs on the grid, 4 to 6 inches from the heat. Cover the grill and adjust the vents. Grill about 10 to 15 minutes, turning twice. The hot dogs should brown and be cooked through.

Heat the rolls quickly, about 1 to 2 minutes on each side. Put a hot dog in each roll and top with hot caramelized onions. Serve immediately with mustard and pickles or relish.

Hot Tip

Chicken or turkey dogs come in many flavors, including Italian, herb spiced, and cheese. Use the ones that you prefer. They usually have less saturated fat than beef and pork dogs, and are very tasty.

Pesto Chicken

Yield: 6 to 8 servings

Grill: 25 to 30 minutes

Level: Easy

At the Ready: Hickory chips soaked 30 minutes and drained (optional), long-handled tongs, meat thermometer

³/₄ cup vegetable oil

³/₄ cup dry white wine

¹/₄ cup lime juice

4 cloves garlic, peeled and smashed

¹/₃ cup minced fresh cilantro

2 frying chickens, about 2¹/₂ pounds each, cut in half, backbones removed (have the guy at the meat counter do this)

2 cups prepared pesto sauce (homemade or store-bought)

Pine nuts for garnish

To make the marinade, mix together the oil, wine, lime juice, garlic, and cilantro. Set the chicken in a glass bowl or shallow glass container. Pour the marinade over the chicken. Turn several times so that all of the chicken is covered with the marinade. Cover and refrigerate for 2 to 4 hours. Drain.

Prepare the grill for indirect heat. When the coals are medium hot, scatter the drained wood chips over them. Sear the chicken a few minutes on each side. Cover the grill, adjust the vents, and grill the chicken, turning 2 to 3 times during cooking, for about 25 to 35 minutes, or until the juices run clear or a meat thermometer inserted in the thickest part of the thigh registers 180°F. Brush the chicken with half of the pesto during the last 5 or 10 minutes of grilling. Remove the chicken to a cutting board. Let it rest 10 minutes. Cut the chicken into quarters. Brush with the remaining sauce and sprinkle with pine nuts. Serve hot.

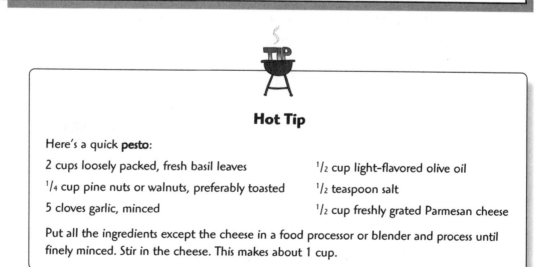

Hot Tip

Here's a quick **pesto**:

2 cups loosely packed, fresh basil leaves

¹/₄ cup pine nuts or walnuts, preferably toasted

5 cloves garlic, minced

¹/₂ cup light-flavored olive oil

¹/₂ teaspoon salt

¹/₂ cup freshly grated Parmesan cheese

Put all the ingredients except the cheese in a food processor or blender and process until finely minced. Stir in the cheese. This makes about 1 cup.

Grill-Roasted Turkey Breast

Yield: 6 to 8 servings

Grill: About 1^1/$_4$ hours

Level: Easy

At the Ready: Aluminum foil, water pan, pecan pieces or aromatic wood of choice, soaked 30 minutes and drained (optional)

Tangerine Marinade:

1 cup red wine

^{1}/$_2$ cup tangerine juice or orange juice

^{1}/$_4$ cup chopped fresh basil or 2 tablespoons dried basil

^{1}/$_2$ teaspoon black pepper

1 3- to 3^1/$_2$-pound boneless turkey breast

^{3}/$_4$ cup barbecue sauce

^{3}/$_4$ cup grape jelly

In a small bowl mix together the wine, juice, basil, and pepper. Set the turkey in a glass bowl or large self-sealing plastic bag.

Pour the marinade over the turkey. Seal the bag and turn it several times so that all areas of the turkey are coated with the marinade. Set the turkey in a glass dish. Refrigerate for 4 to 6 hours. Drain.

Prepare the grill for indirect heat. In a bowl blend together the barbecue sauce and jelly. Brush the turkey breast with the sauce. When the coals are medium hot, sprinkle pecan pieces over them. Set the turkey on a sheet of aluminum foil, and place it on the grill over the water pan. Cover the grill, adjust the vents, and grill the turkey breast for 1 to 1^1/$_4$ hours, or until the juices run clear when you pierce the turkey with the tip of a knife. If you're using a charcoal grill, replenish the grill with lit coals as necessary. Rotate the turkey several times during grilling.

Remove the turkey breast to a cutting board, cover with foil and let rest for 10 to 12 minutes. Slice and serve. This is good with chutney or cranberry sauce and garlic mashed potatoes.

Turkey Burgers with Dried Cranberries

Yield: 6 servings

Grill: 10 to 12 minutes

Level: Easy

At the Ready: Long-handled spatula, grill screen, oil for brushing, and a brush

These are great with grilled sweet potato wedges on the side.

2 pounds ground turkey
1 large onion, minced
1 egg
³/₄ cup dried cranberries

1 teaspoon ground sage
Salt and pepper to taste
6 onion hard rolls, split

In a large mixing bowl, blend together the ground turkey, onion, egg, dried cranberries, sage, salt, and pepper. Shape into 6 equal patties. Put the patties on a plate, cover with plastic wrap and refrigerate until ready to grill.

Prepare the grill for direct heat. Oil or spray a grill screen. When the coals are medium hot, set the burgers on the grill screen, and set that on the cooking grid. Cover the grill and adjust the vents. Grill about 10 to 12 minutes, turning once. When the burgers are almost ready, heat the rolls on the grill, just 1 or 2 minutes, long enough to warm them.

Set each burger in a warmed roll. Serve hot with grilled sweet potato wedges or chips, sliced tomatoes, and/or sweet and sour pickles.

Hot Tip

Dried cranberries, cherries, and strawberries are relatively new items in supermarkets. If you like, you can substitute chopped walnuts or raisins for the dried cranberries.

Yogurt-Marinated Turkey Legs

Yield: 6 servings

Grill: 50 to 60 minutes, or until a thermometer inserted in the thickest part of the thigh registers 180°F

Level: Intermediate

At the Ready: Long-handled tongs, apple wood chips or twigs soaked 30 minutes and drained (optional), water pan, small sharp knife, aluminum foil, meat or instant thermometer

2 cups lowfat plain yogurt or sour cream

1/4 cup lime juice

4 green onions, trimmed and minced

4 cloves garlic, peeled and minced

1 tablespoon ground cumin

1/2 teaspoon salt

6 turkey legs, about 10 to 12 ounces each, washed and patted dry

Chopped fresh cilantro for garnish

Put the yogurt in a mixing bowl. Blend in the juice, onions, garlic, cumin, and salt.

Put the turkey legs in a shallow glass dish. Cover them with the yogurt marinade. Cover with plastic wrap and refrigerate for 6 hours or longer.

Prepare the grill for indirect heat. When the coals are medium hot, set the turkey drumsticks, still covered with some of the yogurt, on a piece of aluminum foil on the grill. Cover the grill and adjust the vents. Grill until the turkey is fork tender and the juices run clear, about 50 to 60 minutes. Turn the turkey pieces every 10 to 15 minutes. If you are using a charcoal grill, replenish the grill with lit coals at least once, or as necessary.

Serve hot with salsa and warm flour tortillas. Garnish with chopped fresh cilantro.

Grilled Quail

Yield: 6 servings

Grill: 10 to 15 minutes

Level: Advanced

At the Ready: Cooked orzo, and a long-handled spatula

Quail are available at some large supermarkets, specialty butcher shops, many Vietnamese markets, and from shops specializing in wild game.

3/4 cup vegetable oil

1/2 cup cider vinegar

1 tablespoon water

1 teaspoon dried rosemary

1 teaspoon dried thyme

1/4 teaspoon ground pepper

1/4 cup minced fresh chives

12 butterflied quail, washed and patted dry

In a bowl whisk together the oil, vinegar, water, rosemary, thyme, pepper, and chives. Have ready 3 large self-sealing bags. Put 4 quail in each bag. Divide the marinade among the bags. Seal securely, and turn the bags several times to coat the quail. Set the bags in a large bowl and marinate the quail for 2 hours in the refrigerator. Drain.

Prepare the grill for direct heat. Oil or spray a grill screen. When the coals are medium hot, set the quail on the grill screen and set that on the cooking grid. Cover the grill and adjust the vents. Grill the quail for 6 minutes, then turn them over. Grill another 8 or 9 minutes or until the joints move easily and the juices run clear.

Serve the quail hot over cooked orzo that is tossed with chopped pecans and currants.

What's What

Orzo is rice-shaped pasta. It is available in some large supermarkets. If your market doesn't carry it, substitute any small pasta.

Hot Tip

To butterfly quail, use a pair of kitchen scissors or poultry shears to cut the backbone out of the quail. Open the quail to butterfly position, then press on the breast bone until the bone cracks and the quail lies flat. Better yet, ask the butcher to do this.

The Least You Need to Know

➤ Chicken is one of the most versatile foods for grilling.

➤ Turkey or chicken white meat is low in fat.

➤ Large pieces of poultry must be cooked over indirect heat.

Chapter 20

Fish

In This Chapter

➤ Swordfish in Buttermilk Marinade

➤ Tarragon-Scented Striped Bass

➤ Red Snapper with Olive Salad

➤ Halibut Steaks au Poivre

➤ Orange Roughy with Salsa

➤ Bluefish Piccata

➤ Minted Flounder on Lime Slices

➤ Grilled Whitefish with Spinach Pasta and Fontina Cheese

➤ Mackerel with Tangerine Brushing Sauce

➤ Salmon Steaks with Asian Marinade

➤ Very Simply Salmon

➤ Red Snapper Margarita

➤ Scrod with Grilled Apple Slices

Fish is too often ignored among the stars of the grill. Lean, sophisticated, and flavorful, it's actually one of the best foods to grill. Thanks to modern air transportation, you can walk into your fish market and have a wide selection of everything from frozen shrimp to farm-raised trout to Alaskan halibut.

Fish generally is cooked until it "flakes"—that is, when you prod it with a fork, it begins to separate into slices. For fish to cook until it flakes does not mean that it should be dry, so be careful, because it does dry out quickly if left on the grill too long. It's best to remove the fish when it is still not quite opaque all the way through the center. It finishes cooking after you remove it from the heat.

In general, fish requires 10 minutes of cooking time per inch of thickness. In other words, you grill a 1-inch-thick swordfish steak for 10 minutes, a $^1/_2$-inch-thick white-fish fillet for 5 minutes. Obviously, this is only a general rule, since fish varies in density. You'll still need to keep an eye on it.

When grilling a long fish fillet, fold the narrow part (the tail section) under the fish. This helps even out the thickness of the fish so it cooks more uniformly.

We have used readily available fish in these recipes, but if the fish we call for is not available, or doesn't look as fresh as it should, you can substitute. Ask the fishmonger for ideas, but you can also use these suggested substitutions as a guide. The fish in a given listing can all substitute for each other:

➤ Swordfish, shark, tuna, marlin

➤ Striped bass, grouper, halibut, orange roughy, rockfish, tilefish, ocean perch, or red sea bass

➤ Red snapper, black sea bass, grouper, halibut, mahi mahi, or rockfish

➤ Halibut, snapper, mahi mahi, yellowtail, or black sea bass

➤ Orange roughy, striped bass, black sea bass, perch, sole, catfish, or tilapia

➤ Bluefish, mackerel

➤ Flounder, sole, or tilapia

➤ Whitefish, rainbow trout, salmon

➤ Scrod, cod, haddock, or flounder

Swordfish in Buttermilk Marinade

Yield: 6 servings

Grill: About 8 minutes

Level: Intermediate

At the Ready: Long-handled spatula, oil for brushing, grill screen, brush

Swordfish has a firm texture and a mildly distinct flavor. You can substitute shark or tuna.

3 cups buttermilk
2 teaspoons Tabasco sauce
6 swordfish steaks, cut $^3/_4$-inch thick, rinsed and patted dry

In a bowl mix together the buttermilk and the Tabasco sauce. Divide the marinade into 2 large self-sealing plastic bags. Add three swordfish steaks to each bag and seal securely. Turn each bag several times. Set the bags on a flat dish and marinate in the refrigerator for 2 hours. Drain the fish and pat dry with paper toweling.

Prepare the grill for direct heat. Oil or spray a grill screen. When the coals are medium hot, set the fish on the grill screen and set that on the cooking grid. Cover the grill and adjust the vents. Grill the fish 4 minutes. Turn and continue grilling another 4 minutes, or until the fish is opaque and flakes easily when prodded with a fork.

Remove the fish from the grill and set on individual plates.

Hot Tip

Buttermilk is a great marinade. It's acidic enough to tenderize foods, and rich enough to give them a wonderful flavor. Despite its name, it is actually low in fat.

Tarragon-Scented Striped Bass

Yield: 6 servings

Grill: About 4 to 6 minutes

Level: Easy

At the Ready: 1 cup dried tarragon or basil, soaked in water 5 minutes and drained (optional), vegetable oil for brushing, long-handled spatula, basting brush, fresh tarragon if available

Striped bass is a lowfat, medium-firm fish with a mild flavor. You can substitute orange roughy or black sea bass in this recipe.

6 striped bass fillets, rinsed and patted dry

Olive or canola oil

Fresh or dried tarragon

Salt and pepper to taste

Balsamic vinegar

continues

continued

Prepare the grill for direct heat. Oil the cooking grid. When the coals are medium hot, sprinkle the herbs over them. Brush the fish lightly with oil, put a few tarragon sprigs on top, and sprinkle with salt and pepper. Set the fish on the cooking grid. Cover the grill and adjust the vents. Grill the fish about 4 to 6 minutes, or until it is opaque and flakes easily when prodded with a fork.

Remove the fish from the grill with a long-handled spatula and set on individual plates. Sprinkle it with balsamic vinegar.

Don't Get Burned!

Do not turn delicate fish such as bass when grilling it; it will fall apart.

Red Snapper with Olive Salad

Yield: 6 servings

Grill: About 8 minutes

Level: Easy

Olive Salad
$^1/_2$ cup extra-virgin olive oil
2 tablespoons chopped fresh parsley
1 tablespoon lemon juice
$^1/_3$ cup pitted chopped olives (use a mixture of flavorful black and green olives)

6 red or Pacific snapper fillets, about 6 to 7 ounces each, rinsed and patted dry

At the Ready: Olive oil or vegetable oil for brushing, grill screen, brush, long-handled spatula, 3 or 4 handfuls of dried grapevine twigs, soaked in water 30 minutes and drained (optional)

To prepare the salad, mix all the ingredients in a small glass bowl. Cover and refrigerate until ready to serve. Bring the salad to room temperature before serving.

Check the fish for any visible bones, and remove them with tweezers.

Prepare the grill for direct heat. Brush the snapper pieces on both sides with oil and arrange the fillets on an oiled or sprayed grill screen. When the coals are medium hot, set the fish and grill screen on the cooking grid. Cover the grill and adjust the vents. Grill the fish 3 to 4 minutes, then turn with a long-handled spatula. Continue cooking for 3 to 4 minutes, or just until the fish is opaque and flakes easily when prodded with a fork. It should still be moist in the thickest part.

Transfer the fish to plates and serve with a spoonful of the olive salad. Serve hot.

Halibut Steaks au Poivre

Yield: 6 servings

Grill: About 6 to 8 minutes

Level: Easy

At the Ready: Long-handled spatula, grill screen, brush

Halibut is a sweet-flavored fish with a moderately high fat content, which makes it especially suitable for grilling.

2 tablespoons black peppercorns, crushed
2 tablespoons green peppercorns, crushed
2 teaspoons dried basil
6 halibut steaks, about $^3/_4$-inch thick, rinsed and patted dry
Vegetable or olive oil

Put the crushed black and green peppercorns in a small bowl. Mix in the basil. Brush the halibut steaks with oil. Sprinkle them with the peppercorn rub and press the peppercorns to adhere to the fish. Set the fish on a glass plate and cover loosely with plastic wrap. Refrigerate for 1 hour. Remove the covering.

Prepare the grill for direct heat. Oil or spray a grill screen. When the coals are medium hot, set the halibut steaks on the grill screen, and set that on the cooking grid. Cover the grill and adjust the vents. Grill 4 minutes, then turn the fish over. Continue grilling for 2 to 3 minutes or until the fish flakes easily when prodded with a fork.

Remove the fish to individual plates. Serve hot.

Hot Tip

If you only have whole peppercorns on hand, crack them by placing them between 2 sheets of waxed paper and pressing down with a rolling pin to crush them.

Orange Roughy with Salsa

Yield: 6 servings

Grill: 6 to 8 minutes or until done to taste

Level: Easy

At the Ready: Oil for brushing, grill screen, brush

4 large tomatoes, chopped
1 medium red onion, peeled and minced
$3/4$ cup chopped fresh cilantro, divided
3 tablespoons lime juice
3 jalapeño peppers, seeded and minced
3 cloves garlic, peeled and minced
$1/4$ teaspoon salt
2 pounds orange roughy, divided into 6 portions, rinsed and patted dry

To make the salsa, toss together the tomatoes, onion, $1/2$ cup of the cilantro, lime juice, peppers, garlic, and salt. Cover and refrigerate. Toss again before serving, and taste to adjust the seasonings.

Brush the fish on both sides with oil and sprinkle with $1/4$ cup cilantro. Prepare the grill for direct heat. Oil or spray a grill screen. When the coals are medium hot, place the fish on the grill screen and set it on the cooking grid. Grill the fish 3 to 4 minutes, turn it over and continue cooking 3 minutes or until the fish is just opaque and flakes easily when prodded with a fork. It should still be moist in the thickest part. Transfer the fish to plates and serve it topped with the salsa.

Bluefish Piccata

Yield: 6 servings

Grill: 8 to 10 minutes, or until done to taste

Level: Easy

At the Ready: Grill screen, oil for brushing, brush, long-handled spatula; 1 cup dried basil, soaked in water for 5 minutes and squeezed dry (optional)

2 tablespoons olive oil
3 cloves garlic, minced
1 cup dry white wine
$^1/_3$ cup lemon juice
$^1/_4$ cup capers, drained
$1^3/_4$ to 2 pounds bluefish, cut into 6 pieces, rinsed and patted dry
$^1/_2$ cup shredded Romano or Parmesan cheese

Heat the olive oil in a small frying pan over medium heat. Add the garlic and cook, stirring, until soft, about 1 to 2 minutes. Add the wine, lemon juice, and capers. Bring the mixture to a boil, stirring often. Remove from heat and allow to cool. Use the sauce at room temperature.

Brush the bluefish with oil. Prepare the grill for direct heat. Oil or spray a grill screen. When the coals are medium hot, set the bluefish on the grill screen, then set that on the cooking grid. Grill the fish 4 minutes. Turn it over and continue cooking about 4 or 5 minutes, or until the fish is opaque, yet still moist in the thickest part, and flakes easily when prodded with a fork.

Transfer the fish to individual plates or to a platter. Spoon the sauce over the fish, sprinkle with cheese, and serve.

What's What

Nicknamed "bulldog of the ocean" for its tenacity, the bluefish is a coastal Atlantic Ocean fish with fine-grained, fatty flesh that makes it great on the grill.

Minted Flounder on Lime Slices

Yield: 6 servings
Grill: 5 to 7 minutes

Level: Easy
At the Ready: Lime slices, oil for brushing, grill screen and brush, food processor or blender, long-handled fork

Flounder has a delicate flavor and a fine texture. You can substitute sole.

Mint Butter
$^1/_2$ cup (1 stick) butter, at room temperature
$^1/_4$ cup fresh mint sprigs, stems discarded
1 tablespoon crème de menthe liqueur
1 tablespoon grated lime peel

6 limes, cut into thin slices
6 flounder fillets, about 6 to 8 ounces each
Fresh mint sprigs

Cut the butter into small pieces and place it in a food processor or blender. Add the mint, crème de menthe, and lime peel. Process until the ingredients are pureed and smooth. Spoon the butter into a small bowl or a crock and cover it with plastic wrap. If you are grilling the fish right away, leave the butter at room temperature. Otherwise, refrigerate it and bring to room temperature before serving.

Prepare the grill for direct heat. Oil or spray a grill screen. When the coals are medium hot, put the lime slices on the grill screen. Brush the fish with oil and set a mint sprig on top of each fillet. Arrange the fish directly on the lime slices. Set the grill screen on the cooking grid. Cover the grill and adjust the vents. Grill 4 to 5 minutes, check the fish, and continue grilling until the fish flakes easily when prodded with a fork.

Remove the fish and the lime slices to individual plates. Serve the fish hot and pass the mint butter to be dabbed on the fish.

Hot Tip

Peppermint or spearmint is very easy to grow. In fact, mint can choke out your garden if you don't contain it. Chop up extra mint, put it in small self-sealing bags, and freeze it for winter use.

Grilled Whitefish with Spinach Pasta and Fontina Cheese

Yield: 6 servings

Grill: 6 to 8 minutes

Level: Easy

At the Ready: The cooked, drained pasta; oil for brushing; brush; grill screen; long-handled spatula

You can substitute salmon or haddock for the whitefish in this recipe.

1 pound spinach pasta

$^1/_4$ cup ($^1/_2$ stick) butter, cut in small pieces, at room temperature

6 ounces fontina cheese, crumbled

2 tomatoes, diced

1 cup nonfat sour cream, or plain nonfat yogurt

$^1/_2$ cup chopped fresh cilantro

$^1/_2$ teaspoon pepper

$1^1/_2$ pounds whitefish fillets, washed and patted dry

Salt and paprika to taste

Cook the pasta according to package directions in a large pot of salted boiling water. Drain. When ready to assemble, rewarm the pasta by putting it in a strainer and running it under hot water for a minute or two. Put it in a serving bowl, and toss it with the butter, crumbled cheese, tomatoes, sour cream or yogurt, cilantro, and pepper.

Prepare the grill for direct heat. Oil or spray a grill screen. When the coals are medium hot, set the fish on the grill screen and sprinkle it with salt and paprika. Put the screen on the cooking grid. Cover the grill and adjust the vents. Grill the fish 6 to 8 minutes, turning once, or until it is opaque and flakes easily when prodded with a fork. Remove the fish to a plate. Break the fish into pieces and toss it with the pasta. Serve the pasta salad warm or at room temperature.

Hot Tip

To keep from running between the stove and the grill, you can cook pasta a bit ahead of time. Then just "refresh" it by putting the cooked pasta in a strainer and running it under hot water for a minute or two.

Mackerel with Tangerine Brushing Sauce

Yield: 6 servings

Grill: 6 to 8 minutes

Level: Easy

At the Ready: $1/2$ cup dried rosemary soaked in water 5 minutes and drained (optional), oil for brushing, brush, long-handled spatula

Mackerel has a high fat content and a rich flavor that's nicely offset by the citrus. This is good with grilled tomatoes and green onions.

1 cup tangerine or orange juice

1 teaspoon minced garlic

3 mackerel, about 1 pound each, cleaned and split in half (butterflied—ask your fishmonger to do this for you)

1 can (11 ounces) mandarin oranges, drained

Prepare the grill for direct heat. Oil the cooking grid. Mix the tangerine juice with the garlic. Brush the fish on both sides with the juice mixture. When the coals are medium hot, sprinkle them with the drained rosemary if desired. Set the fish on the cooking grid. Cover the grill and adjust the vents. Grill the fish 3 minutes, then turn them over and continue grilling for 3 to 5 minutes or until the fish flake easily when prodded with a fork.

Remove the fish to a working tray. Remove the center bone and cut each half down the middle. Set each piece on a dish and scatter mandarin orange pieces over the fish. Serve immediately. This is good with grilled tomatoes (page 127).

Salmon Steaks with Asian Marinade

Yield: 6 servings

Grill: About 7 minutes

Level: Easy

At the Ready: Long-handled spatula, oil for brushing, grill screen, brush

If you can get alder chips, use them in this recipe. Use 3 cups of the alder chips or wood pieces, soaked in water for 30 minutes and drained.

Asian Marinade

$3/4$ cup light (reduced-sodium) soy sauce

$3/4$ cup mirin (Japanese cooking wine)

$1 1/2$ cups chicken broth

3 tablespoons sugar

1 lime, cut in thin slices

6 salmon steaks, each about $3/4$-inch thick, washed and patted dry

In a bowl, combine the soy sauce, mirin, chicken broth, sugar, and lime slices. Place the salmon steaks in a glass dish and brush both sides with the marinade. Pour extra marinade over the fish. Cover the salmon lightly and refrigerate for 1 hour. Turn the fish once. Drain.

Prepare the grill for direct heat. Oil or spray a grill screen. When the coals are medium hot, set the salmon steaks on the grill screen and set that on the cooking grid. Cover and grill 4 minutes, then turn and grill about 3 minutes longer, or until the fish flakes easily when prodded with a fork.

Very Simply Salmon

Yield: 6 servings

Grill: About 7 minutes

Level: Easy

At the Ready: Salad dressing for brushing, and a basting brush

If you like, scatter some apple wood chips onto the coals for some extra flavor.

6 salmon steaks, each about $^3/_4$-inch thick, washed and patted dry

$^1/_4$ cup oil and vinegar salad dressing (or any vinaigrette-style dressing that's a family favorite)

Salt and pepper to taste

Prepare the grill. Brush the salmon steaks with the dressing. Sprinkle with salt and pepper. When the coals are medium hot, set the fish on the grill about 4 to 6 inches from the heat. Cover and grill about 7 minutes, turning once. Brush salmon steaks again as you turn them. Grill until the fish flakes easily when prodded with a fork. Serve.

What's What

Salmon is a cold water fish from both the Atlantic and Pacific Oceans. The salmon of the Northwest has five species, with sockeye, chinook and coho being the most popular varieties. These days, most of the salmon in the markets is farm-raised.

Red Snapper Margarita

Yield: 6 servings

Grill: About 8 minutes

Level: Easy

At the Ready: Lime wedges, oil for brushing, grill screen, brush, long-handled fork, 3 cups mesquite chips, soaked in water 30 minutes and drained (optional)

Margarita Marinade

$^3/_4$ cup orange juice concentrate, thawed (don't add water)

$^1/_4$ cup tequila

$^1/_2$ cup lime juice

2 tablespoons olive oil

1 clove garlic, peeled and smashed

6 red or Pacific snapper fillets, about 6 to 8 ounces each, washed and patted dry

In a bowl, combine the orange juice concentrate, tequila, lime juice, olive oil, and garlic. Put the fish in a flat glass dish or 2 large self-sealing plastic bags. Cover with marinade. Cover and marinate for 1 hour in the refrigerator. Drain.

Prepare the grill for direct heat. Oil or spray a grill screen. When the coals are medium hot, set the fish on the grill screen and set that on the cooking grid. Cover the grill and adjust the vents. Grill the fish for 4 minutes, turn it over and grill it another 4 minutes, or until it flakes easily when prodded with a fork. Remove the fish to a serving platter. Serve hot with lime or orange wedges. This is good with salsa and grilled asparagus.

Hot Tip

To make an easy orange or pineapple salsa, use your favorite salsa recipe and substitute chopped orange or pineapple for the tomatoes.

Scrod with Grilled Apple Slices

Yield: 6 servings

Grill: 6 to 8 minutes

Level: Intermediate

At the Ready: Grill screen, oil for brushing, brush, long-handled spatula

Snapper can be substituted for the scrod in this recipe. While the apples are grilling you can sprinkle them with a small amount of sugar mixed with cinnamon for additional flavor.

6 scrod fillets, about 6 to 8 ounces each, rinsed and patted dry
2 oranges, thinly sliced
4 large Granny Smith apples, peeled, cored, and sliced
Melted butter or margarine for brushing apple slices
Sage and nutmeg

Prepare the grill for direct heat. Brush the scrod pieces on both sides with oil. Oil or spray a grill screen. When the coals are medium hot, set the orange slices on the grill screen. Set it on the cooking grid 4 to 6 inches from the heat, then set the fish atop the orange slices. Cover the grill and adjust the vents. Grill about 6 minutes. Continue cooking until the fish turns opaque and flakes easily when prodded with a fork. It should remain moist in the thickest part. While the fish is cooking brush the apple slices with butter and set them on the screen. Grill the apples on both sides, until they are tender and just beginning to brown.

Serve the fish on individual plates surrounded with grilled apples. Sprinkle both lightly with sage and nutmeg. Serve hot.

The Least You Need to Know

➤ Lean yet flavorful, fish is one of the best choices for grilling.

➤ Cook fish for 10 minutes per inch of thickness, or until it begins to flake.

➤ When a particular fish is unavailable, you usually can easily substitute another variety.

Chapter 21

Shellfish

In This Chapter

➤ Sea Scallops and Mashed Potatoes with Jalapeño Mayonnaise

➤ Sea Scallop Kebabs

➤ Soft-Shell Crabs on the Grill

➤ Soft-Shell Crabs with Garlic Crumbs

➤ Whole Maine Lobsters

➤ Lobster Tails with Sherry Sauce

➤ "Poor Man's Lobster" (Monkfish) with Grapefruit Relish

➤ Coastal Shrimp in Beer

➤ Prawns with Honey Brushing Sauce

➤ Down Maine Clambake

➤ Crab Cakes

Sweet and nutty or deliciously briny, shellfish are irresistible on the grill. Like other varieties of fish, shellfish are usually low in fat and calories, easy to eat, quick to cook, easy to clean up after, and absolutely delicious. Shellfish, along with fish, are indeed the food of the future.

To impart an intriguing flavor to shellfish, toss a half cup of dried herbs of your choice, soaked and drained, onto the coals. And try serving the shellfish with lime wedges, rather than the usual lemon, for a bit more wake-up flavor.

Shellfish such as shrimp, lobster, or clams overcook and toughen very quickly. So watch carefully, and don't leave the grill unattended. Crustaceans such as shrimp are done when they turn opaque; shellfish in the shell are done as soon as the shells pop open.

Some shellfish, such as many crabs, whole lobsters, and most mollusks, are sold live. They're very perishable. Shellfish that is not alive, such as shucked oysters, cleaned crabs, or lobster that the fishmonger has butterflied for you, is even more perishable and should be kept very cold and cooked the same day you buy it. Always thaw frozen shellfish in the refrigerator.

Sea Scallops and Mashed Potatoes with Jalapeño Mayonnaise

Yield: 6 servings

Grill: About 7 to 8 minutes

Level: Intermediate

At the Ready: Long-handled spatula, grill screen, oil for brushing, a brush

Mashed Potatoes

6 large golden potatoes, peeled and quartered

2 tablespoons unsalted butter

$^1/_3$ cup half-and-half or plain lowfat yogurt

$^1/_2$ teaspoon salt

$^1/_4$ teaspoon white pepper

$1^1/_2$ cups regular or reduced-fat mayonnaise

3 jalapeño peppers, carefully seeded and chopped

2 pounds sea scallops, washed gently and patted dry

Put the potatoes in a large saucepan and cover them with water. Bring to a boil, reduce the heat to a simmer and continue cooking for about 20 minutes, or until the potatoes can be easily pierced with a fork. Drain. In a nonstick frying pan, cook the potatoes over medium heat for 4 minutes, shaking and stirring often with a wooden spoon. (This step is optional, but helps get rid of excess moisture so the potatoes are fluffier.) Transfer the potatoes to a mixing bowl and mash them with a masher or fork. Whip the potatoes with a wire whisk, adding the butter, half-and-half, salt, and pepper as you whip. Continue whipping until the potatoes are free from lumps. Serve hot.

In a bowl, mix the mayonnaise with the peppers. Cover and refrigerate until serving time. Stir before serving.

Prepare the grill for direct heat. Oil or spray a grill screen. When the coals are medium-hot, set the grill screen on the cooking grid. Brush the scallops with oil and place them on the screen. Grill, uncovered, about 4 minutes. Turn them over and continue grilling for 3 to 4 minutes, or until the scallops lose their translucency and are just firm to the touch. Set the hot potatoes in the center of individual plates. Put the scallops in the center of the potatoes. Top with a dab of the mayonnaise.

Serve hot. This is good with grilled asparagus (see page 124) and/or tomatoes (page 127).

Don't Get Burned!

Be careful when you seed and chop hot peppers, like jalapeños. Wash your hands thoroughly afterwards, and be careful not to rub your eyes; the capsaicin in pepper is a powerful irritant. Some people prefer to wear latex or rubber gloves when handling chiles.

Sea Scallop Kebabs

Yield: 6 servings

Grill: 7 to 8 minutes

Level: Intermediate

At the Ready: 6 long metal skewers, grill screen, oil for brushing, brush, ¹/₃ cup dried tarragon or sage leaves soaked in water for 5 minutes and squeezed dry (optional)

8 slices bacon, cut crosswise into thirds
24 sea scallops, rinsed and pat dry
24 cherry tomatoes, washed

2 limes, thinly sliced
2 teaspoons dried tarragon or
2 tablespoons fresh tarragon

Place the bacon pieces in a large skillet. Cook over medium heat, turning once, until the bacon is cooked through but not crisp. Remove from the heat and drain on paper towels.

continues

continued

Thread the scallops and bacon pieces, tomatoes, and lime slices onto the skewers, alternating the ingredients. Secure the bacon by threading both ends of each piece through the skewer.

Prepare the grill for direct heat. Oil or spray a grill screen. When the coals are medium hot, scatter the soaked tarragon or sage over them if desired. Set the grill screen on the cooking grid. Brush the scallops with oil and sprinkle with tarragon. Place them on the screen and grill, uncovered, about 3 minutes. Turn them over and continue grilling for 3 to 4 minutes or until they lose their translucency and are just firm to the touch.

Serve hot with a green salad sprinkled with walnuts and chopped pears.

Don't Get Burned!

Metal skewers can get hot on the grill. Have a pot holder or heatproof gloves handy when you're ready to turn the kabobs.

Soft-Shell Crabs on the Grill

Yield: 6 servings

Grill: 6 to 8 minutes

Level: Easy

At the Ready: Oil for brushing, long-handled spatula, and 6 long metal skewers

Grilled soft-shell crabs are a longtime favorite in Barbara's family.

12 cleaned soft-shell crabs (have the fishmonger clean them)

$1/2$ cup (1 stick) butter, melted and cooled

2 lemons or limes, sliced

Brush the crabs with a little of the melted butter and thread 2 crabs lengthwise on each skewer.

Prepare the grill for direct heat. When the coals are medium hot, set the threaded crabs on the grill, 4 to 6 inches from the heat. Grill the crabs, uncovered, for 3 minutes, turn them over, and continue to grill until they turn reddish, about 3 to 4 minutes longer. Serve the crabs hot with the remaining melted butter, lemon or lime slices, cornbread, and a salad.

What's What

Wonderfully sweet *soft-shell crabs,* which are available from May to October, are regular East Coast blue crabs that are gathered right after they molt (shed their shells). The crunchy new shell is completely edible and, as a bonus, is rich in calcium.

Don't Get Burned!

Soft-shell crabs are sold live. It's easiest to let the fishmonger clean them (remove the face portion, gills, and sand receptacle under the mouth)—but be sure to serve them the same day you buy them. They're very perishable, and can spoil quickly.

Soft-Shell Crabs with Garlic Crumbs

Yield: 6 servings

Grill: About 6 minutes

Level: Easy

At the Ready: Long-handled spatula, brush

1^{1}/$_{2}$ cups seasoned bread crumbs

5 cloves garlic, peeled and minced very fine

^{1}/$_{2}$ cup finely minced fresh parsley or cilantro

^{3}/$_{4}$ cup (1^{1}/$_{2}$ sticks) butter, divided, melted and cooled

12 cleaned soft-shell crabs

continues

continued

In a mixing bowl, toss the crumbs with the garlic, parsley, and all but about ¹/₄ cup of the butter. (The remainder is for brushing the crabs.) Set aside.

Prepare the grill for direct heat. Brush the crabs with butter. When the coals are medium hot, set the crabs on the cooking grid. Grill them, uncovered, for 3 minutes, turn them over, and continue grilling until they turn reddish, about 3 to 4 minutes longer.

Remove the crabs to individual dishes and sprinkle them with the crumbs. Serve hot with a lettuce salad and warm rolls.

Whole Maine Lobsters

Yield: 4 servings

Grill: 8 to 10 minutes

Level: Easy

At the Ready: Basting brush, disposable bib for each guest as well as lobster crackers, picks, and damp finger towels

Buy the lobsters within an hour or two of when you will grill them. Have the fishmonger split the lobster lengthwise (butterfly it) and clean out the stomach and intestinal vein. Keep them very cold until grilling. If you cannot grill them until later, you'll have to buy the lobsters whole and cut and clean them yourself (see Chapter 13).

1 cup (2 sticks) butter, at room temperature, cut into pieces

2 tablespoons lemon juice or lime juice

2 tablespoons finely grated lemon or lime peel

2 tablespoons finely minced fresh parsley

4 Maine lobsters, about 1¹/₂ pounds each

Reserve about 3 to 4 tablespoons of the butter to brush the lobsters. Put the remaining softened butter in a mixing bowl. With the back of a wooden spoon smash the butter to soften it. Stir in the juice, peel, and parsley. Spoon the flavored butter into a serving crock or shallow dish. Cover and let stay at room temperature for up to 1 hour, or refrigerate until needed, then let stand 30 minutes to warm up before serving.

Brush the cut side of each lobster with butter. Prepare the grill for direct heat. When the coals are medium hot, put the lobsters, shell side up, on the cooking grid. Cover the grill and adjust the vents. Grill the lobsters 8 to 10 minutes, or until the meat is opaque and just starts to separate from the shell. Do not overcook them.

Remove the lobsters from the grill and serve immediately with the citrus butter. Garnish with lemon or lime wedges. Use bibs, lobster crackers, picks and finger towels. Serve with grilled corn (see page 124) and garlic bread.

Hot Tip

If you have a choice, buy a hard-shelled lobster as opposed to a soft-shelled lobster because the hard one has more meat. The female lobsters are more flavorful because of the roe (eggs).

Lobster Tails with Sherry Sauce

Yield: 6 servings

Grill: 6 minutes

Level: Easy

At the Ready: Basting brush, lobster forks

Lobster tails usually arrive frozen at the market. Defrost them in the refrigerator before grilling. You will notice that the lobster shell color can vary from a mottled brown to dark red.

$^3/_4$ cup (1$^1/_2$ sticks) butter, at room temperature, cut in pieces

$^1/_4$ cup half-and-half

$^1/_4$ cup dry sherry

$^1/_4$ teaspoon ground nutmeg

$^1/_4$ teaspoon ground cinnamon

6 lobster tails

Reserve about $^1/_4$ cup of the butter to brush the lobster tails. Put the remaining softened butter in a mixing bowl. With the back of a wooden spoon, mash the butter until soft. Stir in the half-and-half, sherry, nutmeg, and cinnamon. Spoon the flavored butter into a serving crock or shallow dish. Cover and let stay at room temperature for up to 1 hour, or refrigerate for later use. Bring to room temperature before serving.

Using scissors or a small, sharp knife, cut through and remove the tough outer membrane from the lobster tail meat. Brush the lobster tails with softened butter.

continues

continued

Prepare the grill for direct heat. When the coals are medium hot, put the lobster tails, shell side up, on the cooking grid. Cover the grill and adjust the vents. Grill the tails 6 to 8 minutes, or until the meat is opaque and starts to separate from the shell. Do not overcook the lobster, as the meat will toughen.

Set each tail on a dinner plate. Pass the flavored butter at the table for guests to help themselves. Serve with lobster forks.

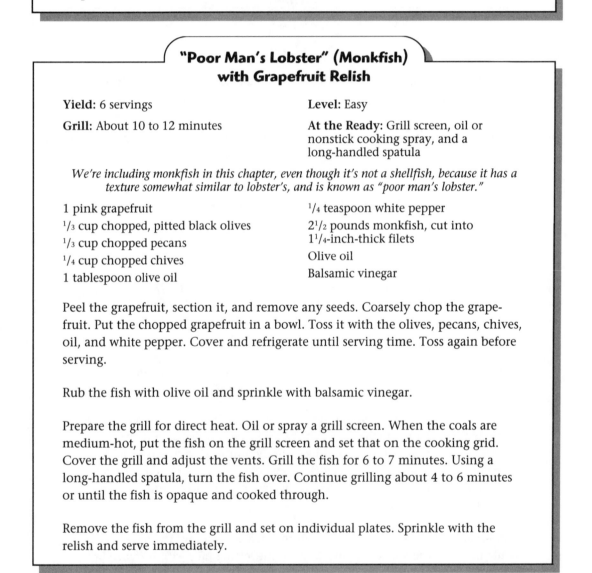

"Poor Man's Lobster" (Monkfish) with Grapefruit Relish

Yield: 6 servings

Grill: About 10 to 12 minutes

Level: Easy

At the Ready: Grill screen, oil or nonstick cooking spray, and a long-handled spatula

We're including monkfish in this chapter, even though it's not a shellfish, because it has a texture somewhat similar to lobster's, and is known as "poor man's lobster."

1 pink grapefruit

$1/3$ cup chopped, pitted black olives

$1/3$ cup chopped pecans

$1/4$ cup chopped chives

1 tablespoon olive oil

$1/4$ teaspoon white pepper

$2^1/2$ pounds monkfish, cut into $1^1/4$-inch-thick filets

Olive oil

Balsamic vinegar

Peel the grapefruit, section it, and remove any seeds. Coarsely chop the grapefruit. Put the chopped grapefruit in a bowl. Toss it with the olives, pecans, chives, oil, and white pepper. Cover and refrigerate until serving time. Toss again before serving.

Rub the fish with olive oil and sprinkle with balsamic vinegar.

Prepare the grill for direct heat. Oil or spray a grill screen. When the coals are medium-hot, put the fish on the grill screen and set that on the cooking grid. Cover the grill and adjust the vents. Grill the fish for 6 to 7 minutes. Using a long-handled spatula, turn the fish over. Continue grilling about 4 to 6 minutes or until the fish is opaque and cooked through.

Remove the fish from the grill and set on individual plates. Sprinkle with the relish and serve immediately.

Coastal Shrimp in Beer

Yield: 6 servings

Grill: 5 to 6 minutes

Level: Easy

At the Ready: Long-handled spatula, grill screen, oil for brushing, basting brush, barbecue sauce (see Index), empty bowls for shells, and finger wipes

2 pounds extra-large shrimp, shells left on (and deveined if preferred)

2 cans (12 ounces each) light beer

Vegetable oil

2 teaspoons celery seed

1 teaspoon cayenne

Wash the shrimp and pat it dry. Pour the beer into a deep bowl and add the shrimp. Cover and marinate for 1 hour in the refrigerator. Drain.

Prepare the grill for direct heat. Oil or spray a grill screen. Brush the shrimp with oil. Mix the celery seed and cayenne together in a small bowl. Sprinkle the shrimp with the spice mixture. When the coals are medium hot, put the shrimp on the grill screen and set it on the grid, 4 to 6 inches from the heat. Cover the grill and adjust the vents. Grill 5 to 6 minutes, turning once, or until opaque. Do not overcook.

Serve immediately. Have empty bowls on the table for the shells, and provide moist paper wipes. Serve with barbecue sauce (use one of the sauce recipes in this book, or your favorite bottled sauce) for dipping.

Prawns with Honey Brushing Sauce

Yield: 6 servings

Grill: About 8 minutes

Level: Easy

At the Ready: Oil for brushing, grill screen, long-handled spatula, and 3 cups oak, maple, or hickory chips soaked 30 minutes and drained (optional)

1 cup orange juice

3 tablespoons honey

1 tablespoon vegetable oil

2 teaspoons grated white horseradish, or to taste

24 prawns, shelled and deveined

In a small bowl, stir together the orange juice, honey, oil, and horseradish. Wash the prawns and pat dry. With a small paring knife, cut partway through the underside of each prawn. Do not cut all the way through. Flatten them into a slight butterfly shape, then brush the prawns with the sauce.

continues

continued

Prepare the grill for direct heat. Oil or spray a grill screen. When the coals are medium hot, scatter the drained chips over them. Put the prawns on the grill screen and set it on the cooking grid. Cover the grill and adjust the vents. Grill the prawns about 3 to 4 minutes, then turn them over. Continue grilling another 4 to 5 minutes, until the prawns are opaque but not overcooked.

Put the hot prawns on individual plates and serve immediately.

What's What

Just what are *prawns*, anyway? The term can refer to several creatures. One is a member of the lobster family, and another is a mostly freshwater crustacean that looks like a cross between a shrimp and a lobster. Chances are, though, that the "prawns" in your supermarket are just jumbo shrimp.

Down Maine Clambake

Yield: 4 servings

Grill: About 12 minutes for corn, 8 minutes for onions, and 5 minutes for clams (have the gas grill on high for the clams)

Level: Easy

At the Ready: Oil for brushing, grill screen, long-handled spatula

Organization is critical in this recipe. Make sure you have the corn, onions, and clams together at the grill.

4 ears of corn, shucked and cut into three pieces each

2 large white onions, peeled and cut in ¹/₂-inch slices

3 dozen medium clams, washed

1 cup (2 sticks) melted butter

Lemon wedges

Prepare the corn and onions and wash the clams, discarding any open ones.

Prepare the grill for direct heat. Oil or spray a grill screen. When the coals are medium hot, set the grill screen on the cooking grid. Brush the corn and onions with some of the melted butter and set them on the screen. Cover the grill and adjust the vents. Grill the onions about 8 minutes or until golden, turning once. Grill the corn about 12 minutes, rotating every 3 minutes; it will char slightly. Arrange the clams on the screen. Cover and grill about 5 minutes. Lift the cover to see if the clams have popped open. If not, cover and grill a few minutes longer until they have opened. Discard any clams that won't open.

Serve the corn, onions, and clams with melted butter, lemon wedges, garlic bread, and coleslaw.

Tasty Tidbit

A traditional clambake is a delicious experience. First, you dig a pit in the sand, and heat the charcoal in that. Then you grill the corn, potatoes, clams, and lobsters. Everyone eats messily and happily, drinking beer and enjoying the cool sea breeze.

Crab Cakes

Yield: 6 servings

Grill: 8 to 10 minutes

Level: Intermediate

At the Ready: Butter or oil for brushing, grill screen, basting brush, long-handled spatula

Obviously, these are best with real crabmeat. Use fresh, pasteurized, or frozen and thawed crabmeat. King crab is nice, but you can substitute blue crab or snow crab. If real crabmeat is simply too rich for your wallet, you can even use imitation "krab" (a mixture of pollock and flavorings) instead.

2 tablespoons butter or margarine	1 cup mashed potatoes, cooled
4 green onions, chopped	$^1/_2$ teaspoon salt
$^1/_2$ cup chopped red or green bell pepper	$^1/_4$ teaspoon cayenne pepper
1 egg white, lightly beaten	$^1/_4$ cup regular or reduced-fat mayonnaise
$1^1/_2$ cups fresh bread crumbs	Tartar sauce (page 149, or use store-bought)
1 pound king crabmeat, flaked (discard any shell pieces)	

continues

continued

Heat the butter in a frying pan and cook the onions and pepper over medium heat until tender, about 5 minutes, stirring occasionally. Transfer the cooked vegetables to a mixing bowl. Stir in the egg white, crumbs, crabmeat, mashed potatoes, salt, cayenne, and mayonnaise.

Shape the mixture into 12 crab cakes and set them on a plate. Cover and refrigerate for at least 45 minutes before grilling.

Prepare the grill for direct heat. Oil or spray a grill screen. When the coals are medium hot, place the crab cakes on the grill screen and set it on the cooking grid. Cover the grill and adjust the vents. Grill the crab cakes 4 to 5 minutes, turning once. When done, the cakes will be firm and browned on the outside and cooked and moist in the center.

Serve the crab cakes hot, with tartar sauce.

The Least You Need to Know

➤ Most shellfish are low in fat and calories.

➤ Be careful not to overcook shellfish, which will quickly turn tough.

➤ Shellfish are highly perishable, and should be cooked as soon as possible after you purchase them.

Chapter 22

Vegetables and Grains

In This Chapter

➤ Pizza Crust

➤ Buffalo Cheese and Tomato Sauce Pizza

➤ Asparagus and Mushrooms with Sage Brushing Sauce

➤ Mixed Grilled Vegetables in a Pita Pocket

➤ Tortellini Vegetable Salad

➤ New Potatoes with Garlic and Cilantro

➤ Mixed Greens Topped with Grilled Vegetables

➤ Baked Potatoes with Vidalia Onions

➤ Grilled Tomatoes and Green Onions

➤ Baby Artichokes with Rosemary

This chapter, which runs the gamut from pizza to baby artichokes with rosemary, is one of our favorites. Not only do we love vegetables, but we feel they're vastly underused on the grill. Grilling vegetables and grains opens a world of creativity. For example, you can use the pizza crust recipe, or buy a prepared crust, and grill assorted toppings—whatever your family likes— to go on it.

Another of our favorite "tricks" is to grill vegetables that are in season, personal favorites, and/or complementary to the rest of the meal, and toss them with cooked pasta (tortellini or ravioli is especially nice) and a little salad dressing.

If you're grilling meat as the main course, it's downright silly not to throw some vegetables or bread on the grill as well. Grilling gives vegetables and breads such as pizza those wonderfully smoky undertones. Although nearly any vegetable can be grilled, starchy and/or "meaty" vegetables or those with some sweetness do best over charcoal.

Pizza Crust

Yield: 2 crusts, about 10 to 12 inches each

Level: Advanced

Grill: About 6 to 10 minutes (may take a few minutes longer on the gas grill)

At the Ready: Food processor or electric mixer with dough hook

For a taste sensation try adding $1/2$ cup pesto sauce to the finished dough, perhaps 2 or 3 tablespoons of chili powder, or 3 or 4 tablespoons of crumbled dried oregano, basil, or rosemary.

$2^3/_4$ cups all-purpose flour, divided

1 package quick-rising yeast

$1/_2$ teaspoon salt

1 scant cup warm water

2 tablespoons warm olive oil

In a food processor combine $2^1/_2$ cups of the flour, the yeast, and the salt. With the machine running, pour the warm water and olive oil through the feed tube.

The dough will come together into a ball in about 8 seconds.

Alternately, you can mix the dough with an electric mixer fitted with the dough hook. Mix the dough on low speed for 3 to 4 minutes, or until it forms a smooth ball.

Remove the dough from the bowl and place on a lightly floured cloth or board using the remaining $1/_4$ cup of flour. Knead until smooth, a few minutes. Set the dough in a bowl, cover with a damp warm towel and let the dough rise in a warm area of the kitchen for 30 minutes or until it has doubled in size. Punch the dough down and divide it in half. You are now ready to roll out the pizza dough. See the next recipe for instructions on shaping the dough and one idea for pizza—but remember, when it comes to pizza, your personal tastes are of the utmost importance, so use what you like, and improvise.

This dough can be made ahead of time and refrigerated for up to 24 hours, or frozen for up to 3 months. If it's refrigerated, let it stand at room temperature for about 2 to 3 hours, or until doubled. If frozen, let it stand at room temperature for about 4 to 6 hours, or until it doubles.

Hot Tip

If time or lack of skill is a problem, use defrosted frozen bread dough. It is available at large supermarkets in the frozen food section. Or, just use a prepared pizza crust. Add the toppings and warm the pizza on the grill (with the baking tiles set on a pan or a grill screen and with the grill covered).

Buffalo Cheese and Tomato Sauce Pizza

Yield: 8 servings, enough for 2 pizzas

Grill: About 3 minutes for the crust and 5 to 6 minutes with the topping

Level: Intermediate

At the Ready: Baking tiles for the grill, grill screen, cornmeal, pizza paddle (or use the back side of a cookie sheet sprinkled with cornmeal), olive oil for brushing, and a brush

It is perfectly natural to cook a pizza on the barbecue grill. After all, for centuries pizzas were cooked over wood—and still are in many restaurants or bakeries.

Tomato-Herb Sauce

1 can (28 ounces) crushed tomatoes, drained

¹/₄ cup tomato paste

2 tablespoons crumbled dried oregano

1 tablespoon crumbled dried basil

¹/₄ teaspoon pepper

1 recipe Basic Pizza Crust (see page 220)

1 pound buffalo milk mozzarella cheese, sliced thin

¹/₄ cup grated Asiago or other sharp cheese

To make the sauce, put the drained tomatoes in a bowl. Mix in the tomato paste, oregano, basil, and pepper. Taste, and adjust the seasonings.

Roll out each half of the dough to a 10- or 12-inch circle.

Prepare the grill for direct heat. When the coals are medium hot, set the tiles on a grill screen (or on a cookie sheet), and place on the cooking grid. Preheat the tiles for about 5 minutes.

continues

continued

Brush the dough lightly with olive oil. Transfer the pizza crust (on a paddle sprinkled with cornmeal or on the back of a cookie sheet sprinkled with corn-meal) to the tiles or to a second oiled grill screen set on the tiles (the grill screen makes it easier to lift the pizza from the grill).

Grill the crust for about 3 minutes. Remove the crust. Brush it again with olive oil, and lay the mozzarella slices over it. Drizzle with the tomato sauce and sprinkle with the Asiago cheese. Return the pizza to the grill screen. Cover the grill and adjust the vents. Grill the pizza for about 3 minutes, then rotate it a half turn to ensure even cooking. Continue grilling for about 2 to 3 minutes, or until the topping is heated through and the crust is firm. Cut and serve the pizza while it is hot.

Don't Get Burned!

Be sure to rotate the pizza during grilling so that it will cook evenly.

Asparagus and Mushrooms with Sage Brushing Sauce

Yield: 6 servings

Grill: About 4 to 8 minutes

Level: Easy

At the Ready: Grill screen, oil for brushing, basting brush, long-handled spatula, and $1/2$ cup dried sage leaves soaked in water 5 minutes and drained (optional)

$1/4$ cup olive oil

3 tablespoons balsamic, red wine, or tarragon vinegar

2 cloves garlic, peeled and minced

1 teaspoon grainy mustard

1 tablespoon minced fresh sage or $1/2$ teaspoons dried crumbled sage

Salt and pepper

$1/2$ pounds asparagus, ends snapped off, washed

1 pound white, brown, or portobello mushrooms, cleaned

6 large plum tomatoes, seeded and chopped

1 small onion, peeled and chopped

In a small bowl, whisk together the oil, vinegar, garlic, mustard, sage, $1/2$ teaspoon salt, and $1/2$ teaspoon pepper. Prepare the vegetables and brush them liberally with the sauce. Set aside.

Toss together the tomatoes and onion in a bowl. Season with salt and pepper to taste. Set aside.

Prepare the grill for direct heat. Oil or spray a grill screen. When the coals are medium hot, set the marinated vegetables on the grill screen and place it on the cooking grid. Grill the asparagus and the mushrooms, uncovered, for 2 or 3 minutes on each side, brushing them again with sauce as you turn them. Continue grilling until they are done to taste, another few minutes on each side.

Remove the vegetables to a serving platter and sprinkle them with the chopped tomato and onion mixture. Serve hot.

Mixed Grilled Vegetables in a Pita Pocket

Yield: 6 servings

Grill: About 6 to 10 minutes

Level: Intermediate

At the Ready: Grill screen, oil for brushing, basting brush, long-handled spatula, and aluminum foil

2 large red bell peppers, seeded and cut in $1/2$-inch strips

2 large green or yellow bell peppers, seeded and cut in $1/2$-inch strips

2 large, ripe tomatoes, cut in $1/2$-inch slices

1 large onion, cut in $1/2$-inch slices

6 pita breads

2 jalapeño peppers, seeded and chopped

1 clove garlic, peeled and minced

$1/4$ cup cider vinegar

Prepare the grill for direct heat. Oil or spray a grill screen. When the coals are medium hot, set the grill screen on the cooking grid. Brush the bell peppers, tomatoes, and onion with oil and set them on the grill. Grill the vegetables, uncovered, 3 to 4 minutes on each side or until they are tender. The tomato will warm and cook first, the bell peppers and onions will take a few minutes longer, and should be removed when they are tender and beginning to brown.

Warm pita breads on the grill about 1 minute on each side or only until warm. Cut in half.

continues

continued

Put the vegetables in a mixing bowl. Toss them with the jalapeño peppers, garlic, and cider vinegar. Using a large spoon, gently stuff the warm pita bread with the grilled vegetable mixture or serve the vegetables with the pita bread on the side. Serve immediately.

Hot Tip

Grilled vegetables are fine as a side dish, but for an even more fun lunch or first course, stuff them into pitas, wrap them in tortillas, or roll them up in a big deli wrap.

Tortellini Vegetable Salad

Yield: 6 servings

Level: Intermediate

Grill: 20 minutes (cover a gas grill for the eggplant and leave uncovered if you like for the remaining vegetables)

At the Ready: Grill screen, oil or nonstick cooking spray, brush, and a long-handled spatula

³/₄ cup red wine

Olive oil

3 shallots, minced

1 tablespoon chopped fresh mint, or 1¹/₂ teaspoons dried mint

1 medium-small eggplant, trimmed and thinly sliced lengthwise

18 cherry tomatoes, trimmed and washed

1 red onion, peeled and cut in ¹/₂-inch slices

1 cup sliced salami

1 pound tortellini, cooked according to package directions

2 teaspoons minced fresh thyme

1 teaspoon minced fresh marjoram

1 teaspoon minced fresh mint

¹/₄ cup chopped fresh parsley

³/₄ cup stuffed green olives

Prepare the dressing by putting the wine in a small bowl. Whisk in ¹/₂ cup olive oil, a few drops at a time, then the shallots and mint. Cover and refrigerate until ready to serve. Whisk again before serving.

Prepare the grill for direct heat. Oil or spray a grill screen. When the coals are medium hot, set the grill screen on the cooking grid. Brush the eggplant with olive oil and place it on the grill screen. Cover the grill and adjust the vents. Grill for 10 to 12 minutes, turning once. Brush the remaining vegetables with oil. Uncover the grill and add the tomatoes, onion slices, and salami to the grill screen (do not remove the eggplant). Grill the vegetables, uncovered, allowing another 8 to 10 minutes for the eggplant and 3 to 4 minutes per side for the tomatoes and onions. The vegetables should be tender and beginning to brown. The salami needs to cook only for a minute or two per side, just to warm it.

Rewarm the cooked tortellini under hot running water. Put it in a serving bowl. Toss it with the thyme, marjoram, mint, parsley, eggplant, tomatoes, onions, salami, olives, and the dressing. Serve immediately.

New Potatoes with Garlic and Cilantro

Yield: 6 servings

Grill: About 10 minutes

Level: Easy

At the Ready: Grill screen, vegetable oil for brushing, basting brush, and a long-handled spatula

2 to 2$^1/_4$ pounds new potatoes, scrubbed
Olive oil

4 cloves garlic, peeled and minced
$^1/_4$ cup minced fresh cilantro

Cook the potatoes in boiling water or in the top of a vegetable steamer just until fork tender, about 13 to 15 minutes. Remove, drain and cool the potatoes. Cut them in half. Brush them with olive oil and sprinkle with the garlic.

Prepare the grill for direct heat. Oil or spray a grill screen. When the coals are medium hot, set the grill screen on the cooking grid. Arrange the potatoes on the screen. Cover the grill and adjust the vents. Grill the potatoes until they are hot and browned, turning once or twice. This should take about 10 minutes, or longer if you like them browner.

Remove the potatoes to a serving bowl and sprinkle with the cilantro. Serve hot.

What's What

New potatoes are very young, small, unblemished potatoes. You'll find them at farmers markets and some supermarkets and natural-food stores, usually in the spring. Stores often label small potatoes "new potatoes," but genuine new potatoes are tiny and tender.

Mixed Greens Topped with Grilled Vegetables

Yield: 6 servings

Level: Easy

Grill: About 8 to 10 minutes (if using a gas grill, cook uncovered)

At the Ready: Grill screen, oil for brushing, brush, a long-handled spatula, and a salad spinner

12 cups torn mixed salad greens, such as red leaf lettuce, Boston lettuce, and arugula

2 tablespoons chopped fresh tarragon or 1 tablespoon dried tarragon

Salt and black pepper to taste

Cider Vinegar Dressing

$^{1}/_{4}$ cup olive oil

$^{1}/_{4}$ cup cider vinegar

3 tablespoons orange juice

1 tablespoon honey mustard

3 cloves garlic, peeled and smashed

2 medium zucchini, washed, trimmed, cut lengthwise into thin slices

18 cherry tomatoes, trimmed and washed

1 bunch green onions, trimmed

Olive oil

Wash and spin dry the mixed salad greens and put them in a salad bowl. Sprinkle with the fresh tarragon, salt, and pepper. (If you're using dried tarragon, add it to the dressing.) Set aside.

In a small bowl, whisk together the oil, vinegar, orange juice, and mustard. Stir in the garlic and the tarragon (if you're using the dried herb). Set aside.

Prepare the grill for direct heat. Oil or spray a grill screen. When the coals are medium hot, set the grill screen on the cooking grid. Brush the zucchini, tomatoes, and green onions with oil and arrange them on the grill screen. Grill the vegetables, uncovered, for 2 or 3 minutes. As they cook, turn them over as necessary. The onions will take the longest to grill and the zucchini will cook the quickest. Remove the vegetables as they become tender and begin to brown.

Decoratively arrange the grilled vegetables over the salad and serve immediately. Pass the dressing on the side.

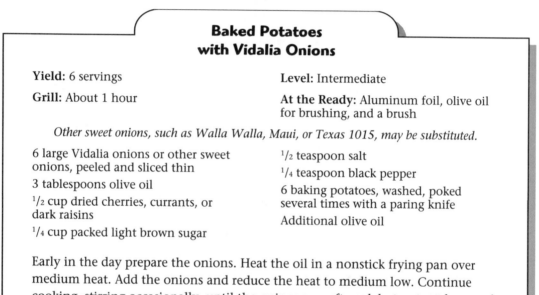

Baked Potatoes with Vidalia Onions

Yield: 6 servings

Grill: About 1 hour

Level: Intermediate

At the Ready: Aluminum foil, olive oil for brushing, and a brush

Other sweet onions, such as Walla Walla, Maui, or Texas 1015, may be substituted.

6 large Vidalia onions or other sweet onions, peeled and sliced thin

3 tablespoons olive oil

$^1/_2$ cup dried cherries, currants, or dark raisins

$^1/_4$ cup packed light brown sugar

$^1/_2$ teaspoon salt

$^1/_4$ teaspoon black pepper

6 baking potatoes, washed, poked several times with a paring knife

Additional olive oil

Early in the day prepare the onions. Heat the oil in a nonstick frying pan over medium heat. Add the onions and reduce the heat to medium low. Continue cooking, stirring occasionally, until the onions are softened, but not yet browned. Stir in the dried cherries, brown sugar, salt, and pepper. Continue cooking, slowly, until the onions are a golden color. Remove from the heat and allow to cool. If the rest of the recipe is not to be prepared for several hours, place the onion mixture in a bowl, cover with plastic wrap and refrigerate. Reheat to serve.

Rub each potato with oil and double wrap the potatoes individually in aluminum foil.

Prepare the grill for direct heat. When the coals are medium hot, set the potatoes directly on the coals (if using charcoal) or on the cooking grid (if using gas). Cover the grill and adjust the vents. Using long-handled tongs, turn the potatoes every 10 or 15 minutes. Cook about 1 hour, or until they are fork-tender. If you're using a charcoal grill, replenish the grill with lit coals as necessary.

continues

continued

Carefully remove the foil from each potato, and set a potato on each plate. Slit the potato lengthwise, squeeze it open and spoon the hot glazed onions over the top. Serve immediately.

Hot Tip

For no more tears, slice onions under cold running water. It also helps to refrigerate the onions first, or pop them in the freezer for 15 minutes just before cutting if they are at room temperature.

Tasty Tidbit

The Vidalia, a very sweet, mild onion, is available in the spring. These onions grow in southeastern Georgia, and the name "Vidalia" can be used only by the 13 counties between Macon and Savannah, and parts of seven other counties. The Vidalia gets its name from the first county from which this onion was shipped.

Grilled Tomatoes and Green Onions

Yield: 6 servings

Grill: About 4 to 6 minutes and

6 medium tomatoes, cut in half crosswise
12 green onions, trimmed

Level: Easy

At the Ready: Long-handled spatula

olive oil

Olive oil
2 tablespoons snipped fresh dill or basil

Brush the cut side of the tomatoes and the onions with olive oil. Sprinkle the tomatoes and onions with the dill or basil.

Prepare the grill for direct heat. Oil or spray a grill screen. When the coals are medium hot, set the grill screen on the cooking grid. Place the tomatoes and green onions on the screen. Leaving the grill uncovered, grill the tomatoes about 4 minutes and the onions for 3 minutes on each side. The onions should be tender and starting to brown, and the tomatoes should soften but not be mushy. Remove the vegetables from the grill and serve.

What's What

The slender "green onions" sold in supermarkets often are really scallions. True green onions are slightly bulbous on the bottom (and often are larger than scallions), while scallions are straight up and down. We use the term "green onion" rather than "scallion" throughout this book because that's the way they're labeled in supermarkets.

Baby Artichokes with Rosemary

Yield: 6 servings

Grill: 10 to 12 minutes

Level: Easy

At the Ready: Dressing; long-handled tongs; $1/2$ cup dried mint soaked for 5 minutes and drained (optional)

12 fresh baby artichokes
3 tablespoons lemon juice
$1/4$ cup olive oil
3 tablespoons red wine vinegar

$1/4$ teaspoon pepper
2 tablespoons chopped fresh rosemary
1 teaspoon minced garlic

Trim the stems from the artichokes, cut the artichokes in half lengthwise, and immediately place them in a large bowl of cold water to which you've added the lemon juice. Let them soak for 15 minutes.

continues

continued

In a bowl mix together the olive oil, vinegar, pepper, rosemary, and garlic. Drain the artichokes, pat them dry, and toss them with the dressing. Let the artichokes marinate for 1 hour, then drain.

Prepare the grill for direct heat. When the coals are medium hot, set the artichokes directly on the cooking grid. Grill them, uncovered, for 10 minutes, turning once, or until cooked through.

The Least You Need to Know

➤ Vegetables are too seldom chosen for the grill, and can inspire great creativity.

➤ To make full use of the fired-up grill, put some vegetables on the grid alongside the meat main course.

➤ Starchy and/or "meaty" vegetables fare best on the grill.

230

Chapter 23

Sweet Stuff

In This Chapter

➤ Glazed Mixed Fruit Grill

➤ Blueberry-Apple Cobbler on the Grill

➤ Wine-Brushed Pears

➤ Warm Apple Cinnamon Slices with Cheddar Cheese

➤ Fruit Kebabs on Grilled Chocolate Pound Cake

➤ Campfire-Style S'Mores

➤ Honeyed Papaya Strips with Warm Brie

➤ Apricots Topped with Raspberries and Raspberry Sherbet

➤ Grilled Angel Food Cake and Pineapple

Now that you've fired up the grill for the rest of your meal, why not grill the dessert as well? After the coals have begun to cool down from the main course, they're the perfect temperature for grilling nearly any fruit, and even cake.

The taste of slightly burnt sugar is irresistible. Just ask any kid (or adult) who's eaten roasted marshmallows. However, the sugar content is also the reason that fruits and other sweet foods can scorch easily on the grill. When you're grilling your dessert, don't get distracted and wander off.

For a really simple dessert, grill wedges of papaya or cantaloupe, top with a scoop of vanilla yogurt, and sprinkle with granola.

Don't Get Burned!

Make sure you cook your dessert on a clean grid. Chocolate pound cake just doesn't go with barbecue sauce or flecks of fish skin. To ensure your dessert is pristine, place it on a clean grill screen, then set that atop the grid. You may also want to give the grid a quick once-over with a wire brush to remove any of the larger bits of the previous course.

Glazed Mixed Fruit Grill

Yield: 6 servings

Grill: About 4 minutes

Level: Easy

At the Ready: Oiled grill screen, long-handled spatula

Vary the fruits according to your taste and seasonal availability. Peeled and cored fresh pineapple is available at most large supermarkets.

3 large peaches
3 to 4 tablespoons brandy (optional)
$1/4$ cup peach jam
2 to 3 tablespoons water
6 medium bananas

Melted butter
$1/2$ cup packed dark brown sugar, or to taste
1 fresh peeled and cored pineapple
6 scoops peach ice cream or pineapple sherbet

Peel the peaches, cut them in half, and discard the pits. Sprinkle with the brandy if desired. Melt the jam in a small pan with the water, stirring constantly until the jam melts. Brush the peach halves with the cooled melted jam. Set on a plate.

Peel the bananas and leave them whole. Brush them lightly with melted butter and sprinkle with half of the sugar. Drain the pineapple and if it is not already sliced, cut it into $1/2$-inch slices. Sprinkle the pineapple slices with the remaining sugar.

After you have grilled your meal and while the coals are still hot, place the fruit on an oiled grill screen and set it on the grid. Grill the fruit, uncovered, for just a few minutes, until it is warmed through and beginning to brown. Remove each piece of fruit as it is done. Divide the warm fruit among dessert plates and set a scoop of ice cream or sherbet in the center. Serve immediately.

Hot Tip

To peel peaches, let them soak in boiling water for 30 seconds to 1 minute, then plunge them into a bowl of ice water. Remove the peaches with a slotted spoon. You should be able to easily pull or rub the skin off.

Blueberry-Apple Cobbler on the Grill

Yield: 6 servings

Grill: 20 to 30 minutes

Level: Intermediate

At the Ready: Large pot holders, baking tiles

For extra crunch and flavor add ³/₄ cup chopped pecans to the topping. For a faster cobbler, you can use a can of apple pie slices or peach pie slices.

5 large Granny Smith or Golden Delicious apples

3 cups fresh blueberries

2 tablespoons lemon juice

¹/₂ cup (1 stick) butter, at room temperature

¹/₂ cup sugar

1 cup all-purpose flour

³/₄ cup regular rolled oats

1 teaspoon ground cinnamon

Butter a 9-inch cast iron frying pan.

Peel and core the apples and thinly slice them. You should have about 6 cups of apples. Wash and pick over the blueberries, discarding any shriveled ones.

In a large bowl, toss together the blueberries and the apples. Sprinkle with the lemon juice and toss the fruit again. Set aside.

Cut the butter into ¹/₂-inch pieces. Using a food processor or a bowl and a fork, mix together the butter, sugar, flour, oats, and cinnamon to make moist crumbs. Arrange the fruit on the bottom of the prepared pan. Sprinkle the crumbs over the fruit.

continues

233

continued

When the coals are cooling but still hot, set the baking tiles on a grill screen and set it on the grid. Place the frying pan on the tiles. Cover the grill, adjust the vents, and grill for about 20 to 30 minutes, or until the topping is golden and the fruit is hot. Spoon the cobbler into individual dessert bowls and top with sweetened whipped cream or vanilla ice cream.

Hot Tip

If you do not have a cast-iron frying pan, you can make this cobbler in a heavy-duty 9-inch cake pan. Do not use a thin pan, or it may scorch.

Wine-Brushed Pears

Yield: 6 servings

Level: Easy

Grill: About 4 to 6 minutes

At the Ready: Oiled grill screen, pot holders or barbecue mitts, long-handled spatula, basting brush, dinner fork

Apples can be substituted for the pears. They will take slightly longer to cook. The apples, too, are done when they are fork tender.

¹/₂ cup sugar
¹/₂ cup red wine
1 cinnamon stick

6 ripe but firm pears, preferably *Bosc* or *Anjou*

Sweetened whipped cream or vanilla frozen yogurt

Mint leaves for garnish (optional)

Mix the sugar, wine, and cinnamon together in a small saucepan. Bring to a boil over medium heat and simmer for 5 minutes. Stir occasionally. Let cool.

Peel and core the pears, and cut them in half lengthwise. Brush them generously with the wine mixture.

When the coals are cooling down but still hot, set the pear halves, cut side down, on an oiled grill screen and set that on the grid. Grill the pears, uncovered, for 2 minutes, then turn them and continue grilling for 2 to 3 minutes, or until soft but not mushy. Brush the pears liberally with the wine mixture as they grill. To test for doneness, remove one pear using the pot holders or a spatula, then insert a fork; if it goes in easily, the pear is done.

To serve, set each pear on a dessert plate and top with sweetened whipped cream or vanilla frozen yogurt. Garnish with mint leaves if desired.

What's What

You'll generally see three pear varieties in your supermarket: the *Bartlett,* whose juicy, slightly grainy flesh is great for eating out of hand; the *Bosc,* which has a slender neck, russet skin, and tart-sweet flavor; and the *Anjou,* a firm, sweet, yellowish-green winter pear. All three varieties are good raw or cooked, but the Bosc best keeps its shape during cooking.

Warm Apple Cinnamon Slices with Cheddar Cheese

Yield: 6 servings

Grill: About 4 minutes

Level: Easy

At the Ready: Oiled grill screen

6 large, firm apples

$^1/_4$ cup orange juice

$^1/_2$ cup sugar

1 teaspoon ground cinnamon

$^1/_4$ cup butter, melted and cooled

$^1/_2$ pound wedge of cheddar cheese, wrapped in aluminum foil

$^1/_2$ cup chopped walnuts and or raisins

Peel and core the apples, and slice them into rounds. Put the sliced apple rounds in a bowl and sprinkle with the orange juice. Mix the sugar and cinnamon together and toss with the apples. Drizzle the butter over the apple mixture and toss again.

Wrap the cheddar cheese in aluminum foil.

continues

continued

When the coals are still hot but cooling down, set an oiled grill screen on the cooking grid. Put the apples on the grill screen.

Grill the apple slices, uncovered, about 2 minutes on each side or until they're warm and beginning to brown. Set the covered cheese on the grill and cook for 1 to 2 minutes on each side. You want the cheese to be just warm and slightly softened. Remove the apples and divide them among individual dessert plates. Sprinkle with the nuts or raisins. Slice the warmed cheese and arrange it on the plates with the apples. Serve immediately.

Tasty Tidbit

Our inspiration for this recipe comes from New England, where it long has been a tradition to pair apple pie with wedges of cheddar cheese.

Fruit Kebabs on Grilled Chocolate Pound Cake

Yield: 6 to 8 servings

Grill: About 4 to 6 minutes

Level: Intermediate

At the Ready: 6 or 8 short bamboo skewers, soaked in water and drained; oiled grill screen; pot holders; long-handled spatula; chocolate sauce

If you're pressed for time or lack baking skills, you can prepare this recipe with a store-bought pound cake and bottled chocolate sauce.

Chocolate Pound Cake

$1^3/_4$ cups cake flour

$1/_3$ cup unsweetened cocoa

$1/_2$ teaspoon salt

$1/_2$ teaspoon baking powder

10 tablespoons ($1^1/_4$ sticks) unsalted butter, at room temperature

$1^1/_4$ cups sugar

3 eggs

1 teaspoon vanilla

$3/_4$ cup sour cream

Chocolate Sauce

2 ounces unsweetened chocolate

2 tablespoons unsalted butter

1 cup sweetened condensed milk

Fruit

6 plums

3 large ripe peaches

$^3/_4$ teaspoon vanilla

Regular milk as needed

Melted butter

To make the cake, first grease or spray a 9-x-5-x-3 inch nonstick loaf pan. Preheat the oven to 350°F.

Sift the flour, cocoa, salt, and baking powder together. Set aside.

Cream the butter in the large bowl of an electric mixer until light, about 1 to 2 minutes. Add the sugar and continue beating for about 2 minutes. Add the eggs, one at a time; beat well after each addition. Mix in the vanilla. Add about a third of the flour mixture, then half the sour cream, beating about 20 seconds after each addition. Repeat. Then add the remaining flour and beat just until it's mixed in.

Pour the batter into the prepared pan. Bake it on the center rack of the oven for about 1 hour and 10 minutes, or until a toothpick inserted in the center comes out dry and clean. Cool the cake on a rack for 5 minutes. Run a knife around the inside edges of the pan and turn the cake out of the pan. Cool the cake on a wire rack, right side up.

To make the sauce, coarsely chop the chocolate. Place it and the butter in a small glass microwave-proof dish. Microwave on medium high for 45 seconds to 1 minute, stirring once. Stir until the chocolate is smooth and cooled. Using a spatula, scrape the chocolate and butter into a bowl. Mix in the condensed milk and vanilla. If the sauce is too thick, thin it with a little regular milk. Cover the sauce with plastic wrap and store it in the refrigerator until ready to serve. The sauce can be served warm or at room temperature.

Cut the plums in half and remove and discard the pits. Cut the peaches in half, remove and discard the pits, and cut each peach half into 2 or 3 wedges. Thread the fruit on the skewers and brush lightly with melted butter.

Cut 6 to 8 slices, $^1/_2$ to 1 inch thick, from the pound cake. Brush the cake slices lightly on both sides with melted butter.

continues

continued

When the coals are medium hot or cooling down, set the skewers on an oiled grill screen and set it on the grid. Grill, uncovered, for a few minutes on each side. You just want the fruit to warm through. While the fruit warms, grill the cake for just 1 minute on each side, being careful not to burn it as it cooks quickly. The cake should have a slight crust.

To assemble, set a slice of cake on each dessert plate. Place a fruit kabob on top of it or to the side. Drizzle the cake and the fruit with chocolate sauce. Serve immediately.

Tasty Tidbit

Pound cake was so named because it originally was made of a pound each of flour, eggs, sugar, and butter.

Campfire-Style S'Mores

Yield: 8 servings

Grill: 4 to 8 minutes

Level: Easy

At the Ready: Lightly buttered aluminum foil, long-handled spatula

6 milk chocolate bars, 5 ounces each

16 squares cinnamon or chocolate graham crackers

2 cups marshmallow fluff or 16 large marshmallows

1 cup good-quality peanut butter

Set half of a chocolate bar on 1 graham cracker. Set a mound of marshmallow fluff on top or use 2 marshmallows in the center over the chocolate. Dab 1 tablespoon of the peanut butter on top. Press the second graham cracker into place, making a sandwich. Wrap each sandwich securely in lightly buttered aluminum foil.

After you have grilled dinner, and while the coals are still hot but cooling down, set the sandwiches on the cooking grid. Grill, uncovered, for about 2 to 4 minutes on each side. Turn them over using a long-handled spatula. Remove one s'more and carefully unwrap to check if it is done to perfection: that is, the chocolate is runny and the marshmallows are soft. Serve immediately.

Honeyed Papaya Strips with Warm Brie

Yield: 6 servings

Grill: About 4 minutes

Level: Easy

At the Ready: Oiled grill screen, long-handled spatula, cheese knife

1 ripe papaya, about 1 to 1^1/$_2$ pounds
^{1}/$_4$ cup (^{1}/$_2$ stick) butter, melted and cooled
^{1}/$_2$ teaspoon cinnamon

^{1}/$_4$ cup honey
^{1}/$_2$ pound ripe Brie, or to taste

Peel the papaya and cut it in half lengthwise. Scoop out and discard the seeds. Cut the papaya halves into lengthwise slices. Stir the butter with the cinnamon and honey. Brush the papaya slices with the mixture. Wrap the Brie securely in aluminum foil.

After you have grilled your dinner and the coals are beginning to cool down, set an oiled grill screen on the cooking grid. Arrange the papaya slices on the grill screen. Grill the papaya uncovered, about 1 to 2 minutes on each side. The papaya should be warm but not mushy, and starting to brown. Put the Brie bundle on the grill at the same time and heat about 1 to 2 minutes on each side. The Brie should be warm, soft, and beginning to run when you cut through the rind.

Serve the warm papaya slices with wedges of cheese. Grapes are good served with this dessert.

Apricots Topped with Raspberries and Raspberry Sherbet

Yield: 6 servings

Grill: About 4 minutes

Level: Easy

At the Ready: Long-handled spatula, raspberries, sherbet, oiled grill screen, long-handled brush

1¹/₂ cups fresh raspberries, rinsed
Sugar
24 ripe apricots

Melted butter
6 scoops of raspberry sherbet

Sprinkle the raspberries with a little sugar and place them at grillside.

Wash the apricots, cut them in half, and remove and discard the pits.

When the coals are still hot but starting to cool down, set an oiled grill screen on the grid. Brush the apricot halves lightly with melted butter and sprinkle them with 3 tablespoons of sugar. Arrange them on the screen. Grill, uncovered, for about 2 minutes on each side, until they begin to brown.

Arrange the apricots on individual dessert plates and sprinkle with the raspberries. Top each serving with a scoop of raspberry sherbet and serve immediately.

Grilled Angel Food Cake and Pineapple

Yield: 6 servings

Grill: 2 minutes for the cake, 5 minutes for the pineapple

Level: Easy

At the Ready: Oiled grill screen, melted butter, basting brush

6 (¹/₂-inch-thick) slices fresh pineapple
Melted butter for brushing

6 slices prepared angel food cake
¹/₄ cup packed dark brown sugar

While the coals are still hot but cooling down, brush the pineapple with melted butter, set it on an oiled grill screen, and set that on the cooking grid. Grill the pineapple, uncovered, for 5 to 6 minutes, turning once. Brush the cake slices on both sides with melted butter. Grill the cake for just 1 minute on each side, being careful not to burn it as it cooks quickly. The cake should have a slight crust.

Set a slice of cake on each plate along with a slice of pineapple. Sprinkle the pineapple with brown sugar. Serve. This is good with vanilla ice cream.

Hot Tip

Instead of sprinkling pineapple with brown sugar, you can drizzle a prepared chocolate sauce over it. Pineapple and chocolate are an excellent combination.

The Least You Need to Know

➤ The ideal time to grill most desserts is after you've cooked the main course, when the coals are still hot but cooling down a bit.

➤ Sugar burns quickly, so keep an eye on sweets as they cook.

➤ Make sure the grill screen is very clean before you put your dessert on it.

Chapter 24

Smoked Foods

In This Chapter

➤ Smoked Shrimp with Chili-Orange Mopping Sauce

➤ Individual Smoked Whitefish

➤ Whole Smoked Salmon with Pecans and Dried Cherries

➤ Carolina-Style Slow Smoked Pulled Pork

➤ Smoked Beef Short Ribs

➤ Mesquite-Smoked Turkey Thighs

➤ Smoked Turkey Sausages

➤ Honey-Brushed Smoked Chicken with Mandarin Orange Sauce

➤ Smoked Pork Sandwiches with Bourbon Barbecue Sauce

Smoking—or barbecuing, if you prefer—is the long, slow cooking that makes traditional barbecued foods so justifiably famous.

It's definitely a do-ahead process. In fact, smoked foods usually taste even better after they've sat in the refrigerator for a day or two.

Because smokers can differ, follow the manufacturer's directions for setting up and cooking. Smoked foods taste much better if cooked over pure charcoal rather than briquets. Under no circumstances should you use lighter fluid or instant-lighting briquets when you're smoking foods.

To give smoked foods an intriguing flavor undertone, add aromatics such as a thinly sliced orange, lime, or lemon; or a bit of whole allspice or chopped fresh ginger to the water pan.

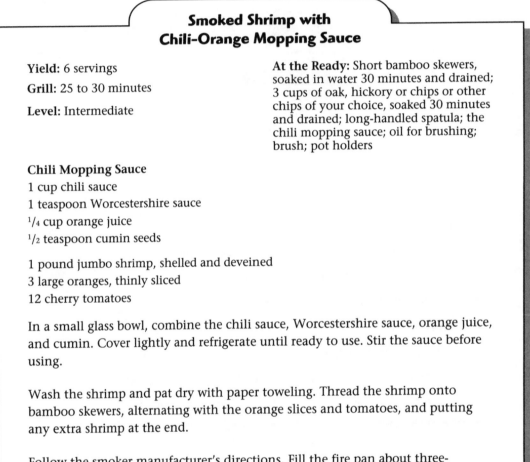

Smoked Shrimp with Chili-Orange Mopping Sauce

Yield: 6 servings

Grill: 25 to 30 minutes

Level: Intermediate

At the Ready: Short bamboo skewers, soaked in water 30 minutes and drained; 3 cups of oak, hickory or chips or other chips of your choice, soaked 30 minutes and drained; long-handled spatula; the chili mopping sauce; oil for brushing; brush; pot holders

Chili Mopping Sauce
1 cup chili sauce
1 teaspoon Worcestershire sauce
$^1/_4$ cup orange juice
$^1/_2$ teaspoon cumin seeds

1 pound jumbo shrimp, shelled and deveined
3 large oranges, thinly sliced
12 cherry tomatoes

In a small glass bowl, combine the chili sauce, Worcestershire sauce, orange juice, and cumin. Cover lightly and refrigerate until ready to use. Stir the sauce before using.

Wash the shrimp and pat dry with paper toweling. Thread the shrimp onto bamboo skewers, alternating with the orange slices and tomatoes, and putting any extra shrimp at the end.

Follow the smoker manufacturer's directions. Fill the fire pan about three-quarters full of hardwood charcoal and heat the coals until ashen. Arrange the drained chips over the hot coals. Fill the water pan of the smoker about three-quarters full with hot water, add any aromatics, and set the pan in place in the smoker carefully, using thick pot holders.

Brush the cooking grid with oil. Mop (brush) the shrimp amply with sauce. Grill the kebabs 2 to 3 minutes. Turn and mop again. Grill 2 to 3 minutes longer or until the shrimp are white in color and just firm to the touch. Do not overcook or the shrimp will become tough.

Place one kebab on each plate and pass any remaining mopping sauce (be sure to reheat it thoroughly first). You might want to make extra sauce to pass at the table. Serve with raw vegetables such as sliced red or green bell peppers, sliced celery, sliced carrots, and green onions.

Hot Tip

You can use this recipe for an appetizer or an entree. If you decide to use it as an entrée, double it by using long, 12-inch, wooden bamboo skewers, soaked in water for 30 minutes and drained, and use double the amount of shrimp, tomatoes, and orange slices on each kebab.

Individual Smoked Whitefish

Yield: 6 servings

Smoke: 45 minutes to 1 hour

Level: Intermediate

At the Ready: Vegetable oil for brushing, brush, cherry, apple or other fruit chips or dry twigs, soaked in water 30 minutes and drained, and large, thick pot holders

You can substitute salmon for the whitefish. Put any extra lime slices in the water pan for extra flavor. You can make your own Tartar Sauce (page 149) or use the store-bought variety.

6 small whitefish, about 6 to 8 ounces each, cleaned, scaled, heads and tail intact
3 limes, thinly sliced

Wash the whitefish and pat dry with paper toweling. Brush them with oil. Arrange lime slices in the cavity of the fish (the opening where the fish was slit and gutted).

continues

continued

Follow the smoker manufacturer's directions. Fill the fire pan about three-quarters full of hardwood charcoal and heat the coals until they are ashen. Arrange drained twigs or chips over the hot coals. Fill the water pan of the smoker about three-quarters full with hot water, add any aromatics, and set the pan in place in the smoker carefully using large, thick pot holders.

Brush the cooking grid with oil. Set the fish on top and cover. Smoke for 45 minutes to 1 hour, or until the fish flakes easily when prodded with a fork and the skin is a golden smoky color. The fish is good served warm or at room temperature. Set 1 fish on each plate and serve with tartar sauce.

Whole Smoked Salmon with Pecans and Dried Cherries

Yield: 6 servings

Smoke: $2^1/_2$ to 3 hours

Level: Intermediate

At the Ready: Vegetable oil for brushing, brush, barbecue mitts or pot holders, dried pecan shells, alder wood, cherry, maple or hickory twigs or chips, soaked in water for 30 minutes and drained, 1 lemon, sliced, to put in water pan as an aromatic (optional)

1 whole salmon, about $3^1/_2$ pounds, cleaned, head discarded
2 to 3 tablespoons olive or vegetable oil
Juice of 2 lemons
1 bunch of marjoram (optional)
1 cup chopped pecans
1 cup dried cherries

Wash the salmon and pat it dry with paper towels. Mix the oil and lemon juice together, and rub the outside and the cavity of the salmon with the mixture. Lay the sprigs of marjoram evenly in the fish cavity (the opening where the fish was slit and gutted). This helps add more flavor. Refrigerate the salmon until the smoker is ready.

Follow the smoker manufacturer's directions. Fill the fire pan about three-quarters full of hardwood charcoal and heat the coals until ashen. Arrange drained twigs or chips over the hot coals. Fill the water pan of the smoker about three-quarters full with hot water, add any aromatics, and set the pan in place in the smoker carefully using barbecue mitts or pot holders. Float the lemon slices in the water pan.

Set the salmon on an oiled cooking grid. Cover and smoke the salmon for $2^1/_2$ to 3 hours or until the fish flakes easily when prodded with a fork and the skin turns a smoky color. Remember to replenish the wood chips and charcoal as necessary during smoking.

Remove and discard the skin from the salmon. Sprinkle the fish with the pecans and the dried cherries. This is good hot or cold.

Hot Tip

You can make a quick sauce for this by mixing $^1/_2$ cup mayonnaise and $^1/_2$ cup plain yogurt with 2 tablespoons minced oregano and half of the pecans and cherries.

Carolina-Style Slow Smoked Pulled Pork

Yield: 8 servings

Grill: About 7 to 8 hours

Level: Intermediate

At the Ready: Meat thermometer, apple or cherry chips or dry twigs, soaked in water 30 minutes and drained, barbecue mitts or large pot holders

$^1/_4$ cup dark brown sugar
1 tablespoon chili powder
$^1/_2$ teaspoon salt
1 teaspoon ground cumin
Dash cayenne
1 teaspoon ground ginger
$^1/_2$ teaspoon cloves
$4^1/_2$- to 5-pound pork butt or Boston butt
$^1/_2$ cup prepared mustard
1 cup apple juice (for basting)

continues

continued

Carolina Sauce
1 cup cider vinegar
$1/4$ cup sugar
3 dashes Tabasco sauce, or to taste

To make the rub, combine the sugar, chili powder, salt, cumin, cayenne, ginger, and cloves. Brush the meat with the mustard, and then rub with the spice mixture. Put the meat in a glass bowl and refrigerate for $1^1/2$ to 2 hours.

Follow the smoker manufacturer's directions. Fill the fire pan about three-quarters full of hardwood charcoal and heat the coals until the smoker reaches 225°F. Scatter the apple twigs over the hot coals. Fill the water pan of the smoker about three-quarters full with hot water and set the pan in place in the smoker carefully using barbecue mitts or pot holders.

This is a long slow "smoke"; figure on 8 hours or so. Set the pork butt on the oiled cooking grid, cover, and smoke until the pork registers 180°F with an instant-read thermometer inserted in the thickest part of the meat, without touching bone. Wrap the pork in aluminum foil after about 6 hours, or if the outside starts to look dry. Brush it with the apple juice several times during the last hour of smoking. Replenish the charcoal and water as necessary to keep a constant heat of about 225°F.

To prepare the Carolina sauce, use a glass mixing bowl and combine the vinegar, sugar, and Tabasco. Stir well.

Remove the pork to a board, cover with aluminum foil and let rest for 15 minutes. Discard any fat. Using 2 forks, pull apart the pork in shreds. Sprinkle a small amount of the Carolina sauce over the meat for extra flavor. Serve the pulled pork hot in a warm bun, accompanied by coleslaw and all the trimmings, including spicy baked beans and pickles.

Hot Tip

This is a good idea for a Fourth of July celebration. You can even prepare the pork the day before if you like. It takes most of a day to cook this, so be prepared. Serve with coleslaw, lightly warmed buns, relish, and salad.

Smoked Beef Short Ribs

Yield: 6 servings

Grill: 1¹/₂ hours

Level: Intermediate

At the Ready: Aluminum foil to wrap ribs, marinade, large pot holders or barbecue mitts, a brush, and hickory, pecan, or cherry chips or twigs soaked in water 30 minutes and drained

The smoking time depends on the thickness of the ribs, the heat of the coals and the temperature the day that you are grilling.

Pink Grapefruit Sauce

¹/₃ cup dark brown sugar

1 ¹/₄ cups pink grapefruit juice

2 cloves garlic, peeled and smashed

1 tablespoon dried oregano, crumbled

1 teaspoon ground cinnamon

5 to 6 pounds beef chuck ribs, cut into individual ribs

To make the sauce, combine the sugar, grapefruit juice, garlic, oregano, and cinnamon in a bowl, and mix well.

Place the ribs in a glass dish and brush with the sauce. Cover and marinate for 2 hours, turning one or two times. Drain.

Follow the smoker manufacturer's directions. Fill the fire pan about three-quarters full of hardwood charcoal and heat the coals until ashen. Arrange drained chips or twigs over the coals. Fill the water pan of the smoker about three-quarters full with hot water, add any aromatics, and set the pan in place in the smoker carefully using barbecue mitts or pot holders.

continues

continued

Wrap the ribs, 4 or 5 together, in a double layer of aluminum foil, sealing the packages securely. Continue until all of the ribs have been wrapped. Set the ribs on the grill and cover. Smoke the ribs for 1 hour, replacing water and twigs as necessary. Uncover the ribs during the last 30 minutes of grilling and brush with your favorite barbecue sauce. The meat should be fork tender. Serve hot with hush puppies or corn bread.

Hot Tip

Wrapping the ribs in foil ensures that they'll stay moist.

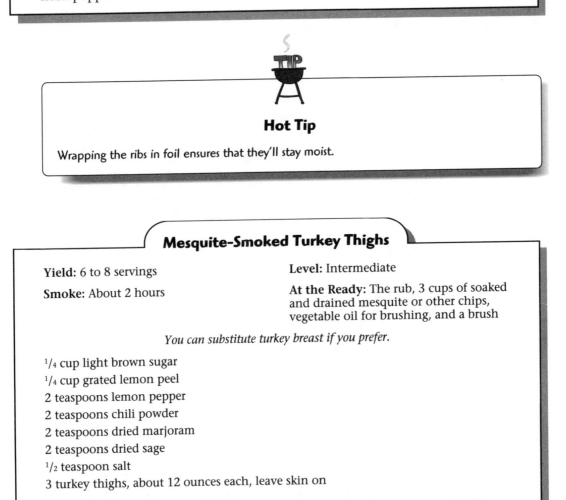

Mesquite-Smoked Turkey Thighs

Yield: 6 to 8 servings

Smoke: About 2 hours

Level: Intermediate

At the Ready: The rub, 3 cups of soaked and drained mesquite or other chips, vegetable oil for brushing, and a brush

You can substitute turkey breast if you prefer.

$^1/_4$ cup light brown sugar

$^1/_4$ cup grated lemon peel

2 teaspoons lemon pepper

2 teaspoons chili powder

2 teaspoons dried marjoram

2 teaspoons dried sage

$^1/_2$ teaspoon salt

3 turkey thighs, about 12 ounces each, leave skin on

In a small glass bowl mix together the sugar, lemon peel, lemon pepper, chili powder, marjoram, sage, and salt.

Wash and dry the turkey thighs with paper towels. Brush the turkey with oil and rub it all over with the spice mixture. Set the turkey in a glass dish and let stand in the refrigerator for 1 hour.

Follow the smoker manufacturer's directions. Fill the fire pan about three-quarters full of hardwood charcoal and heat the coals until ashen. Arrange the drained chips over the hot coals. Fill the water pan of the smoker about three-quarters full with hot water, add any aromatics, and set the pan in place in the smoker carefully using barbecue mitts or pot holders.

Brush the cooking grid with oil. Set the turkey thighs on the grid, cover and smoke for about 2 hours or until the turkey juices run clear and the meat is fork-tender. Replenish the coals and wood chips as necessary during grilling.

Remove the turkey to a cutting board. Let it stand for 15 minutes. Slice the turkey and serve hot, warm or cold. This is good with salsa and grilled vegetables, or try a black and white bean salad with chili powder seasoning.

Smoked Turkey Sausages

Yield: 6 servings

Grill: About 40 to 50 minutes

Level: Intermediate

At the Ready: 3 tablespoons allspice as an aromatic for the water pan, barbecue mitts or large pot holders, 3 cups hickory chips, soaked in water 30 minutes and drained

12 turkey sausages, regular or Italian
Yellow hot dog mustard
Ketchup
Pickles
1 can (16 ounces) sauerkraut, drained
12 hot dog rolls

Follow the smoker manufacturer's directions. Fill the fire pan about three-quarters full of hardwood charcoal and heat the coals until ashen. Arrange the drained chips over the hot coals. Fill the water pan of the smoker about three-quarters full with hot water and add the allspice. Set the pan in place in the smoker carefully, using barbecue mitts or pot holders.

continues

continued

Stick the sausages with a fork several times. Set the sausages on top of the cooking grid and cover the smoker, adjusting the vents. Smoke the sausages about 40 to 50 minutes, turning twice or as necessary. The sausages will turn a golden color and should be cooked through. Remove the sausages to individual plates. Serve them with mustard, ketchup, pickles, sauerkraut, and hot dog rolls that have been warmed on the grill.

Honey-Brushed Smoked Chicken with Mandarin Orange Sauce

Yield: 6 to 8 servings

Smoke: About 70 minutes

Level: Intermediate

At the Ready: Barbecue mitts or large pot holders, dried plum twigs, or other twigs or chips of your choice, soaked in water 30 minutes and drained; long-handled fork, and vegetable oil for brushing

The Orange Sauce can be prepared ahead of time and reheated. For extra flavor, you can add 2 tablespoons of grated orange peel or orange liqueur.

2 chickens, about 3 or $3^1/_2$ pounds each, cut in half (see section on butterflying chickens in Chapter 12)

$^3/_4$ cup wildflower or other honey

$^1/_3$ cup stone-ground mustard

Orange Sauce

2 cans (11 ounces each) mandarin orange segments, with the liquid

$^1/_3$ cup unsalted butter

1 medium onion, peeled and minced

$^1/_2$ cup chicken broth

$^1/_2$ teaspoon salt

5 tablespoons sugar

Wash the chickens and pat dry with paper toweling. In a small bowl, mix the honey with the mustard. Brush the chickens with the mixture on all sides. Refrigerate the chickens until the smoker is ready.

Follow the smoker manufacturer's directions. Fill the fire pan about three-quarters full of hardwood charcoal and heat the coals until ashen. Arrange the drained twigs over the hot coals. Fill the water pan of the smoker about three-quarters full with hot water, add any aromatics, and set the pan in place in the smoker carefully using barbecue mitts or pot holders.

Set the chickens on the oiled cooking grid. Cover and smoke for about 70 minutes, or until the chicken legs move easily and the juices run clear. Replenish the charcoal and drained wood chips as necessary during smoking.

While the chicken is smoking, prepare the Orange Sauce. Puree the orange segments with their juice in a food processor fitted with the steel blade. Set aside. Heat the butter and cook the onions over medium heat until soft, about 5 minutes. Stir in the orange puree, chicken broth, salt, and sugar. Simmer over medium heat for 10 to 15 minutes or until the sauce thickens slightly. Taste and adjust the seasonings. Reheat before serving.

Remove the chickens to a cutting board. Let stand for about 10 minutes. Cut the chicken if desired and serve hot and pass the sauce.

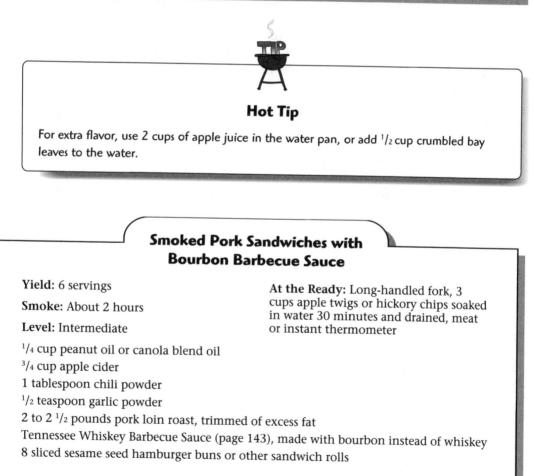

Hot Tip

For extra flavor, use 2 cups of apple juice in the water pan, or add $^1/_2$ cup crumbled bay leaves to the water.

Smoked Pork Sandwiches with Bourbon Barbecue Sauce

Yield: 6 servings

Smoke: About 2 hours

Level: Intermediate

At the Ready: Long-handled fork, 3 cups apple twigs or hickory chips soaked in water 30 minutes and drained, meat or instant thermometer

$^1/_4$ cup peanut oil or canola blend oil
$^3/_4$ cup apple cider
1 tablespoon chili powder
$^1/_2$ teaspoon garlic powder
2 to 2 $^1/_2$ pounds pork loin roast, trimmed of excess fat
Tennessee Whiskey Barbecue Sauce (page 143), made with bourbon instead of whiskey
8 sliced sesame seed hamburger buns or other sandwich rolls

continues

continued

Combine the oil, cider, chili powder, and garlic powder. Pour into a glass dish large enough to hold the pork loin. Place the pork in the marinade and turn several time so that all surfaces are coated with the marinade. Cover, and refrigerate. Marinate the pork for 5 to 6 hours, turning occasionally. Drain.

While the pork is marinating, prepare the sauce and refrigerate it.

Follow the smoker manufacturer's directions. Fill the fire pan about three-quarters full of hardwood charcoal and heat the coals until ashen. Arrange the drained chips over the hot coals. Fill the water pan of the smoker about three-quarters full with hot water, add any aromatics, and set the pan in place in the smoker carefully using barbecue mitts or pot holders.

Set the pork on the lowest rack. Brush it lightly with the sauce. Cover, adjust the vents and smoke the pork for about 2 hours. Rotate it 2 or 3 times and brush it with the sauce during the last 15 minutes of smoking. Check for doneness after $1^1/_2$ hours. The pork is done when the juices run clear when meat is cut, and an instant read thermometer registers 180°F when inserted in the thickest part of the meat.

Transfer the pork to a cutting board and let it stand 5 minutes. Thinly slice the meat. Arrange the sliced pork in heated rolls and drizzle with the remaining sauce. Serve the pork sandwiches hot, accompanied by baked beans, hush puppies, and coleslaw.

Tasty Tidbit

In southern Illinois, this pork is smoked with apple twigs and apple cider for its unique flavor.

The Least You Need to Know

➤ Smoking is the process by which most famous barbecued foods are cooked.

➤ Smoked foods improve in flavor as they "age."

➤ It's best to use real charcoal, rather than briquets, when smoking foods.

What's Wrong, and How to Fix or Prevent It

Burner flame on gas grill is too yellow.

➤ If the burner is new, it's probably just burning off machine oil. Don't worry.

➤ If it's not new, consult the owner's manual or call the manufacturer. You may need to adjust something.

Gas grill makes noise.

➤ A bit of a "whoosh" as the gas flows in is normal.

➤ Ticking and slight pinging are normal as the elements expand and contract with heat.

➤ Excessive rattling or vibrating may mean something's loose. Consult the owner's manual, or call the manufacturer.

Ignition sparks, but burner(s) on gas grill won't light.

➤ Burners may be clogged. Bend a paper clip straight, and dig out any crud in the burner holes.

➤ If that doesn't work, consult the manufacturer.

Charcoal won't light.

➤ Use a charcoal chimney.

➤ Use an electric fire starter.

➤ Use solid starters.

➤ Use kindling—crumpled newspaper, twigs, pine cones—under the charcoal. Add a teaspoon of vegetable oil to the newspaper to help it catch.

Charcoal won't stay lit or burns slowly.

➤ Make sure it's piled in a pyramid shape.

➤ Open the grill vents.

It's windy.

➤ Use the lid to shield the grill as much as possible.

➤ Use a charcoal chimney, electric starter, or solid starters to get the coals lit.

➤ Be sure the grill is covered during cooking.

➤ If fire flares, close the bottom vents.

It's raining.

➤ Forget cooking in the pouring rain. Put everything in the oven or under the broiler.

➤ If it's drizzling, allow extra time for lighting charcoal and preheating the grill, and for cooking. Cover the grill during cooking.

Fire keeps flaring up.

➤ Trim fats from food before cooking.

➤ Move the food so it's not directly over the coals.

➤ Cover the grill.

➤ Close the bottom vents.

Food drops into the coals.

➤ Put the food on a grill screen, or a piece of oiled foil with holes punched in it.

Food sticks.

➤ Clean the cooking grid.

➤ Make sure the grid and/or the food is oiled. If you're cooking fish, both the grill and the fish need to be oiled.

➤ "Preheat" the grid by putting it over the coals a few minutes before you put the food on it.

Food is nicely browned on outside, still raw on inside.

➤ Coals are too hot. They should be covered with a layer of ash before you start cooking.

➤ Food hasn't cooked long enough. Before you remove foods from the grill, insert an instant-read thermometer or cut into a slice to be sure it's cooked through.

➤ The sugar in the sauce burned. When you're using a sugary sauce, baste with it toward the end of the cooking time, or turn the food frequently.

➤ To salvage food in this condition, finish cooking it in the microwave. Cut off any burnt parts, and serve the food with a sauce.

Food is burnt and/or dry.

➤ The coals are too hot.

➤ It was cooked too long.

➤ To salvage burnt food, cut off the burnt parts, slice, and cover with a sauce.

➤ Next time, don't answer the phone while you're grilling.

Food is "grimy" looking.

➤ Clean the grill.

➤ Use separate sets of tongs for food and for charcoal.

➤ Use a better grade of charcoal.

➤ When you lift the lid up, pull it to the side rather than straight up.

Food doesn't brown nicely.

➤ The coals are too cool. They should be covered with ash, but still faintly glowing.

Meat is tough (applies to slow-cooking cuts like brisket or ribs).

➤ Food needs to be cooked longer.

➤ Coals are too hot—keep the temperature for slow-smoked foods at about 225°F.

Food tastes smoky and bitter.

➤ Use fewer wood chunks or chips.

➤ Use a milder smoking wood (for example, pecan instead of mesquite).

Food has an unpleasant chemical flavor.

➤ Don't use lighter fluid.

➤ If you do use it, let the coals burn to ash with the grill lid open, so volatile fumes can escape.

Glossary

Anjou   A firm, sweet, yellowish-green winter pear.

Aromatic   An herb, spice, or other ingredient that you sprinkle onto the coals or into the drip pan to perfume the smoke and enhance a food's flavor.

Ash catcher   A metal tray or container that is attached to the bottom of a charcoal grill to collect ashes.

Ashen   *See* Medium hot coals.

Barbecue   Often used broadly to mean cooking over wood or out of doors. But serious barbecuers use it to mean slow-cooking meats over a low fire. *See also* Grill *and* Smoke.

Bartlett   A pear variety with juicy, slightly grainy flesh.

Baste   To brush or drizzle a sauce or other liquid on a food during cooking. It helps to keep food moist.

Big Green Egg   Trade name for a charcoal grill made of ceramic. It is inspired by the Japanese *kamado.*

Bluefish   A coastal Atlantic Ocean fish with fine-grained, fatty flesh that makes it great on the grill.

Boil   To cook a liquid on medium high or high heat until the liquid is very active, with large bubbles breaking the surface.

Boning knives   Knives with thin, curved blades designed to cut meat off the bone.

Bosc   A slender-necked, russet pear with a sweet-tart flavor.

Briquets   A mixture of charcoal and other substances, molded into uniform pillow shapes that are designed to catch fire easily.

Buffalo wings   Chicken wings that are marinated in a spicy rub, grilled, and served with a blue cheese dip. Named for Buffalo, New York, where they originated.

Burner   The heating element in a gas grill. Burners commonly are made of stainless steel, and often are shaped like an "H."

Butterfly   To cut a food most, but not all of the way through, so that it can be flattened, like butterfly wings. Butterflied meats and poultry absorb marinade better and cook faster on the grill.

Carving knives   Knives with very long, fairly thin blades that are strictly for slicing.

Charcoal   Often used as a generic term for any fuel made of burnt wood. But true charcoal is actually *hardwood* that has been burned down to eliminate volatile gases and reduce its water content so it does not smoke.

Charcoal chimney   A large metal can that has a heatproof handle, an interior plate to hold charcoal, and a ventilated bottom. You put coals in the pan and light it from the bottom; the bottom coals ignite, and in turn ignite the other ones.

Chef's knives   All-purpose chopping and slicing utensils with thick, heavy blades.

Chop   To roughly cut food into fairly small pieces, using a chef's knife or food processor. To chop onions, peppers, and similar vegetables, lift and drop the blade of the knife rapidly, using a bit of a rocking motion.

Coals   Generic grilling term that refers to the heat source, whether it's briquets, true charcoal, or gas heating elements. *See also* Medium hot coals; Red hot coals.

Cooking grid   The wire rack in the grill that you put food on.

Core   To remove the woody or seedy center of a fruit, such as a pear, apple, or pineapple. If you don't have a special tool called a corer, the easiest way to do this usually is to cut the fruit in half lengthwise, and cut out the core.

Crustaceans   Ocean and freshwater creatures that wear their skeletons on the outside of their bodies. Popular edible crustaceans include lobster, shrimp, prawns, and crawfish.

Dice   To cut a food into little cubes, about $1/2$ inch or smaller. It's neater than chopping, and is often used for hard foods such as carrots. To dice, you slice the food one way, then the other way to make small squares.

Direct heat   A method in which the food is cooked right over the heat source. It is used with most foods, unless they are very thick or large pieces.

Dressed   Scaled, gutted, and ready to cook (as applied to fish).

Drip pan   A pan put directly under the food when cooking by indirect heat or smoking. Usually you partly fill it with water or another liquid.

Dust   A fine, powdery *rub*.

Elephant garlic   A relative of the leek that looks like giant garlic, and tastes like mild garlic. It's a good choice for the grill.

Finishing sauce   A barbecue sauce or other liquid that is served alongside the meat at the table, and may also be used to baste the meat in the last few minutes of cooking. Also called table sauce.

Firebox, fire pan   The part of the grill that holds the charcoal, wood, or briquets. In most wood-fired smokers, the firebox is separate from the cooking chamber.

Flake   As applied to fish, to separate into sections. When fish is cooked through, it flakes when you prod it gently with a fork.

Gas grill   A grill that is fueled by propane or, less often, natural gas.

Glowing   *See* Red hot coals.

Grate   To shred a food such as ginger or cheese by rubbing it against the holes on a grater. Used interchangeably with shred.

Grill   To cook foods relatively quickly over a medium-hot fire. It's a quicker process than barbecuing or smoking.

Grilling basket   Hinged, long-handled flat wire baskets into which you put delicate foods, such as fish or vegetables, to make turning them on the grill easier.

Grill-roasting   *See* Indirect heat.

Grill screen   A portable metal grid designed to sit atop the grill's cooking grid. It has mesh or small holes to keep foods such as sliced onions and shrimp from falling through the wires of the grid.

Hardwood   The solid, compact wood of various trees. Hardwoods commonly used in grilling include oak, cherry, maple, hickory, and mesquite (which is actually a shrub).

Hardwood charcoal   *See* Charcoal.

Heat distributors   The "briquets" or bars in a gas grill that help spread the heat from the burners. They can be made of metal, pumice stone, or ceramic.

Heterocyclic amines (HCAs)   Chemicals that are formed when protein foods are cooked over high heat. They may be harmful to human health.

Hibachi   A rectangular tabletop grill with a stand, rather than legs, so it won't tip over, and a fairly heavy cooking grid that's often adjustable.

Indirect heat   A method in which food is placed away from the heat source, so that it cooks more slowly. This is the grilling equivalent of roasting, and is usually used with larger cuts of meat or poultry that is whole.

Jerk   A seasoning mixture traditionally used to flavor slow-cooked pork in Jamaica. Its ingredients vary, but it always contains Jamaican pimento, or allspice. Other common ingredients include chiles, ginger, thyme, and garlic.

Kamado   In Japan, a bell-shaped grill made of ceramic. In the United States, it's a trademarked name for a similar ceramic grill, modeled after the Asian type.

Kettle   A round grill with a dome-shaped bottom and lid. Developed and sold by the Weber-Stephens Company, it is the most commonly sold form of charcoal grill.

Lemongrass   A citrusy herb that looks a bit like a tough scallion. It is widely used in marinades and sauces in Southeast Asia.

Marinade   An acid-containing liquid in which raw foods are soaked. *See also* Marinate.

Marinate   Traditionally, to tenderize and flavor meats by soaking them in a liquid, usually a mixture of acid and oil, for a long time—anywhere from an hour to overnight. We use the term "marinate" a bit more broadly, to also include foods that are rubbed with a spice mixture and allowed to stand.

Meats   *See* Medium; Medium rare; Medium well; Well done.

Medium   As applied to meats, pinkish in the center, with an internal temperature of 155°F.

Medium hot coals   Coals that have burned, then become covered with a fairly thick layer of ash. Most foods are grilled over ashen, or medium hot, coals.

Medium rare   As applied to meats, still quite pink in the center, but warm, with an internal temperature of 145°F.

Medium well   As applied to meats, brown in the center, but still juicy, with an internal temperature of 160°F.

Mince   To chop into very fine pieces. Garlic, ginger, and herbs are often minced.

Mollusks   Spineless creatures that live inside hard shells. Popular edible mollusks include clams, oysters, scallops, and mussels.

Mop   A small utensil with a cotton string top. It's designed for applying a thin sauce to foods. As a verb, *mop* is the same as *baste*.

Mopping sauce   A liquid added to foods to add moisture and flavor. Also called basting sauce or sopping sauce.

New potatoes   Very young, small, unblemished potatoes.

Oil or spray   To rub the cooking grid lightly with a vegetable oil (use a brush or a paper towel for this), or to spray it with a nonstick cooking spray.

Orzo   Rice-shaped pasta.

Paella   A Spanish rice dish with numerous variations. It usually includes seafood, poultry, and meats, and is flavored with saffron.

Paring knives   Knives with short blades suitable for peeling and other detail work.

Peel   To remove the skin of a fruit or vegetable. The easiest way to peel hard vegetables such as carrots or potatoes is with a vegetable peeler. The easiest way to peel soft fruits such as peaches or tomatoes is to put them in boiling water briefly (see Chapter 14). We also use *peel* to refer to the colored part of the rind in citrus fruits.

Pig pickin'   The classic barbecue style in the Carolinas. Slow-cooked pork is pulled into shreds, then moistened with a vinegary sauce and served on buns.

Pit   To remove the large seed in a fruit such as a plum or peach. Cut the fruit in half lengthwise, the pry out the seed.

Polycyclic aromatic hydrocarbons (PAHs)   Substances formed when the fatty juices from meat drip into the heat source. They may be dangerous to human health.

Portobello, portabella   An extra-large, cultivated brown mushroom. The caps are often cooked on the grill.

Prawns   A broad term that can refer to a member of the lobster family, or to a freshwater crustacean. Most seafood labeled "prawns," however, is just jumbo shrimp.

Process   To grind, chop, or blend foods in a blender or food processor.

Propane   A colorless, flammable gas that's a component of petroleum and natural gas. It burns more cleanly than gasoline, and is the most common fuel used to run gas grills.

Rare   As applied to meat, still red in the center and soft to the touch, with an internal temperature of 130 to 135°F.

Red hot coals   Coals that are still burning brightly orange. At this point, they may have only a thin coating of ash. Charcoal at this temperature is suitable for searing meats and for quickly cooking shellfish.

Rotate   To turn food clockwise or counterclockwise, without turning it over.

Rotisserie   A long rotating rod, or spit, with prongs on either end to hold the food in place. At one end is a small motor, which rotates the rod with the food on it, helping larger cuts of meat and poultry to cook more evenly.

Rub   A mixture of spices used to flavor meats for barbecuing. It forms an oily crust that helps seal in juices.

Salmon   A cold water, fatty fish that's very popular for grilling. It comes from both the Atlantic and Pacific oceans, but these days most of the salmon in the markets is farm-raised.

Sear   To quickly brown over high heat. Searing meats and poultry helps form a crust on the surface, sealing in the juices.

Simmer   To cook foods at just below a boil. The liquid will have small bubbles coming to the surface, but will be "calmer" than a boiling liquid.

Skewer   A thin metal or wooden rod that's used to hold chunks of food.

Slice   To cut crosswise or lengthwise through a food to make thin, fairly large pieces.

Smoke   To cook foods very slowly over a low fire, with wood chips or chunks added to produce fragrant smoke.

Smoker   A specialized grill fired by wood, charcoal, gas, or electricity. The food sits far away from the heat source, so that it cooks very slowly and absorbs more of the flavor from the cooking wood or the wood chunks or chips added to the coals. The *water smoker* is a common variant.

Smoking woods   Chips or chunks of unburnt wood that are soaked and scattered onto the charcoal (or heat diffusers in a gas grill) to produce an aromatic smoke.

Soft-shell crabs   Regular East Coast blue crabs that are gathered right after they molt (shed their shells). The crunchy new shell is eaten right along with the meat.

Softwoods   The resinous woods of conifer trees such as pine, spruce, fir, and cedar. They are unsuitable for cooking or smoking woods, but fine for kindling.

Solid starter   Squares of a nontoxic wax that sit under the briquets. As they burn, they ignite the charcoal.

Trim   To cut off and discard parts of a food that you don't normally eat. That includes such things as the woody bottoms of asparagus, the ends of green beans, or the fat and gristle on meats.

Trout   Various species of a freshwater fish that's commonly grilled. Much of the rainbow trout in the markets is farm-raised.

Turn   To use a spatula or tongs to flip a food onto its other side.

Vent   An opening on the top, side, or bottom of a grill or smoker that's designed to let air in and smoke out. Adjusting the vents can change the cooking temperature.

Water smoker   A tall, cylindrical grill with a firebox, a water pan, and one or two cooking grids. The food sits above the water pan, which is between it and the heat source, allowing the food to cook slowly.

Well done   As applied to meats, completely brown through the center, with little juice and an internal temperature of 165°F.

Resources

Information

Here's where you can learn all you want to, and probably more, about barbecue. Consider this a bibliography as well; many of these Web sites were used as research resources for this book.

Weber-Stephen Products Co.
200 East Daniels Rd.
Palatine, IL 60067-6266
1-800-GRILL-OUT, toll-free hot line for grilling questions, operates April 1 through Labor Day *only*. "Live" 8 A.M. to 6 P.M. Central Time; taped messages the rest of the time.
www.weberbbq.com
Makers of charcoal and gas grills and accessories. The company's superb Web site offers tons of information about grilling and entertaining.

Barbecue'n
www.barbecuen.com
Excellent, comprehensive Web site devoted to grilling and barbecuing—but mostly the latter. Also includes extensive lists of grill manufacturers, and on-line shopping for accessories.

The Lexington Collection
www.ipass.net/~lineback/lex.htm
All about Southern barbecue and Carolina pig pickin'.

U.S. Department of Agriculture
Food Safety and Inspection Service
Meat and Poultry Hot Line
1-800-535-4555
www.fsis.usda.gov
"Live" Monday to Friday, from 10 A.M. to 4 P.M., Eastern Time. Recorded messages the rest of the time.
Agency responsible for meat and poultry safety.

U.S. Food & Drug Administration
Center for Food Safety and Applied Nutrition
Food Information and Seafood Hot Line:
1-800-FDA-4010 (or 202-205-4314 in the Washington, D.C., area)
"Live" noon to 4 P.M. Eastern Daylight Time, Monday through Friday; recorded messages the rest of the time.
www.vm.cfsan.fda.gov
Agency responsible for general food safety and seafood safety.

Barbecue Industry Association (BIA)
710 East Ogden, Suite 600
Naperville, IL 60563-8603
(630) 369-2404
www.bbqind.org
Trade association that keeps track of grilling trends and statistics.

Bibliography

In addition to most of the Web sites mentioned above, we also relied on these books and articles for information:

Bennett, Bev, and Virginia Van Vynckt. *The Dictionary of Healthful Food Terms*. Barron's Educational Series, 1997.

Grunes, Barbara. *The Beef Lover's Grill Book*. Contemporary Books, 1991.

Grunes, Barbara, and Phyllis Magida. *Poultry on the Grill*. Dell Publishing, 1989.

Grunes, Barbara, and Phyllis Magida. *The Complete Fish on the Grill*. Contemporary Books, 1994.

Herbst, Sharon Tyler. *The New Food Lover's Companion,* 2d ed. Barron's Educational Series, 1995.

Jamison, Cheryl Alters, and Bill Jamison. *Texas Home Cooking*. Harvard Common Press, 1993.

Lawrence Livermore National Labs. "Marinating and Heterocyclic Amines." www-bio.llnl.gov/mutagens/html/fd.marinade.html (World Wide Web). Cited August 25, 1998.

Product Information and Mail Order

Equipment and Accessories

Barbecue Renew
Moss Bay Commerce Center
731 Kirkland Ave.
Kirkland, WA 98033
(425) 828-0637
www.grillparts.com
On-line tips and ordering of gas grill parts.

Barbeques Galore
15041 Bake Parkway, Suite A
Irvine, CA 92618
1-800-GRILL-UP
www.bbggalore.com
Chain of barbecue equipment superstores in the United States and Australia. Call or visit the Web site to find out if there is a store in your area.

Big Green Egg
3414 Clairmont Road
Atlanta, GA 30319
(404) 321-4658
www.biggreenegg.com
Makers of a charcoal grill/smoker made of ceramic.

Char-Broil
PO Box 1300
Columbus, GA 31902-1300
1-800-241-8981 (orders)
1-800-252-8248 (customer service)
www.grilllovers.com
Makers of gas, charcoal, and electric grills.

Chef's Catalog
3215 Commercial Ave.
Northbrook, IL 60062-1920
(847) 480-9400
1-800-338-3232 (orders only)
www.chefscatalog.com
Purveyor of a wide variety of kitchen tools, cookware, and utensils.

Frontgate
2800 Henkle Dr.
Lebanon, Ohio 45036-8899
1-800-626-6488 (orders)
1-800-537-8484 (questions)
www.frontgate.com
Upscale grills and accessories for entertaining. Offers a grilling-specific catalog in addition to the main catalog.

Grill Parts Distributors
6150 49th St. North
St. Petersburg, FL 33709
1-800-4GRILLS
www.gasgrills.com
Company that specializes in supplying parts for over 20 brands of gas grills.

The Kamado Company
2224 Rice Ave.
West Sacramento, CA 95691
1-888-KAMADOS
www.kamado.com
Makers of a charcoal grill/smoker made of ceramic.

Peoples Woods
75 Mill Street
Cumberland, RI 02864
1-800-729-5800, or (401) 725-2700 (in Rhode Island)
www.peopleswoods.com
Manufacturers and purveyors of Nature's Own pure hardwood charcoal, as well as a variety of smoking woods, some exotic. Available in kitchenware and natural-foods stores, or by mail order.

Traeger Industries
1385 E. College St.
P.O. Box 829
Mt. Angel, OR 97362
1-800-872-3437, or (503) 845-9234
www.traegerindustries.com
Manufacturers of wood pellet grills.

Foodstuffs

American Spoon Foods
1668 Clarion Ave.
P.O. Box 566
Petoskey, MI 49770-0566
1-888-735-6700 (orders)
1-800-222-5886
www.spoon.com
Barbecue and marinating sauces, chutneys and relishes, and other condiments.

Culver Duck Farms
12215 County Road 10
Middlebury, IN 46540
1-800-825-9225, or (219) 825-9537
www.culverduck.com
Sells ducks and duck parts, including boneless breasts.

Mo Hotta Mo Betta
P.O. Box 4136
San Luis Obispo, CA 93403
1-800-462-3220
www.mohotta.com/index2.html
Wide selection of spicy barbecue sauces, salsas, and marinades.

Penzeys, Ltd.
W19362 Apollo Dr.
Muskego, Wisconsin 53150
(414) 679-7207
www.penzeys.com
Wide variety of spices and seasonings, including various barbecue rubs.

Peppers
2009 Highway One
Dewey Beach, DE 19971
1-800-998-FIRE, or (302) 227-4608
www.peppers.com
Restaurant with "the world's largest collection of hot sauces," and online catalog and ordering of spicy marinades and sauces, mustards, and other condiments.

Index

A

allspice, about, 36
almost beef Stroganoff, ideas for leftovers, 136
aluminum foil, about, 28
angel food cake, grilled, and pineapple (recipe), 240
antipasti, grilled (recipe), 162–63
appetizer recipes, 151–63
    Crostini, 161
    Five-Minute Mussels, 153
    Focaccia, 157
    Garlic Pita Chips, 157
    Glazed Polish Sausage, 153–54
    Greek Cheese with Garlic Pita Chips, 156–57
    Grilled Antipasti, 162–63
    Grilled Garlic Potato Skins, 160
    Spicy Chicken Dogs, 154–55
    Sweet and Sour Lamb Ribs, 155–56
    Turkey Sausage on a Stick, 152–53
    Walnut-Stuffed White Mushrooms, 159
apple(s)
    about, 128
    recipes with
        blueberry-, cobbler on the grill, 233–34
        cinnamon and, warm, with cheddar cheese, 235–36
        grilled, scrod with, 205
        pork chops with, 173
apricot(s)
    sauce, whole grilled chicken with (recipe), 181–82

topped with raspberries and raspberry sherbet (recipe), 240
aprons, about, 32
aromatic, definition of, 36
artichoke(s)
    about, 124
    recipes with
        baby, with rosemary, 229–30
        hearts, in Grilled Antipasti, 162–63
Asian-inspired salad, ideas for leftovers, 134
Asian-style sweet potatoes, ideas for leftovers, 136
asparagus
    about, 124
    ideas for leftovers, 136
    and mushrooms with sage brushing sauce (recipe), 222–23

B

Baby Artichokes with Rosemary (recipe), 229–30
baby back ribs, grilling tips for, 104
bagel spread, ideas for leftovers, 135
Baked Potatoes with Vidalia Onions (recipe), 227–28
baking tiles or stones, about, 32
balsamic vinegar, 39
bananas, about, 128
barbecue, family, suggested menu for, 79
barbecue glasses, about, 32
barbecue sauce
    about, 41, 97–98, 130

bourbon, smoked pork sandwiches with (recipe), 253–54
molasses, chicken pieces with (recipe), 183–84
Tennessee whiskey (recipe), 142
basil, about, 36, 130
bass, striped, tarragon-scented (recipe), 195–96
basting
    brushes, 24–25
    definition of, 61
    sauces, 97
bay leaves, about, 36
beef. *See also* Meat
    how much to buy when entertaining, 76
    ideas for leftovers, 133–34
    and peppers, about, 133
    recipes
        Beer-Basted Short Ribs, 171–72
        Cheeseburger Deluxe, 170–71
        Flank Steak Strips on Salad Greens with Lemongrass Mopping Sauce, 169
        Grilled Sliced Meat Loaf with Chopped Tomatoes, 167
        Jerk Strip Steaks, 168
        Skirt Steak with Grilled Peppers and Shallot Marinade Sauce, 166
        Smoked Beef Short Ribs, 249–50
beer-basted short ribs, 171–72
    coastal shrimp in, 215
beets, about, 124
beverages for party, 78–79
Big Green Egg, The, 20

bison, how much to buy when entertaining, 76
Blueberry-Apple Cobbler on the Grill (recipe), 233–34
Bluefish Piccata (recipe), 199
boil, definition of, 43
botulism, about, 58, 70
bourbon barbecue sauce, smoked pork sandwiches with (recipe), 253–54
bread(s)
    about, 129
    Buffalo Cheese and Tomato Sauce Pizza (recipe), 221–22
    Crostini (recipe), 161
    Focaccia (recipe), 157
    Pizza Crust (recipe), 220
brie, warm, honeyed papaya strips with (recipe), 239
briquet(s)
    about, 48–50, 52
    amount of, 52
brisket, grilling tips for, 103, 104
broiler/fryer, grilling tips for, 111
Buffalo Cheese and Tomato Sauce Pizza (recipe), 221–22
Buffalo wings, grilling tips for, 111
bugs, fending off, 66
build-your-own pits, 20
burger(s)
    grilling tips for, 99–100
    press, about, 31
    recipes
        beef, cheese, deluxe, 170–71
        lamb, 175
        turkey, with dried cranberries, 189
    safety issues for cooking, 101–2
    vegetarian, about, 130
burritos, instant, about, 133
buttermilk marinade, swordfish in (recipe), 194–95

C

Caesar salad, about, 133
Cajun Spice Rub (recipe), 142
cake
    angel food, grilled, and pineapple (recipe), 240
    pound, about, 129
    pound, chocolate, grilled, fruit kebabs on (recipe), 236–38
Campfire-Style S'Mores (recipe), 238–39
Campylobacter jejuni, about, 69
candles, about, 32
canola oil, about, 41
cantaloupe
    about, 128
    in Grilled Antipasti (recipe), 162–63
Cantonese-Style Sweet and Sour Chicken Breasts (recipe), 180–81
capon, grilling tips for, 112
caramelized onions, chicken dogs with (recipe), 186
Carolina-Style Slow Smoked Pulled Pork (recipe), 247–48
carrots, about, 124
cart, about, 29
cast-iron griddle, about, 32
charcoal
    about, 48–54
    dividers or holders, about, 26
    grills, 13–16
cheese, recipes with
    brie, warm, honeyed papaya strips with, 239
    buffalo, and tomato sauce pizza, 221–22
    cheddar, warm apple cinnamon slices with, 235–36
    fontina, spinach pasta and, grilled whitefish with, 201
    Greek, with garlic pita chips, 156–57
Cheeseburger Deluxe (recipe), 170–71
cherries, dried, whole smoked salmon with pecans and (recipe), 246–47

chicken
    Caesar, about, 133
    grilling tips for, 107–8
    noodle soup, about, 132
    recipes
        Cantonese-style Sweet and Sour Chicken, 180–81
        Chicken Dogs with Caramelized Onions, 186
        Chicken Pieces with Molasses Barbecue Sauce, 183–84
        Chicken Yakitori, 182–83
        Ginger Marinade for Chicken, 145–46
        Honey-Brushed Smoked Chicken with Mandarin Orange Sauce, 252–53
        Paella, 184–85
        Pesto Chicken, 187
        Spicy Chicken Dogs, 154–55
        Whole Grilled Chicken with Apricot Sauce, 181–82
    salad, about, 132
    sausages, grilling tips for, 113
    slaw, about, 133
    tea-smoked, 113
    wings, grilling tips for, 111
chili
    ideas for leftovers, 134
    -orange mopping sauce, smoked shrimp with (recipe), 244–45
chips, garlic pita (recipe), 157
    Greek cheese with (recipe), 156–57
chives, about, 36
chocolate pound cake, grilled, fruit kebabs on (recipe), 236–38
chop(s)
    definition of, 43
    lamb, Greek-style (recipe), 174
    lamb rib, with fresh mint (recipe), 174–75
    pork, with apple slices (recipe), 173

cilantro
about, 36
garlic and, new potatoes
with (recipe), 225
cinnamon
about, 37
apple, slices, warm, with
cheddar cheese (recipe),
235–36
citrus fruits, about, 128
citrus juices
as flavoring, 122
tip about, 142
clambake, down Maine
(recipe), 216–17
clams, grilling tips for, 120
Coastal Shrimp in Beer (recipe),
215
cobbler, blueberry-apple, on
the grill (recipe), 233–34
condiment(s)
fat and, 85
shelf, about, 31
cooking bags, about, 30
cooking/prep area, 7–8
core, definition of, 43
coriander, about, 37
corn, about, 124–25
Cornish hen, grilling tips for,
112, 113
crabs
buying, 117
recipes
Crab Cakes, 217–18
Soft-Shell Crabs on the
Grill, 210–11
Soft-Shell Crabs with
Garlic Crumbs, 211
cranberry(ies)
recipes with
dried, turkey burgers with
(recipe), 189
raisin ketchup (recipe),
148
tip about, 145
cross-contamination, preventing, 98
Crostini (recipe), 161
crumbs, garlic, soft-shell crabs
with (recipe), 211
crust, pizza (recipe), 220
crustaceans, grilling tips for,
121–22

cumin, about, 37
cutting boards, about, 26

D

desserts, 231–41
Apricots Topped with
Raspberries and Raspberry
Sherbet (recipe), 240
Blueberry-Apple Cobbler on
the Grill (recipe), 233–34
Campfire-Style S'Mores
(recipe), 238–39
Fruit Kebabs on Grilled
Chocolate Pound Cake
(recipe), 236–38
Glazed Mixed Fruit Grill
(recipe), 232
Grilled Angel Food Cake and
Pineapple (recipe), 240
Honeyed Papaya Strips with
Warm Brie (recipe), 239
Warm Apple Cinnamon
Slices with Cheddar
Cheese (recipe), 235–36
Wine-Brushed Pears (recipe),
234–35
dice, definition of, 43
dill, about, 37
dinner party, suggested menu
for, 80
dogs, chicken
with caramelized onions
(recipe), 186
spicy (recipe), 154–55
Down Maine Clambake
(recipe), 216–17
dried cherries, whole smoked
salmon with pecans and
(recipe), 246–47
dried cranberries, turkey
burgers with (recipe), 189
drip pans, about, 28
duck
grilling tips for, 112, 113
tea-smoked, 113
dust, definition of, 96

E–F

eating/entertainment space,
6–7
E. coli, 68–69, 101
eggplant, about, 125
electric grills, 19
elephant garlic, about, 163
embers, cooking in, 59
entertaining tips, 73–81, 84–87

fajitas, grilling tips for, 103
fats, about, 87
fennel, about, 37
finishing sauces, 97
fire
extinguisher, about, 29
keeping it going, 51
methods of starting the,
49–51
putting it out, 53
starters, about, 27
fish
cakes, ideas for leftovers,
135
fillets, buying, 117
flavors that go well with,
122
forms of, 117
how much to buy when
entertaining, 77
ideas for leftovers, 135
preparation for grilling,
basics of, 115–22
recipes, 193–205
Bluefish Piccata, 199
Grilled Whitefish with
Spinach Pasta and
Fontina Cheese, 201
Halibut Steaks au Poivre,
197
Herb Marinade for Fish,
142
Mackerel with Tangerine
Brushing Sauce, 202
Minted Flounder on Lime
Slices, 200
Orange Roughy with
Salsa, 198
Red Snapper Margarita,
204
Red Snapper with Olive
Salad, 196–97

Salmon Steaks with Asian Marinade, 202–3
Scrod with Grilled Apple Slices, 205
Swordfish in Buttermilk Marinade, 194–95
Tarragon-Scented Striped Bass, 195–96
Very Simply Salmon, 203
storing and handling, 42–43
storing and thawing, 117–18
substitutions among, 119
Five-Minute Mussels (recipe), 153
five-spice, tip about, 145
flake, definition of, 119
Flank Steak Strips on Salad Greens with Lemongrass Mopping Sauce (recipe), 169
flashlight, about, 31
flavored vinegars, about, 40
flounder, minted, on lime slices (recipe), 200
flour tortillas, pork tenderloin in (recipe), 172
Focaccia (recipe), 157
fontina cheese, spinach pasta and, grilled whitefish with (recipe), 201
food, how much to buy when entertaining, 76–77
food holders, about, 30
food thermometer, 26–26
Fourth of July, suggested menu for, 79
free-range chicken, grilling tips for, 111
fried rice, pork, ideas for leftovers, 134
fruit(s). *See also individual fruits*
glazed mixed, grill (recipe), 232
grillable, 127–29
kebabs on grilled chocolate pound cake (recipe), 236–38

G

garbage bags, about, 29
garlic
about, 37, 125

recipes with
and cilantro, new potatoes with, 225
crumbs, soft-shell crabs with, 211
Greek cheese with, 156–57
pita chips, 157
potato skins, grilled, 160
gas grills
about, 16–19
preheating, 52
safety tip about, 65
ginger
about, 130
marinade for chicken or pork (recipe), 145–46
Glazed Mixed Fruit Grill (recipe), 232
Glazed Polish Sausage (recipe), 153–54
gloves, heat-resistant, about, 32
goose, grilling tips for, 112, 113
grains, on the grill, 129
grapefruit relish, "poor man's lobster" (monkfish) with (recipe), 214
grate, definition of, 44
gravy, vegetarian, ideas for leftovers, 136
Greek Cheese with Garlic Pita Chips (recipe), 156–57
Greek-Style Lamb Chops (recipe), 174
Greek-style shrimp, ideas for leftovers, 135
green onions, tomatoes and, grilled (recipe), 228–29
greens
mixed, topped with grilled vegetables (recipe), 226–27
salad, flank steak strips on, with lemongrass mopping sauce (recipe), 169
grill(s)
baskets, about, 31
brush, 24
lifter, about, 29
screen, 24
types of, 12–22
Grilled Angel Food Cake and Pineapple (recipe), 240
Grilled Antipasti (recipe), 162–63

Grilled Garlic Potato Skins (recipe), 160
Grilled Quail (recipe), 190–91
Grilled Sliced Meat Loaf with Chopped Tomatoes (recipe), 167
Grilled Tomatoes and Green Onions (recipe), 228–29
Grilled Whitefish with Spinach Pasta and Fontina Cheese (recipe), 201
grilling techniques, 55–62
cooking in embers, 59
directly to the point, 55–57
indirect cooking, 57–58
rotisserie, 59
smoking, 59–60
versus barbecuing, 4
timetable when entertaining, 75–78
Grill-Roasted Turkey Breast (recipe), 188
ground meats
chicken, grilling tips for, 113
ideas for leftovers, 134
pork sausage, tip about, 152
turkey, grilling tips for, 113

H–I

Halibut Steaks au Poivre (recipe), 197
hardwood, definition of, 48
hats, about, 32
Herb Marinade for Fish (recipe), 142
heterocyclic amines (HCAs), 70–71
hinged cooking grid, about, 29
hoisin sauce, about, 41, 130
Honey-Brushed Smoked Chicken with Mandarin Orange Sauce (recipe), 252–53
honey brushing sauce, prawns with (recipe), 215–16
Honeyed Papaya Strips with Warm Brie (recipe), 239
ice bucket and/or cooler, 27

Individual Smoked Whitefish (recipe), 245–46

J-K

jalapeño mayonnaise, sea
  scallops and mashed potatoes
  with (recipe), 208–9
jerk, definition of, 96
Jerk Strip Steaks (recipe), 168
juices, citrus, tip about, 142

Kamado, 20
kebabs
  fruit, on grilled chocolate
    pound cake (recipe),
    236–38
  sea scallop (recipe), 209–10
  shish (recipe), 176
  tips on making, 61
ketchup
  about, 41
  cranberry raisin (recipe), 148
  tip about, 145
kids, suggested menu for, 81
kiwifruit, about, 128
knives
  about, 26
  tip about, 44

L

lamb
  grilling tips for, 105
  how much to buy when
    entertaining, 76
  ideas for leftovers, 134–35
  recipes
    burgers, 175
    chops, Greek-style, 174
    rib chops with fresh
      mint, 174–75
    ribs, sweet and sour,
      155–56
    rosemary brushing
      marinade for, 147
leftovers, 131–37
  reheating, 132
  storing, 131
legumes, on the grill, 129
lemongrass
  about, 170
  mopping sauce, flank steak
    strips on salad greens with
    (recipe), 169

lighter fluid, about, 50
light strings, about, 32
lime slices, minted flounder on
  (recipe), 200
lobster(s)
  buying, 117
  grilling tips for, 121–22
  recipes
    "poor man's" (monkfish)
      with grapefruit relish,
      214
    tails with sherry sauce,
      213–14
    whole Maine, 212–13
lowfat recipes, list of, 87–89

M

Mackerel with Tangerine
  Brushing Sauce (recipe), 202
Maine clambake, down
  (recipe), 216–17
Maine lobsters, whole (recipe),
  212–13
mandarin orange sauce, honey-
  brushed smoked chicken with
  (recipe), 252–53
mangoes, about, 128
margarita, red snapper (recipe),
  204
marinade(s)
marinades
  basics of, 93–95
  boiling tip about, 145
  ingredients for a simple, 95
  recipes
    Asian, salmon steaks
      with, 202–3
    buttermilk, swordfish in,
      194–95
    ginger, for chicken or
      pork, 145–46
    herb, for fish, 142
    orange or tangerine, for
      poultry or pork, 145
    red wine, for meat, 146
    rosemary brushing, for
      lamb, 147
    sauce, shallot, skirt steak
      with grilled peppers
      and, 166

tangerine, with grill-
  roasted turkey breast,
  188
marinara sauce for leftovers, tip
  about, 135
marinate
  definition of, 44
  tips for meats, 102–3
marjoram, about, 37
mayonnaise
  about, 41
  jalapeño, sea scallops and
    mashed potatoes with
    (recipe), 208–9
meat(s)
  basics of, 99–106
  beef recipes
    Beer-Basted Short Ribs,
      171–72
    Cheeseburger Deluxe,
      170–71
    Flank Steak Strips on
      Salad Greens with
      Lemongrass Mopping
      Sauce, 169
    Grilled Sliced Meat Loaf
      with Chopped Toma-
      toes, 167
    Jerk Strip Steaks, 168
    Skirt Steak with Grilled
      Peppers and Shallot
      Marinade Sauce, 166
    Smoked Beef Short Ribs,
      249–50
  fat content of cuts of, 86
  flavors that go well with,
    105
  ground, ideas for leftovers,
    134
  how much to buy when
    entertaining, 76–77
  lamb recipes
    Greek-Style Lamb Chops,
      174
    Lamb Burgers, 175
    Lamb Rib Chops with
      Fresh Mint, 174–75
    Rosemary Brushing
      Marinade for Lamb, 147
    Shish Kebabs, 176
    Sweet and Sour Lamb
      Ribs (recipe), 155–56
  marinating tips for, 102–3

meat loaf, grilled sliced, with chopped tomatoes (recipe), 167
minimum cooking temperature for, 67
pork recipes
  Carolina-Style Slow Smoked Pulled Pork, 247–48
  Ginger Marinade for Chicken or Pork, 145–46
  Grilled Sliced Meat Loaf with Chopped Tomatoes, 167
  Orange or Tangerine Marinade for Poultry or Pork, 145
  Pork Chops with Apple Slices, 173
  Pork Tenderloin in Flour Tortillas, 172
  Smoked Pork Sandwiches with Bourbon Barbecue Sauce, 253–54
  red wine marinade for (recipe), 146
  storing and handling, 42–43
medium-cooked meat, definitions of, 100
menus, suggested, 79
Mesquite-Smoked Turkey Thighs (recipe), 250–51
microwave, about, 132
mince, definition of, 44
mint, about, 37
Minted Flounder on Lime Slices (recipe), 200
Mixed Greens Topped with Grilled Vegetables (recipe), 226–27
Mixed Grilled Vegetables in a Pita Pocket (recipe), 223–24
molasses barbecue sauce, chicken pieces with (recipe), 183–84
mollusks
  buying, 117
  grilling tips for, 120
monkfish, "poor man's lobster" with grapefruit relish (recipe), 214
monounsaturated fats, about, 87

mushroom(s)
  about, 125–26
  recipes with
    Asparagus and Mushrooms with Sage Brushing Sauce, 222–23
    Grilled Antipasti, 162–63
    Two-Mushroom Dust, 142
    Walnut-Stuffed White Mushrooms, 159
  salad, ideas for leftovers, 136
  shiitakes, about, 142
mussels
  five-minute (recipe), 153
  grilling tips for, 120
mustard, about, 41–42

N-O

nectarines, about, 129
New Potatoes with Garlic and Cilantro (recipe), 225
nonstick cooking spray, about, 41

oil(s)
  about, 40–41
  definition of, 44
olive oil, about, 40
olive salad, red snapper with (recipe), 196–97
onions
  about, 37, 126
  green, about, 37
  recipes with
    caramelized, chicken dogs with, 186
    green, tomatoes and, grilled, 228–29
    vidalia, baked potatoes with, 227–28
orange, recipes with
  chili-, mopping sauce, smoked shrimp with, 244–45
  mandarin, sauce, honey-brushed smoked chicken with, 252–53
  marinade for poultry or pork, 145
Orange Roughy with Salsa (recipe), 198

oregano, about, 37
Orzo, about, 191
oven thermometer, about, 31
oysters, grilling tips for, 121

P

Paella (recipe), 184–85
papaya
  about, 129
  strips, honeyed, with warm brie (recipe), 239
parsley, about, 37
pasta
  seafood, ideas for leftovers, 135
  spinach, and fontina cheese, grilled whitefish with (recipe), 201
pastes, basics of, 95
peaches, about, 129
pears
  about, 129
  wine-brushed (recipe), 234–35
peas, about, 126
pecans and dried cherries, whole smoked salmon with (recipe), 246–47
peel, definition of, 44
pepper(s)
  about, 126
  black, about, 37
  grilled, skirt steak with, and shallot marinade sauce (recipe), 166
  red, about, 37
perishables, about, 42–43
pesto (recipe), 187
Pesto Chicken (recipe), 187
Philly-style sandwich, about, 133
piccata, bluefish (recipe), 199
picnic, suggested menu for, 79
pineapple
  about, 129
  grilled angel food cake and (recipe), 240
  salsa (recipe), 149
pit, definition of, 44
pita chips, garlic (recipe), 157
  Greek cheese with (recipe), 156–57

pita pocket, mixed grilled vegetables in a (recipe), 223–24

pizza
buffalo cheese and tomato sauce (recipe), 221–22
crust (recipe), 220
peel or paddle, about, 32

polenta, about, 129

polycyclic aromatic hydrocarbons (PAHs), 70–71

polyunsaturated fats, about, 87

"Poor Man's Lobster" (Monkfish) with Grapefruit Relish (recipe), 214

pork
chops, grilling tips for, 104
how much to buy when entertaining, 76
ideas for leftovers, 134
recipes
Carolina-Style Slow Smoked Pulled Pork, 247–48
Ginger Marinade for Chicken or Pork, 145–46
Grilled Sliced Meat Loaf with Chopped Tomatoes, 167
Orange or Tangerine Marinade for Poultry or Pork, 145
Pork Chops with Apple Slices, 173
Pork Tenderloin in Flour Tortillas, 172
Smoked Pork Sandwiches with Bourbon Barbecue Sauce, 253–54
spareribs, grilling tips for, 104
tenderloin, grilling tips for, 104

potato(es)
about, 126
and botulism, 58
mashed, ideas for leftovers, 136
recipes with
baked, with vidalia onions (recipe), 227–28

mashed, sea scallops and, with jalapeño mayonnaise (recipe), 208–9
new, with garlic and cilantro (recipe), 225
skins, grilled garlic (recipe), 160
sweet, about, 127

pot holders, 24

poultry
chicken recipes
Cantonese-Style Sweet and Sour Chicken Breasts, 180–81
Chicken Dogs with Caramelized Onions, 186
Chicken Pieces with Molasses Barbecue Sauce, 183–84
Chicken Yakitori, 182–83
ginger marinade for, 145–46
Honey-Brushed Smoked Chicken with Mandarin Orange Sauce, 252–53
Paella, 184–85
Pesto Chicken, 187
Spicy Chicken Dogs (recipe), 154–55
tea-smoked, 113
Whole Grilled Chicken with Apricot Sauce, 181–82
content of cuts of, 86
duck recipes
grilling tips for, 112, 113
tea-smoked, 113
flavors that go well with, 113
-grain salad, about, 133
grilling, 107–14
how much to buy when entertaining, 77
ideas for leftovers, 132–33
minimum cooking temperature for, 67
Orange or Tangerine Marinade for Poultry (recipe), 145
shears, about, 31
quail recipe
Grilled Quail, 190–91

turkey recipes
Grill-Roasted Turkey Breasts, 188
Turkey Burgers with Dried Cranberries, 189
Yogurt-Marinated Turkey Legs, 190
Smoked Turkey Sausages, 251–52
Turkey Sausage on a Stick, 152–53
Mesquite-Smoked Turkey Thighs, 250–51

Prawns with Honey Brushing Sauce (recipe), 215–16

process, definition of, 44

propane, about, 65

pulled pork, Carolina-style slow smoked (recipe), 247–48

Q-R

quail
butterflying, 191
grilled (recipe), 190–91
grilling tips for, 112

raisin, cranberry, ketchup (recipe), 148

rare meat, definition of, 100

raspberries, apricots topped with, and raspberry sherbet (recipe), 240

recipes
lowfat, list of, 87–89
vegetarian, list of, 87–89

Red Snapper Margarita (recipe), 204

Red Snapper with Olive Salad (recipe), 196–97

Red Wine Marinade for Meat (recipe), 146

relish, grapefruit, "poor man's lobster" (monkfish) with (recipe), 214

ribs
grilling tips for, 103
lamb, sweet and sour (recipe), 155–56
short, beef, smoked (recipe), 249–50
short, beer-basted (recipe), 171–72

rice vinegar, about, 40
roast beef sandwich, about, 133
roasts, pork, grilling tips for, 105
rosemary
    about, 38–39, 130
    recipes with
        baby artichokes with, 229–30
        brushing marinade for lamb, 147
rotisserie
    about, 30
    grilling, 59
roughy, orange, with salsa (recipe), 198
rubs
    basics of, 93, 96–97, 141–50
    Cajun spice (recipe), 142
    Two-Mushroom Dust (recipe), 142

S

safety tips, 63–71, 98, 100–102
    about grills, 64–65
    fending off bad bugs, 66
    grilling temperatures, 67–68
    guidelines for meats, 100–102
    keeping food clean, 66
    preventing cross-contamination, 98
sage, about, 39
sage brushing sauce, asparagus and mushrooms with (recipe), 222–23
salad(s)
    poultry-grain, about, 133
    recipes
        greens, flank steak strips on, with lemongrass mopping sauce, 169
        olive, red snapper with, 196–97
        tortellini vegetable, 224–25
salad dressing(s)
    about, 42
    tip about, 136
salmon, recipes for
    smoked, whole, with pecans and dried cherries, 246–47

steaks with Asian marinade, 202–3
    very simply, 203
salmonella, about, 69
salsa(s)
    orange roughy with (recipe), 198
    pineapple (recipe), 149
    tip about, 145
sandwich(es)
    Midwest-style, ideas for leftovers, 134
    Philly-style, about, 133
    roast beef, about, 133
    turkey deli, about, 133
    smoked pork, with bourbon barbecue sauce (recipe), 253–54
saturated fats, about, 87
sauce(s)
    about, 41–42
    recipes for
        apricot, whole grilled chicken with, 181–82
        barbecue, Tennessee whiskey, 142
        beer basting, 171
        bourbon barbecue, smoked pork sandwiches with, 253–54
        chili-orange mopping, smoked shrimp with, 244–45
        honey brushing, prawns with, 215–16
        lemongrass mopping, flank steak strips on salad greens with, 169
        mandarin orange, honey-brushed smoked chicken with, 252–53
        molasses barbecue, chicken pieces with, 183–84
        sage brushing, asparagus and mushrooms with, 222–23
        shallot marinade, skirt steak with grilled peppers and, 166
        sherry, lobster tails with, 213–14

tangerine brushing, mackerel with, 202
tartar, 149
sausage(s)
    grilling tips for, 113
    ideas for leftovers, 134
    recipes for
        Polish, glazed, 153–54
        turkey, on a stick, 152–53
        turkey, smoked, 251–52
scallions, about, 37
scallop(s)
    grilling tips for, 120
    sea, kebabs (recipe), 209–10
    sea, and mashed potatoes with jalapeño mayonnaise (recipe), 208–9
Scandinavian-inspired sandwiches, ideas for leftovers, 135
scoop for briquets, about, 28
Scrod with Grilled Apple Slices (recipe), 205
Sea Scallop Kebabs (recipe), 209–10
Sea Scallops and Mashed Potatoes with Jalapeño Mayonnaise (recipe), 208–9
seafood pasta, ideas for leftovers, 135
sear, definition of, 56
serving utensils, 8
sesame oil, about, 40
shallot marinade sauce, skirt steak with grilled peppers and (recipe), 166
shallots, about, 39
shellfish
    flavors that go well with, 122
    how much to buy when entertaining, 77
    ideas for leftovers, 135
    preparation for grilling, basics of, 115–22
    recipes, 153, 207–18
        Coastal Shrimp in Beer, 215
        Crab Cakes, 217–18
        Down Maine Clambake, 216–17
        Five-Minute Mussels, 153
        Lobster Tails with Sherry Sauce, 213–14

"Poor Man's Lobster" (Monkfish) with Grapefruit Relish, 214
Prawns with Honey Brushing Sauce, 215–16
Sea Scallop Kebabs, 209–10
Sea Scallops and Mashed Potatoes with Jalapeño Mayonnaise, 208–9
Soft-Shell Crabs on the Grill, 210–11
Soft-Shell Crabs with Garlic Crumbs, 211
Whole Maine Lobsters, 212–13
    storing and handling, 42–43
sherbet, raspberry, apricots topped with raspberries and (recipe), 240
sherry sauce, lobster tails with (recipe), 213–14
shiitakes, about, 142
Shish Kebabs (recipe), 176
shore grill dinners, suggested menus for, 80
shrimp
    grilling tips for, 120, 122
    recipes with
        coastal, in beer (recipe), 215
        smoked, with chili-orange mopping sauce (recipe), 244–45
side dishes, how much to buy when entertaining, 77
simmer, definition of, 44
skewers, 25
skillet casserole, ideas for leftovers, 134
Skirt Steak with Grilled Peppers and Shallot Marinade Sauce (recipe), 166
slaw, chicken, about, 133
slice, definition of, 44
small watering can, about, 28
smoked foods, recipes for, 243–55
    Carolina-Style Slow Smoked Pulled Pork, 247–48
    Honey-Brushed Smoked Chicken with Mandarin Orange Sauce, 252–53

Individual Smoked White-fish, 245–46
Mesquite-Smoked Turkey Thighs, 250–51
Smoked Beef Short Ribs, 249–50
Smoked Pork Sandwiches with Bourbon Barbecue Sauce, 253–54
Smoked Shrimp with Chili-Orange Mopping Sauce, 244–45
Smoked Turkey Sausages, 251–52
Whole Smoked Salmon with Pecans and Dried Cherries, 246–47
smoker box, about, 29
smokers, 21–22
S'mores, campfire-style (recipe), 238–39
snapper, red
    margarita (recipe), 204
    with olive salad (recipe), 196–97
soft-shell crabs
    grilling tips for, 122
    recipes
        on the grill, 210–11
        with garlic crumbs, 211
softwood, definition of, 48
soup, chicken noodle, about, 132
soybean curd (tofu), about, 130
soy sauce, about, 42
spareribs, grilling tips for, 104
specialty grills, 20
spice(s)
    about, 36–39
    blends, about, 39
Spicy Chicken Dogs (recipe), 154–55
spinach pasta and fontina cheese, grilled whitefish with (recipe), 201
spray, definition of, 44
spray bottle, about, 28
squab, grilling tips for, 112
squash, about, 127
starter fluid, caution about, 60, 65
steak(s)
    flank, strips on salad greens with lemongrass mopping

sauce (recipe), 169
    grilling tips for, 99–101
    halibut, au poivre (recipe), 197
    jerk strip (recipe), 168
    the most tender, 101
    salmon, with Asian marinade (recipe), 202–3
    skirt, with grilled peppers and shallot marinade sauce (recipe), 166
stews, ideas for leftovers, 134
stir-fry, ideas for leftovers, 134
storage tips for perishables, 42–43
striped bass, tarragon-scented (recipe), 195–96
summer squash, about, 127
sweet and sour
    chicken breasts, Cantonese-style (recipe), 180–81
    lamb ribs (recipe), 155–56
sweet potatoes
    about, 127
    ideas for leftovers, 136
Swordfish in Buttermilk Marinade (recipe), 194–95

T

tabletop and portable grills, 19–20
tacos al carbon, about, 133
tandoor, about, 20
tangerine, recipes with
    brushing sauce, mackerel with, 202
    marinade, for poultry or pork, 145
    marinade, with Grill-Roasted Turkey Breast, 188
tarragon
    about, 39
    -scented striped bass (recipe), 195–96
Tartar Sauce (recipe), 149
    tip about, 145
tea-smoked duck or chicken, 113
temperatures for food while grilling, 67
Tennessee Whiskey Barbecue Sauce (recipe), 142

teriyaki sauce, about, 42
thermometer, instant-read, how to use, 67–68
thyme, about, 39
timetable for entertaining, 75–78
tofu, about, 130
tomato(es)
  about, 127
  chopped, grilled sliced meat loaf with (recipe), 167
  and green onions, grilled (recipe), 228–29
  sauce, buffalo cheese and, pizza (recipe), 221–22
tool holder, about, 28
tools, 24
Tortellini Vegetable Salad (recipe), 224–25
tortillas, flour, pork tenderloin in (recipe), 172
trans fats, about, 87
tray, about, 28
trim, definition of, 44
tropical shrimp salad, ideas for leftovers, 135
tuna salad niçoise, ideas for leftovers, 135
turkey
  deli sandwich, about, 133
  recipes
    breast, grill-roasted, 188
    burgers, with dried cranberries, 189
    legs, yogurt-marinated, 190
    sausage, on a stick, 152–53
    sausages, smoked, 251–52
    thighs, mesquite-smoked, 250–51
  sausage, grilling tips for, 113
  whole, grilling tips for, 108, 109–10
turn, definition of, 44
Two-Mushroom Dust (recipe), 142

V–W

veal
  in Grilled Sliced Meat Loaf with Chopped Tomatoes (recipe), 167
  grilling tips for, 105
vegetable(s). *See also Greens; Vegetarian*
  ideas for leftovers, 136
  not suited for grilling, 127
  oil, about, 41
  recipes, 219–30
    Asparagus and Mushrooms with Sage Brushing Sauce, 222–23
    Baby Artichokes with Rosemary, 229–30
    Baked Potatoes with Vidalia Onions, 227–28
    Grilled Antipasti, 162–63
    Grilled Tomatoes and Green Onions, 228–29
    Mixed Greens Topped with Grilled Vegetables, 226–27
    Mixed Grilled Vegetables in a Pita Pocket, 223–24
    New Potatoes with Garlic and Cilantro, 225
    Tortellini Vegetable Salad, 224–25
  suited for grilling, 124–27
vegetarian
  burgers, about, 130
  recipes, list of, 87–89
  tips for serving to, 86–88
Very Simply Salmon (recipe), 203
vidalia onions, baked potatoes with (recipe), 227–28
vinegars, about, 39–40
vinyl or canvas grill covers, about, 31

Walnut-Stuffed White Mushrooms (recipe), 159
Warm Apple Cinnamon Slices with Cheddar Cheese (recipe), 235–36
warming rack, about, 30
water smokers, 22
well done meat, definition of, 100
whiskey barbecue sauce, Tennessee (recipe), 142
whitefish, grilled, with spinach pasta and fontina cheese (recipe), 201
whitefish, smoked, individual (recipe), 245–46
whole chicken or turkey, grilling tips for, 108, 109, 110
Whole Grilled Chicken with Apricot Sauce (recipe), 181–82
Whole Maine Lobsters (recipe), 212–13
Whole Smoked Salmon with Pecans and Dried Cherries (recipe), 246–47
Wine-Brushed Pears (recipe), 234–35
wine, red, marinade, for meat (recipe), 146
wine list for party, 78–79
wine vinegars, about, 40
winter squash, about, 127
wood chips, tips about, 58, 60
wood smokers, 21
Worcestershire sauce, about, 42
work table, about, 277

Y–Z

yakitori, chicken (recipe), 182–83
Yogurt-Marinated Turkey Legs (recipe), 190

zucchini, in Grilled Antipasti (recipe), 162–63